D1433581

Case studies
in Latin American
political economy

MANCHESTER
UNIVERSITY PRESS

Case studies
in Latin American
political economy

edited by
JULIA BUXTON
AND NICOLA PHILLIPS

Manchester University Press
Manchester and New York

distributed exclusively in the USA by St. Martin's Press

Copyright © Manchester University Press 1999

While copyright in the volume as a whole is vested in Manchester University Press, copyright in individual chapters belongs to their respective authors, and no chapter may be reproduced wholly or in part without the express permission in writing of both author and publisher.

Published by Manchester University Press
Oxford Road, Manchester M13 9NR, UK
and Room 400, 175 Fifth Avenue, New York, NY 10010, USA
http://www.man.ac.uk/mup

Distributed exclusively in the USA by
St. Martin's Press, Inc., 175 Fifth Avenue, New York, NY 10010, USA

Distributed exclusively in Canada by
UBC Press, University of British Columbia, 6344 Memorial Road, Vancouver, BC, Canada V6T 1Z2

British Library Cataloguing-in-Publication Data
A catalogue record for this book is available from the British Library

Library of Congress Cataloging-in-Publication Data applied for

ISBN 0 7190 5457 5 hardback

First published 1999

06 05 04 03 02 01 00 99   10 9 8 7 6 5 4 3 2 1

Typeset
by Northern Phototypesetting Co. Ltd, Bolton
Printed in Great Britain
by Bookcraft (Bath) Ltd, Midsomer Norton

Contents

Tables

Notes on contributors

Jonathan R. Barton is a Senior Research Associate at the School of Development Studies at the University of East Anglia. His publications include *A Political Geography of Latin America* (1997) and 'The North South Dimension of the Environment and Cleaner Technology Industries, *Cepal Review*, 1998. He is currently working on a European Commission project on industry, trade and the environment.

Julia Buxton has recently completed a doctoral thesis on the Venezuelan party system 1989–93 at the London School of Economics and works as a consultant on Venezuelan politics and economics. She is Lecturer in Social Science at Kingston University. Publications include *The Contemporary History Handbook* (ed., 1995) and 'Venezuela, Degenerative Democracy', in *Democratization: The Resilience of Democracy* (forthcoming).

John Crabtree is Latin American Editor at Oxford Analytica. He is also a visiting fellow at the Institute of Latin American Studies at the University of London (1997–98). Formerly a Senior Associate Member at Saint Antony's College Oxford (1994–96), he was also a visiting fellow at the Universidade de Sao Paulo (1990) and the Universidad del Pacifico, Lima (1995–96). He is author of *Peru under Garcia: An Opportunity Lost ?* (1992) and *Fujimori's Peru* (1998) He is currently co-editing a volume on democratisation and economic liberalisation in Bolivia.

Henry Finch is Senior Lecturer in the Department of Economic and Social History at Liverpool University, where he has taught since 1963. His publications in English on Uruguay include *A Political Economy of Uruguay since 1870* (1981), *Uruguay* (1989), *Contemporary Uruguay: Problems and Prospects* (ed., 1989) and *Towards the New Economic Model: Uruguay 1973–1997* (1998).

Colin M. Lewis is Senior Lecturer in Latin American Economic History at the London School of Economics and Political Science and an Associate Fellow of the Institute of Latin American Studies, University of London. His recent publications include *The New Institutional Economics and Third World Development* (edited with John Harriss and Janet Hunter, 1997) and *The Argentine: From Economic Growth to Economic Retardation, 1850s–1980s* (1995). He is currently working on Argentinian economic and social policy during the post-1920s period and will shortly publish a working paper on the history of the Argentinian system of social insurance.

Brian McBeth is closely associated with the work of the Latin American Centre at St Antony's College, Oxford. He is a former director of Schroder Securities Ltd and worked as a stockbroker in the City of London between 1979 and 1989 specialising in oil companies. He now works as an independent consultant on energy and Latin American matters. His publications include *Juan Vicente Gomez and the Oil Companies in Venezuela, 1908–1935* (1983), *British Oil Policy, 1919–1939* (1985), *Petroleum in Venezuela: A Bibliography* (1985), *Colombia* (1993), *Venezuela: The Way Forward* (1995), and *Privatisation: A Strategic Report* (1996).

Francisco Panizza is Lecturer in Latin American Politics at the London School of Economics, and has written extensively on politics and democracy in Latin America. Recent publications include, *The Politics of Human Rights in Brazil* (1998), *Democratization*, vol. 5 No. 4, *Os Direitos Humanos na Polmtica Domestica e, Internacional Brasileira, Politica Internacional 17,* Primavera, Verco (1998), and *Late Institutionalisation and Early Modernisation: The Emergence of Uruguay* (1997).

Sergio Peschard is a doctoral student at the University of Warwick, UK. His research concerns conceptions of the firm in international political economy, particularly co-operative arrangements between firms. He has written papers on 'Firm Networks in the Retail Services Sector: The Mexican Case', and on 'Maquiladoras vs. Growth Triangles: Lessons from the East', and has worked for the Mexican government at the Department of Trade and Industry and in consultancy firms.

Nicola Phillips is Lecturer in Politics and International Studies at the University of Warwick, UK. She received her Ph.D. from the London School of Economics, and her research interests focus principally on international political economy with a particular application to the Latin American region. She has written various papers and book chapters on globalisation and the state in Latin America, the impact of the global crisis on regionalism in South America, and East Asian and Latin American perspectives on the global economic crisis. She is author of 'The Future Political Economy of Latin America', in Richard Stubbs and Geoffrey R. D. Underhill, *Political Economy and the Changing Global Order* (second edition, forthcoming 1999), and her forthcoming book is entitled *Globalisation and State Power in Latin America*.

Howard Handelman is Professor of Political Science and Acting Chair of the Department of Spanish at the University of Wisconsin–Milwaukee. His most recent books include: *Mexican Politics: The Dynamics of Change* (St. Martin's Press, 1997); *Politics in a Changing World* (co-authored, 2nd edition, St. Martin's Press, 1998); *Democracy and its limits – Lessons from Asia, Latin America and the Middle East* (co-edited, University of Notre Dame Press, 1999); *The Challenge of Third World Development*, (2nd edition, Prentice Hall, 2000).

Introduction

JULIA BUXTON
AND NICOLA PHILLIPS

The 1980s and 1990s have seen a profound change in the economic development models pursued by Latin American countries. This is reflected in the move
away from inward-looking, state-led industrial development models introduced
after the Second World War, towards neoliberal market strategies. This transition was influenced by a number of factors, notably the exhaustion of import-
substituting industrialisation (ISI) and the debt crisis, which broke forcefully at
the beginning of the 1980s. International financial actors, specifically the International Monetary Fund (IMF), have played a central directing role in this
economic reorientation. The application of stabilisation and structural adjustment policies has entailed enormous social costs. Privatisation and public
spending restraint have had a critical impact on living standards, reversing the
traditions of extensive state employment, subsidisation and expansionary
economic policies. Further to this, neoliberalism has undermined the structural
underpinnings of the 'populist' political systems which guided Latin American
states through the early stages of democratisation. As a result, contemporary
history points to a conjunction of both economic and political change.

In a number of countries, acceptance of neoliberal economic policies
occurred initially during periods of authoritarian military government. This
prompted enquiry into the 'benefits' of authoritarianism during economic transition. In this interpretation, highly restrictive forms of government were
viewed as the best 'shell' for the application of neoliberalism. Socially unpalat-
able measures could be enforced with minimal resistance from civil society, and
defensive interest-group actions were restricted by the relative insulation of
government. The most enduring influence in this respect was the experience of
Chile under General Augusto Pinochet.

The process of redemocratisation which characterised the 1980s did not
lead to any substantive change in economic direction. If anything, the neoliberal order appeared to have been 'consolidated'. Democracy and political

freedom were increasingly viewed as complementary rather than antithetical counterparts to the economic liberties of the free market. The experience of the Argentine, Uruguay, Brazil and Peru in fact suggested the opposite to the lessons gleaned from Chile, in that democratic governments themselves proved more functionally capable of implementing adjustment than the military regimes. Although interest-group access to economic policy-making remained relatively restricted – revealing a strong element of continuity with the pre-military populist political systems, the legitimacy and accountability requirements of democratic administrations improved the policy-making process. This contrasted with the hierarchical and 'closed' nature of policy making within the military, wherein the absence of feedback and consultation mechanisms led to major economic policy failures, most clearly demonstrated by the Argentine military junta.

Countries which had been spared the experience of authoritarian military intervention – Colombia, Mexico and Venezuela – did not escape the standard neoliberal prescriptions. Extensive state intervention and flawed development models culminated in the same economic slowdown as regional neighbours, leading to the adoption of neoliberalism. As a result, the traditional populist systems have been forced to adapt to a radically different economic environment. The impression at the end of the twentieth century was that democracy and the free market were entrenched, that we had arrived at the 'end of history' with no further debate or ideological challenges ahead. This assessment was based on the peaceful turnover of civilian governments during the 1990s (an unprecedented event in the Argentine), party-political consensus on economic reform and the scope of benefits accruing from stabilisation and structural adjustment measures – including a sharp reduction in inflation, diversification of the economic base and an influx of foreign capital.

As the chapters in this volume illustrate, this is a fundamentally misleading impression. The idea that the limited role of the state is both unchallenged and hegemonic will be revealed over the next decade as a flawed, illogical conclusion. The idea that coherent adjustment policies have even been applied is in itself open to vigorous debate. In addition, the perception of Latin American civil societies as largely passive recipients of adjustment measures, and party politics as consensually predisposed to the 'Washington Consensus', has to be reviewed.[1] Social opposition to the costs of neoliberalism is not only gaining organisational form after years of quiescence, but it is also forging new debates with the state. Pressures for access and accountability, in conjunction with increasing support for the 'new Left', are forcing Latin American governments and their parties into a major re-evaluation of policy positions. As the ideological polarity between the Left and Right breaks down in the post-Cold War period, and as electoral competition intensifies, party systems can be expected to undergo a major realignment.

In this respect, the region is again at a major turning point, facing a new set of challenges to the established order. The new economic direction of 'modern

Latin America' and the unprecedented democratic stability shield traditional problems which have not been overcome. The nature and direction of development have changed, but overall the results are limited. The same problems of gross inequalities and extensive poverty coexist with sustained vulnerabilities in the international economy. Political authoritarianism, limited representation and profound social tensions remain, disguised in the cloak of democratic government. Pretensions to economic modernity, globalisation and regional integration run parallel with antiquated political and institutional forms. This is perhaps the greatest limitation to substantive economic change.

This book examines the diverse experiences of eight Latin American countries. The aim is to be forward-looking, examining recent trends to generate future scenarios. It seeks to provide a country-specific dimension to debates outlined in its sister volume, *Developments in Latin American Political Economy: States, Markets and Actors*.[2] Different methods of analysis and interpretation have led to broadly similar conclusions, pointing to a confluence of obstacles and potential difficulties which lie ahead. Rather than the policy debate having been exhausted, it is evident that major issues have yet to be coherently addressed. It will be impossible for the countries examined in the case studies to bypass these 'new debates'. When they are addressed, it will forge a major change in the political status quo.

The myth and reality of stabilisation and structural adjustment in Latin America

A primary area of concurrence for all the authors is that neoliberalism has largely failed to end Latin America's perennial vulnerability in the international economy. Whilst in the majority of cases mono-export dependence has been replaced (with the exception of Venezuela) by a diversified export strategy, this has failed to alter fundamentally the structural tendency towards economic instability, boom–bust cycles and crisis. A clear example is the case of Chile. Jonathan Barton not only challenges the neoliberal characterisation of the Pinochet regime, but further asserts that Chile's dependence on natural resources effectively remains, and has 'merely shifted from mineral resources to the exploitation of other natural resources'. What emerges is *continuity* in Latin America's historical experience of export dependency: it is only the nature of the exports that has changed. This vulnerability is equally evident in the Argentine and Mexico where, as Colin Lewis in his discussion of the 1991 Convertibility Plan and Sergio Peschard in his analysis of the 'Tequila' crisis observe, a central weakness of the current development strategy is reliance on international capital inflows. While economic stabilisation allowed for the repatriation of native currency – reversing the trend of capital flight which characterised the 1980s, these capital inflows remain acutely responsive to the slightest changes in macroeconomic performance.

A related issue addressed by all the authors is the extent to which Latin

America has actually applied stabilisation and structural adjustment measures. In this respect, political, cultural and institutional constraints on economic policy-making forcefully emerge. In Uruguay, Brazil and Venezuela the governing administrations have encountered institutional obstacles to the application of major reform, which is examined from a number of perspectives. First, constructing congressional support to advance structural changes to the economy has proved problematic. Weak and fragmented party systems, political 'distancing' from unpopular measures in the run-up to elections and entrenched clientelism have impeded reforms. In addition, Brazil, Uruguay and Venezuela further demonstrate what Henry Finch, in his chapter on Uruguay, refers to as 'a widespread belief in the rightness of public provision of public services', or for Francisco Panizza on Brazil, 'an enduring attachment to the idea of an interventionist state'. These two facets have combined to limit major reform, generating enduring fiscal and current account deficits, particularly in Venezuela and Brazil, which have served to limit economic growth. This not only calls into question the extent to which these countries can be said to have applied neoliberalism, but also their room for manoeuvre in the future. Even where political constraints on structural reform have been negligible, progress has been limited. This is most clearly in evidence in John Crabtree's chapter on Peru. Whilst the Fujimori government is credited with streamlining some state institutions, 'in other areas, the quality of state activity was not noticeably improved'. It is not, then, a question of which form of government is the greatest facilitator of neoliberal reform, but rather of the enduring pragmatism which characterises Latin American government and counters the possibilities for coherent economic reform.

All the authors converge on poverty and unemployment as critical issues to be addressed in the future. In no single case can it be said that the benefits of neoliberalism have 'trickled down' to the majority of people. It is increasingly apparent that the reverse has occurred, and that neoliberalism has exacerbated marginalisation and widened an already massive social gulf in each country. It further appears to be the case (most clearly illustrated in the chapters on the Argentine, Mexico and Peru) that privatisation and export-led growth have benefited the elite disproportionately, accelerating income divisions. In addition, as both John Crabtree and Jonathan R. Barton point out, free-market, export-oriented growth is not an adequate 'vehicle' for the generation of employment: rather, neoliberal policies have generated sustained structural problems of under-employment and unemployment.

These factors lead us to a broad consensus that unless the benefits of economic reform are distributed more equitably, the political future looks increasingly unstable. No government can be credited with tackling chronic problems of marginalisation and poverty, even if the political will is seen to be present – most noticeably in Chile and Colombia. Efforts to target assistance have been undermined by bureaucratic incompetence (Venezuela, Colombia) and, where the government has sought to improve social redistribution, a clear trend has been to do this to build personalistic support (as in Peru, in Mexico with PRONASOL, and in Colombia to preclude the President's impeachment) rather than on the basis of rights, social justice and equity. The destabilising implications of mounting poverty and inequality have also to be viewed in the context of a growing labour market (Peru and Venezuela), which will further accelerate social divisions unless there are government efforts to generate employment.

This brings us to a further area of concurrence. All the countries examined are seen to have a 'democratic deficit' (with the exception of Uruguay) which has yet to be overcome. Resolving this in favour of a more open, pluralistic society with adequate channels for the articulation of interests within transparent and accountable institutions will generate enormous tension. Whilst the deficit is largely common to all countries, it is rooted in distinct factors. Limited democratic forms continue to exist either because antiquated and authoritarian civilian practices have been 'frozen' or inadvertently strengthened by military government (Brazil, the Argentine), or because of the continued interference of the military (Chile). In the Mexican and Venezuelan cases, restricted democracy has endured as a result of limited political modernisation and as a remnant of the traditional party-dominated models (of the PRI in Mexico and AD and the COPEI in Venezuela). In contrast to these latter two cases, in Peru the weakness of and popular hostility to the traditional parties facilitated the 'neopopulist' authoritarianism of Fujimori.

The absence of political renovation has led to mounting social alienation and a haemorrhage of talent out of existing parties, whilst efforts to reform through either decentralisation (Mexico, Venezuela and arguably Brazil) or constitutional change (Colombia) have had the unintended consequence of strengthening pre-existing authoritarian tendencies. Limited efforts at political reform have proved to be a highly inadequate response to the demands of a reinvigorated civil society. All the authors agree that neoliberalism and authoritarianism led to the demobilisation and erosion of collective identities, most clearly evident in the decline of organised labour. This is slowly changing. As fears of military reintervention retreat, as hostility to pervasive corruption and limited representation continues to mount, the 'people' are once again becoming part of the Latin American political equation.

Opposition to existing political practices has been expressed in a number of forms, from guerrilla uprisings (the Zapatistas and the EZLN in Mexico) to abstention. A discernible trend is the re-emergence of the Left from the political wilderness of the immediate post-Communist period. In Uruguay, Brazil, Mexico, Venezuela and Chile, the 'reformed' Left has attracted increasing support from those disaffected by neoliberalism. A core appeal is their commitment to democratic reform, and military accountability; a two-pronged attack on the economic and political structures of the 'old model' of the 1980s and 1990s which will radically redefine the party systems at the beginning of the next century. The political consensus on neoliberalism, regional integration and further limiting the role of the state which links the leading parties in all countries is likely to fracture. As organised social opposition acquires an increasingly coherent form, the ability for top-down leadership, decree-led policy making and limited accountability will be constrained by electoral pragmatism. The next sets of elections in each of the countries studied is expected to be a watershed, generating major changes to the political alignments of the past decade. As parties are forced to address critical policy issues, we may witness a re-ideologicalisation of Latin American parties as they compete for an increasingly disaffected support base. In addition, as Francisco Panizza illustrates with reference to Brazil, the issues of democratic reform and economic inequality are implicitly interlinked. Eliminating poverty is not only an ethical issue, it is fundamental for the consolidation and strengthening of democracy.

A policy area which emerges as having enormous resonance in the next century is the issue of regional integration. The 1980s and 1990s will be historically significant for the changes they wrought in the foreign policy of Latin American states. The formation of the Southern Common Market (Mercosur), the North American Free-Trade Agreement (NAFTA) and integration into the General Agreement on Tariffs and Trade (GATT) has had the dual effect of integrating Latin America into the world economy whilst providing an institutional form for the neoliberal model. As the chapters on Uruguay, the Argentine, Mexico and Chile demonstrate, the assumed consensus on membership of these various organisations may yet be open to challenge. Membership of these trading groups carries both benefits and risks to members, the full implications of which have yet to be borne out. The phasing-out of tariff barriers will be a severe test of economic competitiveness and will have a major impact on the functions and dimensions of the state in each country.

The issue of the military is also likely to intensify policy debate. In the case of both Uruguay and the Argentine the authors confer that the military is no longer a threat to the civilian order, yet, as in Chile, where the military remains a central political actor, the question of accountability for atrocities committed continues to divide society. Despite the passage of the 1986 Ley de Caducidad (expiry law) which granted immunity from prosecution to the Uruguayan military, relations between the government and the armed forces continue to be extremely sensitive, a situation with strong parallels in the Argentine. In Chile, where the 1978 General Law of Amnesty declared that military personnel would not be indicted for violations of human rights during the period 1973–78, the Rettig Commission on Truth and Reconciliation set up in 1991 brought the issue of political justice once again to the fore. Burying the military past is proving to be a complicated obstacle to democratic consolidation, for human rights issues continue to divide Chilean, Uruguayan and Argentine society, in turn increasing military intransigence. Until justice is seen to be done, Latin America will continue to look to its past rather than to its future, and relations between the military and society will remain tense.

In looking to the future, it is unlikely that there will be a return to the statist model of the past. However, this is not to say that the debate around the role of the state has been decisively resolved. As Colin Lewis notes in the context of the Argentine, technical doubts about the profundity of institutional transformation, socio-economic problems and global issues remain. Sustaining support for economic reforms and progress on 'deepening' structural adjustment is highly contingent on political modernisation. The maintenance of hierarchical, personalistic and restrictive political practices not only impedes economic development but has alienated civil society. This will make the electorate unwilling to bear the continued costs of economic reforms which are seen as being unfairly distributed. Major policy issues have to be addressed in the immediate future, in what looks likely to be a congested, unstable political environment.

Notes

1 See D. Green, 'The Impact of Neoliberalism', in J. Buxton and N. Phillips (eds), *Developments in Latin American Political Economy: States, Markets and Actors* (Manchester, Manchester University Press, 1999).
2 See n. 1.

1

Brazil

FRANCISCO PANIZZA

During the 1980s and 1990s Brazil experienced a conjunction of political and economic change, from authoritarianism to democracy[1] and from an inward-looking, statist model of economic development towards a more open, market-oriented economy. In this process, democracy was restored and, after a dismal economic performance in the 1980s and early 1990s, economic growth increased in the second half of the decade only to fall again at the end of the decade. These achievements should not be underestimated, but neither should the persistent democratic deficit and the considerable economic problems the country faces on the threshold of the twenty-first century.

Politically, the important democratic advances registered since Brazil returned to democracy in 1985 coexist with a weak and fragmented party system, a lack of proper mechanisms for democratic accountability, important violations of human rights and the persistence of 'traditional' political practices of personalism, patronage and clientelism. Socially, Brazil has a numerically large and well-educated middle class and an active civil society, but the country is also one of the more unequal societies in the world, with wide class and regional disparities. Economically, Brazil has South America's most diverse and advanced industrial sector, as well as a large consumer market, but the economy underperformed in the 1980s and 1990s and economic modernisation has lagged behind other major Latin American nations. The reasons for this contradictory state of affairs will be explored below.

Brazil's transition to democracy: elite accommodation or genuine democratisation?

After more than twenty years of military governments, Brazil returned to civilian rule in March 1985. Although the inauguration of President José Sarney marked the country's return to democracy, it was not until December 1989 that a president was directly elected, and up until January 1999 no popularly elected president had handed office to an equally directly elected successor since President Juscelino Kubitschek handed over the presidency to Jânio Quadros in 1961.

Brazil's path to democracy has been presented as a typical case of 'transition through transaction'.[2] Indeed, the Brazilian transition to democracy was a long and protracted affair, starting with a military controlled process of liberalisation (the so-called *abertura*), which began as far back as the nomination of General Ernesto Geisel as president in 1974, gathered momentum after the dismissal of hard-line army commander General Silvio Frota in 1977 and took over a decade to lead to full democracy. The transition involved both implicit and explicit pacts and accommodation between the military and the civilian opposition. In this process mutual guarantees were established and the rules of the transition agreed. Moreover, the mode of transition allowed a large number of the political elite that had supported the military regime to retain positions of power at federal, state and local levels in the new democratic polity.[3]

The significant degree of elite continuity that characterised Brazil's return to democracy has led some writers to question its true democratic nature. According to this view, Brazil's transition amounted to little more than the transfer of state power from one elite group to another. During this process, everything worked more or less according to a grand plan devised by the military. A leading Brazilian social scientist called this process 'conciliation from above', a concept reminiscent of Barrington Moore's 'modernisation from above'.[4] While elite continuity has been an important constraint to political and economic reform (as analysed below), this view underestimates the importance of the democratic gains made by the Brazilian people in their long journey towards democracy. Far from being the outcome of a political strategy executed with military precision by the country's military rulers, the return to democracy was the result of the progressive unravelling of the military's strategy. The period 1974–85 was marked by significant political and electoral defeats for the military governments of the period. As Cammack notes, the military eventually acquiesced to Tancredo Neves' 1985 victory in the electoral college not because it was the culmination of a successful programme of withdrawal from power, but because the disarray of their own forces and the upsurge of democratic opposition left them with no better option.[5]

Democracy was partly brought by the same forces of modernisation unleashed by the economic transformation promoted by the military regime.[6] When the struggle for democracy gathered momentum in the late 1970s, Brazil was a more industrialised, urban and socially active country than at the time of the military take-over in 1964. Furthermore, the mere size of the country and, more importantly, the specific characteristics of its military regime meant that repression and social control never reached the extremes of other Southern Cone military dictatorships. Thus, when controlled liberalisation started in 1974, the seeds of an active civil society were rooted in the country's social fabric. Lawyers, students, journalists and other social groups spearheaded the campaign for a full democratic opening, playing a prominent role in widening the originally narrow limits of the *abertura*. The mobilisation of social movements was important, not just in terms of their contribution to the ending of military rule, but also because their campaign strengthened the notion that an active citizenship was an essential component of the new democracy. [7]

Democratisation, however, was not just the work of an increasingly active civil society: it also had a specific political dimension. In contrast with other Southern Cone military regimes, through most of their rule, the Brazilian military allowed limited political activity and semi-competitive elections for the Federal Congress, state and local assemblies as part of their strategy of gaining political legitimacy. The electoral rules, however, were designed to favour the official party and to ensure that the military's more radical political opponents did not have a place in the elected bodies. As part of this strategy, hundreds of politicians were exiled or banned from running for office, old political parties were abolished and two new parties were set up in 1965: an official party, the Aliança Renovadora Nacional (ARENA, National Renovation Alliance), later renamed the Partido Democrático Social (PDS, Democratic Social Party); and a tolerated opposition, the Movimento Democrático Brasileiro (MDB, Brazilian Democratic Movement), later renamed Partido do Movimento Democrático Brasileiro (PMDB, Brazilian Democratic Movement Party). While initially in no condition to challenge the military's grip on power, the MDB's leadership made shrewd use of the narrow political space to transform the party from a token opposition force into a broad democratic opposition front. By obtaining significant gains in controlled congressional, state and local elections between 1974 and 1982, the MDB effectively derailed the military's project of transforming the ARENA into an adequate electoral vehicle for perpetuating their rule.

The third aspect of the process of transition which gave it a genuine democratic dimension was popular mass mobilisation. Of particular significance were the São Paulo car-workers' mobilisations of 1977–79, which signalled the emergence of a new trade unionism, free from the corporatist controls imposed upon traditional unions since the 1930s.[8] The resurgence of the union movement placed the São Paulo elite industrial workers at the head of a broad spectrum of social movements, which actively mobilised opposition to the military and laid the ground for the campaign for direct presidential elections in 1984. The campaign, known as the '*Diretas Já*' ('Direct Elections Now'), consisted of a series of mass demonstrations that swept the country between January and April 1984.[9] Although the demonstrators did not achieve their professed goal of forcing direct presidential elections, the mass peaceful protests sapped the regime's residual claims to legitimacy, and decisively contributed to the political climate that led to the defeat of the official party's candidate in the ensuing indirect presidential election.

Brazil's path to democracy encapsulates the confluence of continuity and change that would characterise the so-called New Republic. In this process, elite accommodation and democratic pressure from below converged to shape the new democratic polity. Democratic forces were considerably strengthened by the social and political changes that led to the military's retreat. However, the military's ultimately self-defeating strategy of allowing semi-competitive elections at state and local level while keeping the reins of power firmly concentrated in the Executive, had the unintended consequence of strengthening the hand of traditional oligarchies, which operated at these levels as providers of political support for the official party in exchange for the clientelistic allocation of state funds. Thus, paradoxically, a political regime that had come to power with the mission of modernising Brazil ended up by perpetuating political practices of patronage and clientelism antithetical to democracy and a modern economy.[10]

Political institutions under democracy

In spite of the traumatic circumstances that surrounded his accession to office, the inauguration in March 1985 of José Sarney as the country's first civilian president since 1964 was a landmark in Brazil's political history.[11] The new authorities quickly brought the process or re-institutionalisation to its completion by re-establishing direct elections for all levels of government and legalising the Brazilian Communist parties and other Marxist organisations.[12] The government also abolished party fidelity, erased most legal barriers to the formation of political parties and their representation in Congress, and allowed multi-party alliances in future elections. The suffrage was extended to illiterate citizens for the first time in Brazil's history.[13]

How has the restoration of liberal democratic institutions shaped the working of the new democratic governments? To answer this, it is necessary to examine two separate but related aspects of the country's political life under democracy. The first refers to relations between state actors: while some scholars have stressed the centralising power of the Executive and its ability to impose its will over Congress and other political actors as the defining characteristic of the Brazilian political system, others, in contrast, have highlighted political and organisational fragmentation as a major obstacle for good governance.[14] The second feature which has permeated contemporary Brazilian politics is the contrast between a modern civil society, able to influence political outcomes at crucial points in recent history, and the persistence of more traditional practices of patronage and clientelism which, together with significant levels of corruption, are also a prominent feature of the political system. This section analyses the tension between the forces of centralisation and fragmentation and those of modern democratic practices and traditional forms of political representation.

Historically, the President has been the nodal point of Brazil's state-centred political system. In common with the rest of Latin America, the institution of the presidency combines the functions of head of state and head of government. This double function gives the President a vast array of institutional responsibilities. In addition to its formal attributions, the ascendancy of the President is grounded in three key political dimensions of his or her power. Firstly, in a socially fragmented and regionally divided country with few truly nation-wide institutions, the President can claim a higher level of legitimacy as the directly elected representative of the people. On these grounds, in cases of conflicts of power with other branches of the state, the President can appeal directly to the people, bypassing other political institutions. This centralising, populist dimension of presidential power has been evident at different moments in the country's history, particularly during the personalist rule of Getulio Vargas,[15] the architect of modern Brazil. Since the return to civilian rule, the populist appeal of the presidency has been exemplified by the government of Fernando Collor de Melo (1990–92), a political outsider (or, better said, a pseudo-outsider), with no significant party-political base of support. During the electoral campaign he reached the electorate with the strong backing of the country's main television network, the Rede Globo. He gained the presidency by capitalising on popular disenchantment with the first post-military regime democratic administration and on fears of a triumph of the left-wing candidate, Luiz Inácio Lula da Silva. Once in office, Collor ruled in a highly personalist and idiosyncratic fashion, centralising power in the Executive and seeking to implement an ambitious programme of economic modernisation from the top down, although his political isolation ultimately led to his downfall under accusations of corruption.[16]

The second dimension of presidential power in Brazil is the power of patronage. As head of the public administration, the President has ultimate control over the release of budget funds and discretionary power of appointment of thousands of positions in the public administration and state-owned enterprises. Political appointments are important staging posts in politicians' careers and form part of the clientelistic chain of exchanging political support for politically allocated public goods, which extends from the centre to the furthest outreaches of the Brazilian state. Through the use of patronage powers, the President is able to co-opt members of Congress, as well as state and local politicians, to further his or her political interests.[17] The discretionary appointment of cabinet ministers is also an important attribution of the President. Ministries and state agencies, like the Communications, Transport and Health ministries, are particularly valuable political positions, as they hold large budgets whose funds can be allocated at the discretion of the Minister to foster the political fortunes of allies at state and local levels.

The third dimension of presidential power in Brazil is the Executive's power to control the political agenda. The President has the ability to formulate, initiate and, with important qualifications, to promote the implementation of public policy. The President has command over key technical, administrative and material resources for policy making and implementation. Particularly relevant is the President's access to the expertise and advice of highly qualified technocrats within the upper echelons of the Federal Administration.[18] Under the new democratic polity, economic policy-making has remained top-down, concentrated in the core economic Ministries of Finance and Planning.[19] These ministries are staffed by a powerful and highly influential techno-bureaucracy which has a key role in economic policy-making. The successive stabilisation plans that have characterised economic policy-making in the 1980s and 1990s are an example of how the alliance between the President and a tight group of technocrats has dominated policy making under democracy.[20]

The presidency's accumulation of institutional and political resources has led some scholars to argue that the new democratic environment notwith-standing, the position maintains the core features of the 'imperial presidency', characteristic of the military governments and other authoritarian periods in Brazilian history.[21] However, this notion is misleading, overlooking significant institutional and political constraints to presidential power in contemporary Brazil. As Mainwaring argues, the problems associated with presidentialist regimes are worsened by its interrelation with a multi-party system, as the com-bination makes coalition-building difficult and often leads to political stale-mate.[22] In this respect, Brazil's multi-party system appears as a case in point.

Since Brazil's return to democracy, relations between the Executive and Congress have been complex and prone to gridlock. State, regional and spe-cial interests are strongly represented in Congress, often binding Congressmen together over and above party allegiances. In turn, the party system has made relations between the Executive and Congress difficult to coordinate, as the counterpart to the post-war centrality of the state has been a weak party sys-tem, highly dependent on the state and of limited representative ability.[23] The open-list proportional representation electoral system favours the prolifera-tion of political parties: 18 parties gained congressional representation in the 1998 elections and the largest party won just over 20 per cent of the seats in the Lower House.[24] With the exception of the parties of the Left, parties are catch-all and internally fragmented. Party discipline is poor, as the electoral legislation puts a low premium on party allegiance. The result is a high level of cross-benching, with Congressmen often switching allegiance to parties other than the one under which they were elected, and the parties themselves are prone to mergers and splits. The large number of parties and the lack of intra-party discipline made the system highly fragile and vulnerable to external pressure.[25]

To overcome the lack of a majority party, the President is forced to rely on multi-party alliances to secure parliamentary support. As a general norm, these alliances have taken the form of 'grand coalitions' in which the number of seats held by the parties supporting the government exceed (by a substantial mar-gin) the number of votes necessary to secure a simple parliamentary majority. Two reasons lie behind this; the first concerns the lack of party discipline which makes it necessary to secure an extra number of seats as a cushion against possible defections. The second, and perhaps more important, is that grand coalitions reflect the government's need to take into account the country's regional and state balance of forces in the parliamentary majority.[26]

Brazil is the most truly federal of all Latin American countries and regional differences affect the structure and functioning of presidential coalitions. The Federal Government cannot properly govern without taking into consideration the political balance between the regions and the state hierarchy of power within each region. While there are no state or regional parties in contemporary Brazil, the parties' electoral strength is concentrated in particular states or regions, and some, like the PMDB, are in practice a loose federation of state and regional bosses. Moreover, because of their political and economic importance, certain states assume a *de facto* leading role within their regions. So, the states of Rio Grande do Sul and Bahia are regarded as the natural representatives of the South and the North-East respectively, and their political leaders expect to be awarded a corresponding share of government positions and state resources at federal level.

The balance of forces between the federal government and the states has shifted significantly in different historical periods but, as would be expected, the centralisation of power in the Executive reached one of its peaks during the years of military rule. Authoritarian centralisation contributed to make the struggle for democracy in Brazil not just a fight for free elections but also for devolution of power to states and municipalities. Significantly, free elections for state governors in 1982 were regarded as a milestone in the country's transition to democracy as they preceded by seven years the first direct election for the presidency. The return to democracy has increased the governors' political influence, as they have important political responsibilities within their states and a significant influence in determining how their states' representatives in Congress cast their vote.[27] This gives state governors considerably political clout and makes it politically costly for the federal authorities to ignore their demands.

Historically, financial dependence on the federal government has been one of the foundations of what is known in Brazilian political parlance as the politics of *fisiologismo*, – the trading of parliamentary support for politically allocated financial resources.[28] Democracy did not immediately put an end to state governments' financial dependency on the federal government, as tax revenues continued to be highly centralised in the Union. Moreover, fiscal dependency translated into political dependency, with the release of funds effectively conditional on the good will of the Finance Minister and, ultimately, the President. The 1988 Constitution sought to redress the fiscal imbalance. States and municipalities gained the power to enlarge their tax bases and were awarded a larger share of federal revenues without, however, a corresponding shift in the provision of services from the federal government to the states.[29] The constitutional initiative, however, did not entirely end the states' financial dependence, as most states have continued to run high budget deficits and have been forced to negotiate the rollover of their debts with the federal government.

The Brazilian state is not only divided vertically between the federal government and the states but also horizontally, as fractionalism is a characteristic
of the federal government itself. Ministries are divided among a large number
of parties, with the President often forced to act as a mediator between the
Ministries' competing financial claims and political rivalries. Moreover, divisions at the top filter through all levels of the administration, undermining the
state's internal cohesion.[30] Furthermore, the larger the governmental coalition,
the greater the danger of free-riders and disloyalty. This makes the working of
the coalition dependent on the President's use of selective political and material incentives to keep political allies on board, as well as on the President's ability to maintain a minimum political consensus within the coalition.

Moreover, politics is not constrained within the narrow boundaries of the
state institutions. The working of Brazilian democracy cannot be properly
understood without reference to relations between state and society. Brazilian
society is complex and socially, cultural and regionally diverse. Deep social differences result in different forms of articulation between the state and society.
Thus, an active and modern civil society, in which organisations both challenge
and complement state action, coexist with paternalist and hierarchical relations
of subordination between patrons and clients and with large pockets of social
exclusion, in which the absence of the state has been substituted by a parallel
social order. As Stepan puts it, 'civil society' became the political celebrity of
the *abertura,* firstly because it was explicitly meant to focus on opposition to
the (military) regime and second, because it created bonds between groups
within society which, in another context, might have been antagonistic.[31] The
weak representative capacity of the parties, the traditional mistrust of the state
and the growing complexity and diversity of Brazilian society mean that civic
and non-governmental organisations have continued to play a significant role
in the country's public life. The advent of democracy, however, has changed the
way social organisations operate, deprived social movements of the unifying
cause of opposing the military government and raised new questions about
their role in Brazilian society.

Some of the traditional organisations, such as the Brazilian Lawyers' Association and the Brazilian Journalists' Association, which had a prominent role in
pushing the originally narrow boundaries of the *abertura,* have lost their political centrality and have become more concerned with the defence of their own
corporate interests. More significantly, the Catholic Church, while still playing
an important role as a moral critic of the country's social ills and actively
engaged in supporting social movements in areas such as human rights and land
rights, has also seen its political influence undermined by the Church's own
conservative turn in the 1980s and the strong growth of other Christian
denominations.[32] Labour organisations have also faced problems in adapting to
the democratic social and political environment. The *novo sindicalismo* (new
unionism), which played a prominent role in the return to democracy,
remained a powerful force during the initial years since democratisation. Free

from corporatist constraints and with close links to the Partido dos Trabalhadores (PT, Workers' Party), the Central Únicados Trabalhadores (CUT,
United Workers Congress) established itself as the country's largest and more
militant umbrella trade-union organisation. CUT-affiliated unions are strongly
represented among workers from the public sector, state enterprises, banks and
the traditional industrial heartland of São Paulo state.[33]

However, in the late 1980s and the 1990s, high unemployment, industrial
restructuring and the crisis of the public sector, together with the growth of the
informal sector, undermined the unions' newly found power. In May 1995, a
strike by the powerful Oil Workers' Union was defeated by the government,
seriously weakening union militancy within the public sector. In June 1996 a
general strike called by the three umbrella trade-union organisations in protest
against government economic policies elicited only patchy support, and was
regarded as largely unsuccessful. The failed general strike confirmed the decline
in union power since Brazil's return to democracy and highlighted the problems unions faced in maintaining their influence within the changed economic
conditions and political climate of the 1990s.

The decline in labour's influence has not been matched by a parallel rise in
the political power of collective organised business. While during the initial
years of military rule the private sector strongly backed the military government, at later stages, business organisations and prominent individual entrepreneurs supported the country's return to democracy.[34] The business sector,
however, has had limited influence under democracy (as opposed to its market
power and the influence of individual entrepreneurs), as witnessed by their failure to persuade Congress to quickly pass key constitutional economic reforms.
Several reasons have been advanced to explain the business sector's weak influence with Congress, with attention drawn to the continuous disarticulation of
the country's business organisation.[35] Other contributing factors are the pre-
eminence of particularist over collective demands in Brazilian politics, and the
political autonomy of legislators from their voters and campaign financiers
resulting from the nature of the country's electoral system.[36]

Politically motivated social mobilisations which were an important part of
the political landscape in the 1980s have become less frequent, although mass
demonstrations and social militancy have not entirely disappeared. The process
of drafting the 1988 Constitution illustrates the diversity and complexity of
organised interests in Brazil and the capacity of social movements' to influence
legislation; the weakness of political parties and their combined disarray
regarding the constitution-making process allowed interest groups to actively
pursue their agenda through lobbying, mass demonstrations and direct personal contacts.[37] Mass demonstrations by students and other social sectors were
important in cajoling Parliament into initiating impeachment proceedings
against President Collor de Melo in 1992, and of particular significance in
the late 1990s were the actions of the Landless Peasants' Movement, which
promoted land occupations and the seizure of public buildings to press for

agrarian reform. Moreover, the ability of social organisations to influence the political system cannot be gauged only by their lower mobilising ability. In the 1990s social movements combined their traditional mobilising and campaigning role with a more institutional approach to politics.

In conjunction with the development of a more democratic, diverse and organised civil society, 'traditional' political practices of clientelism, patronage and personalism remain deeply entrenched in Brazilian politics and society.[38] Historically, the poorest sectors of the population have depended on the exchange of politically allocated public goods for political support to gain access to basic state provisions. At the heart of the clientelist networks is the enduring power of regional and local elites acting as power brokers between federal and state forces.[39] Furthermore, the return to democracy has exacerbated the municipal roots of patrimonial politics. The number of mayoralties increased from 4,300 in 1988 to 5,100 in 1996, largely to allow an expansion in the number of available municipal positions.[40] Clientelism, however, is not just a feature of small-town politics and traditional rural elites: it is also an integral part of politics at federal level. After the return to democracy, health and social security provisions continued to be used as a way of channeling benefits as particular favours rather than as legal entitlements.[41] If it can be argued that the retrenchment of the state as a result of neoliberal reforms may reduce opportunities for patronage, limited state resources can actually make the role of their political gatekeepers even more important.

If many within the urban poor still depend on politically allocated state goods for their survival, others have been forced to rely on actors operating not just outside the state but also beyond the legal order. Largely as a product of the same forces of modernisation that contributed to the development of civil society, Brazil has experienced a parallel process of social disorganisation and exclusion. The growth of a vast informal sector, high unemployment and persistently high levels of economic and cultural inequality have led to the emergence of a chasm between a legal and a paralegal social order: while the former is framed by the rule of law and the practices and culture of formal social institutions, the latter has its own forms of private justice, economic activities, political mediation and moral codes of conduct. In poor neighbourhoods deprived of state protection, 'justice' is enforced by self-appointed *justicieiros*, or, more recently, by the organised force of drug gangs and death squads. In these circumstances, the dividing lines between police and policed and between legality and illegality have become blurred as a paralegal network of complicity, collaboration and confrontation develops between police and criminal gangs. Municipal and state politicians, local judges as well as local traders and neighbourhood associations all participate in this parallel universe in which the selective absence and presence of the state has resulted in universal entitlements being substituted by vertical hierarchies of power, backed by private violence unmediated by notions of rights.[42]

The inextricable links between 'traditional' and 'modern' politics and between 'legality' and 'paralegality' are at the core of modern Brazilian politics. This may appear striking, particularly under a government as strongly committed to a programme of economic modernisation as that of President Cardoso. However, the loyalty of the parties that form the seven-party alliance supporting the government in Congress is maintained by 'traditional' practices of state patronage, selective allocation of funds and politically motivated public appointments. Indeed, policies of state modernisation have been promoted by appealing to the 'traditional' practices they are meant to supersede.[43] The persistence of patronage, personalism and clientelism, in parallel with the works of a modernising government backed by a technocratic elite, could be construed as a manifestation of the classical sociological dichotomy between 'modern' and 'traditional' society. It would be mistaken, however, to understand this as a simple duality, or opposite poles of a teleology of modernisation. It is important to emphasise that all actors and institutions, albeit in varying degrees, operate within this dual universe, acting within both realms in dynamic and highly adaptable ways. These practices, which undermine notions of citizenship and a modern culture of rights, are not just remnants of the past. They may be regarded as part of 'traditional' politics, but it is a tradition that is both produced and re-created by the forces of modernity. For want of a better term, these practices can perhaps be understood as a 'reconstituted tradition' or as a 're-traditionalisation'. Rather than being merely atavistic remnants of an undemocratic past, they are part and parcel of the dark underside of Brazil's process of modernisation.[44]

Democratic politics and economic policy

Between 1950 and 1980 Brazil was Latin America's most successful developmental state.[45] Over this period annual gross domestic product (GDP) growth averaged 7.4 per cent, or almost 4.5 per cent in per capita terms. In 1950 nearly two-thirds of the population still lived in rural areas. The primary sector (mostly agriculture) was responsible for approximately a quarter of GDP and employed 60 per cent of the workforce. Primary products represented nearly 90 per cent of total exports, with coffee accounting for 64 per cent. By 1980, less than one-third of the Brazilian population (at 119 million, nearly two and a half times larger than in 1950) lived in rural areas. The industrial sector grew at more than double the average rate for agriculture (8.4 per cent against 4.1 per cent). As a result, industry employed a quarter of the labour force in 1980, against 14 per cent in 1950. Exports of manufactured goods represented nearly 60 per cent of the total in 1980, against 12 per cent in 1950. The stock of foreign investment in the Brazilian economy, estimated at around $1 billion in 1950, had reached nearly $18 billion by 1980.[46]

Throughout the post-war period, the state played a leading direct and indirect role in implementing a highly interventionist model of economic development grounded in the legacy of the Vargas era.[47] The state engaged directly in economic activities through a large number of public enterprises, extended from banking (Banco do Brasil, Banco Nacional de Desenvolvimento Econô-mico, Caixa Econômica Federal) to oil and steel production (Petrobrás, Com-panhia Siderúrgica Nacional) and from mining (Companhia Vale do Rio Doce) to the traditional public utilities (Telebrás, Electrobrás). Indirectly, the state's economic influence was exercised through the whole array of instruments char-acteristic of the policies of ISI such as protective tariffs, fiscal incentives, con-trolled prices, differential exchange rates, direct and indirect subsidies and other forms of non-market allocation of resources. Economic policy was highly centralised as the states-dominated political system and the existence of pock-ets of bureaucratic efficiency provided the government with the necessary embedded autonomy to exercise its leading economic role.

By the late 1970s the highly successful developmental model began to reach its limits. The crisis of the authoritarian regime was accelerated by erratic eco-nomic growth between 1978 and 1980 and deep recession between 1981 and 1983. The economic legacy of the military governments and, more broadly, of the whole post-war economic model, was, however, deeply ambiguous both politically and economically. The return to democracy was greeted with expec-tations of social and economic change. But the critique of the 'old model' was centred on its gross economic inequality, high unemployment and on the mili-tary governments' inability, particularly since the late 1970s, to control infla-tion without affecting economic growth, rather than on the role of the state in economic affairs or the extremely high levels of protectionism.[48]

The enduring influence of developmentalist ideas is illustrated by the eco-nomic and social chapters of the 1988 Constitution, which sanctioned state monopolies in the oil and telecommunications sectors and placed restrictions on foreign investment in mineral extraction, health, telecommunications, and oil exploration and refining. Article 177 established as a federal monopoly the exploration and extraction of oil and natural gas, oil refining and the importa-tion and exportation of oil products. In addition, the Constitution established a generous system of social security and labour rights under the principle of universal coverage, resulting in an extremely rigid legal framework which was consequently difficult to enforce.

Economic policy during the first years of the New Republic was dominated by attempts at implementing an anti-inflationary strategy compatible with economic growth and with political demands to meet the country's massive social debt.[49] During the first democratic administration, economic policy was in the hands of a politically weak president. Elected president Tancredo Neves, who had been the architect of the negotiated transition, died before taking office and his vice president José Sarney was sworn as President for the 1985–90 period. Sarney was a late defector to the democratic opposition. He had been the president of the PDS, the official party of the military regime, and was chosen as Neves's running mate to accommodate the dissidents from the PDS who contributed to Neves' victory in the Electoral College. He had weak legitimacy and no strong personal support, which made him heavily dependent on the backing of the parliamentary leadership of the ruling PMDB, a broad-based party, whose members' only common ground was their past history of opposition to the military. To strengthen his position, Sarney made extensive use of patronage and stressed an abstract commitment to social issues without, however, a coherent economic strategy. Meanwhile inflation was running at 17.5 per cent in January 1986.

The heterodox Cruzado Plan, launched in February 1986, was an attempt at stabilising the economy. The assumption underlying the plan was that Brazil was suffering from 'inertial inflation', or inflationary memory,[50] hence the need for shock treatment to produce a sudden reversal of expectations. The cornerstone of the plan was a temporary wage and price freeze combined with monetary reform and a set of complementary measures to end the indexation of the economy and reduce the public deficit. However, in an attempt to gain political support for the government, the plan included wage bonuses which resulted in an 8 per cent real increase to all wage earners and 15 per cent to those earning up to one minimum wage.[51] The plan was an instant but short-lived success, both politically and economically. The sudden drop in inflation and the increase in real wages were massively popular with the public and brought handsome electoral rewards for the government in the November 1986 parliamentary elections. However, the incorporation of a substantial wage increase was inconsistent with the anti-inflationary strategy and this, together with the government's failure to tackle the fiscal deficit and errors of execution, led to a new upsurge in inflation shortly after the election. Two further stabilisation plans, the so-called Bresser and Summer Plans, were subsequently implemented, but the total discredit brought to the Sarney administration by the failure of the Cruzado and the lack of political support for the proposed new measures meant that the plans had no realistic chance of succeeding.

From the collapse of the Cruzado Plan in late 1986 until the inauguration of Fernando Collor de Melo in March 1990, the economy deteriorated sharply. At this time Brazil was on the verge of hyperinflation, with inflation running at 81 per cent a month.[52] A new radical heterodox plan, the Plano Collor, was set in place on the day of Collor's inauguration. Amongst the plan's key initiatives was a freeze on all financial assets to reduce the economy's liquidity. Prices were frozen, indexation mechanisms were attenuated and thousands of public employees were laid off in an attempt to cut the public deficit. In contrast to Sarney, Collor also sought to introduce fundamental changes in the model of development. He proposed a far-reaching programme of reforms particularly in the areas of trade liberalisation, reduction of state intervention in the economy and privatisation of state assets.[53]

The Plano Collor, however, followed a similar path of the ill-fated Cruzado: a drastic and rapid fall in inflation for a short period after which it surged again, forcing the government to implement a new plan (Collor II) with a much lower credibility threshold. In 1992, President Collor, some of his relatives and a number of his closest associates faced serious allegations of corruption. Fighting for political survival, the government effectively abandoned attempts to pursue economic reform, seeking instead to use public-sector resources to buy political support to prevent the President's impeachment. Political uncertainty and the loss of confidence in the ability of the government to maintain macroeconomic equilibrium led to a resurgence of speculative pressures and inflation rose to 25 per cent per month. Amidst noisy but peaceful demonstrations by students, lawyers and intellectuals, President Collor was forced to step down in October 1992 and resigned when he was about to be impeached in December the same year. His vice president, Itamar Franco, was sworn into office.

The accession of Franco inaugurated a new government whose provisional character was reinforced by the faltering leadership demonstrated by the new head of state. This was expressed by frequent changes in ministerial responsibilities, particularly in the crucial Finance and Planning Ministries, which seriously increased political and economic uncertainty. An economic nationalist rather than a moderniser, Franco placed economic growth, lowering interest rates and attacking poverty as higher priorities than attacking inflation or pushing ahead with the programme of privatisation and other structural reforms. Divisions within his government, lack of parliamentary support for fiscal reform and the government's decision to award wage increases of a rate higher than inflation in the public sector resulted in an increase in the budget deficit which had been reduced by Collor.

With inflation running at 2,148.4 per cent in 1993, Franco appointed Senator Fernando Henrique Cardoso from the left-of-centre Partido da Social Democracia Brasileira (PSDB, Brazilian Social Democracy Party) as Finance Minister. Under Cardoso's guidance, the Government adopted a new economic stabilisation plan, the Plano Real. Launched in March 1994, the Real was, between 1994 and 1998 the country's most successful stabilisation plan since the 1960s. In contrast with previous stabilisation initiatives, the Plano Real was notable for its transparency regarding the measures to be adopted and the timing of their implementation. The plan ruled out the use of price freezes, intervention in contracts or any other type of drastic or unexpected action. In its initial stage, the plan's main strategy was the creation of a fictitious unit of account, the Unidade Real de Valor (URV, Real unit of value), to break inflationary expectations, followed in July 1994 by the introduction of a new monetary unit (the real) that was pegged to the US dollar as an anchor to stabilise prices. The results were immediate and spectacular, both economically and politically. Despite the strong demand that followed the introduction of the real, the monthly inflation rate fell from close to 50 per cent before July to around 2 per cent in the period from August to December. In a matter of weeks, the popularity of Cardoso (who was by then a presidential candidate) jumped from more than 20 points behind his main rival to a commanding lead in opinion polls, resulting in his comprehensive electoral victory in the October 1994 presidential election with 54 per cent of the vote, defeating his nearest rival Luis Inácio Lula da Silva by some 24 points.

Cardoso's success in launching the real and his impressive electoral victory gave him a strong mandate for change. There was widespread expectation that the Cardoso presidency would lead to a new era of political and economic modernisation.[54] The new regime began its efforts to amend the 1988 Constitution and to further liberalise the economy. Shortly after taking office in January 1995, the President sent Congress a set of proposals for constitutional amendments aimed at opening the path to privatisation and economic modernisation. The reforms favoured greater participation for direct foreign investment, especially in the soon to be privatised state enterprises and in public service concessions. The amendments also lifted barriers to domestic and foreign capital participation in the areas of petroleum, navigation, natural gas and telecommunications.

Helped by a booming economy and the President's prestige, the first batch of reforms were approved by Congress (with some modifications) during the first nine months of the new administration. After a slow start, the privatisation programme gathered momentum in 1997 and 1998 with the sale of the giant mining company Vale do Rio Doce and the first electrical power-generating plants, as well as the telecommunications holding Telebrás. Regulatory agencies were created to oversee the petroleum, electricity and telecommunications industries, which had formerly been state monopolies.[55] Between 1990 until the end of 1998 the privatisation programme had raised over $50 billion at federal and state levels. More than eighty firms were transferred to the private sector over the period.[56]

However, the first Cardoso administration faced important obstacles to deepening economic reform. Under the umbrella of 'coalition presidentialism', the government depended on a six-party alliance for support in Congress. Leading the coalition was Cardoso's own PSDB and the conservative *Partido da Frente Liberal* (PFL, Liberal Front Party). Although the government had a comfortable majority on paper, party fragmentation, a lack of discipline and entrenched *fisiologismo* meant that majorities were never secure and needed to be renegotiated for each vote. Majorities were particularly difficult to secure for constitutional amendments which require three-fifths of the votes for their approval and are subject to a complex parliamentary procedure. This proved to be the case with a further package of constitutional reforms, including the reform of the public administration, social security and tax systems. The reforms were sent to Congress in early 1996 and became bogged down in Parliament for almost four years. The Government claimed the delays were natural in a complex political system. However, delays in the approval of the administrative and social security reforms cost the Federal Government dearly. Without the reforms it had no legal powers to reduce the heavy and inefficient bureaucracy or to overhaul the generous public-sector pension system. Moreover, the work of Congress in 1996 and early 1997 was dominated by the discussion of a constitutional reform to allow President Cardoso to stand for re-election, which further delayed the treatment of the other reforms.

Cardoso was duly re-elected as President of Brazil in October 1998, largely due to the enduring popularity of the real, which in 1998 brought inflation down to its lowest level in over 40 years (2.6 per cent). However, the continuous high budget and current account deficits made the economy increasingly vulnerable to external events. The collapse of the Russian economy in August 1998 triggered a massive capital flight which resulted in the loss of $24 billion of the country's international reserves in the last quarter of the year. In a vain attempt to shore up the real the Government agreed with the International Monetary Fund a severe fiscal adjustment in exchange for a $41.5 billion financial assistance package. The IMF agreement, however, proved unable to restore the international markets' confidence in the Brazilian economy. In January 1999, facing further losses in its international reserves, the Government was forced to devalue the real less than two weeks after Cardoso's inauguration of his second presidency on 1 January.

What is the balance of the Brazilian economy in the 1990s? After significantly improving in the second half of the decade, the Brazilian economy ended the 1990s as it started: in economic recession. The drastic fall in inflation since the introduction of the real was an important achievement, which brought not only economic benefits but also significant political and social stability. Incoming direct investment has risen substantially and was estimated to have reached $22 billion in 1998 up from U$ 18.5 billion in 1997 and more than double the recorded sum for 1995–96[57]. However, the Government's failure to bring the public accounts under control, which contributed the collapse of the real, has put in jeopardy the gains in the fight against inflation and incurred a heavy price in terms of falling economic growth at the turn of the century. Economic growth in the 1990s has been volatile and well below Brazil's post-war average. Between 1991 and 1998 Brazil grew at an estimated average of 2.7 per cent a year, higher than the 1.3 per cent recorded in the 1980s, but still below the Latin American average of 3.3 per cent and much lower than the country's 1970s average of 9.4 per cent.[58]

Underlying the statistics there have been significant long-term changes in the country's economic model. The old developmentalist model which still commanded strong political support in the late 1980s, as shown by the 1989 Constitution, has now lost its hegemony which is reflected in policy changes: external tariffs in the late 1990s were a fraction of those at the beginning of the decade. Privatisation gathered pace in the second half of the decade to become one of the largest programmes in the developing world. Moreover, the private sector has undergone a far-reaching process of economic modernisation, making its products more competitive in the international market. However, even if the parameters of ideological consensus have shifted in favour of a more market-oriented economy, the debate about the role of the state is far from settled. The Brazilian state is still much more interventionist than other Latin American states. While there is no way back to the old Vargas legacy, important political arguments remain unsettled on issues such as industrial policy, the further opening-up of the economy, the role of the state's development banks and, above all, social policy.

There is still much progress to be made to fulfill the country's development potential. Arguably, by its very nature, democracy is not the best political shell for radical economic reform. In contemporary Latin America, many governments have sought to bypass resistance to reform through the concentration of power in neopopulist-style rulers who have promoted swift reform with little regard for the rules of parliamentary procedure. Neopopulism, however, failed in Brazil under Collor de Melo. In contrast to Collor's strategy of imposing reform with a maximum autonomy from the country's political parties, President Cardoso has sought to work within the system rather than from its outside, yet political fragmentation, the diversity of regional and economic interests and the persistence of *fisiologismo* have made reform a protracted affair.

At the heart of the government's difficulties to achieve sustainable growth are enduring fiscal and current account deficits which constrain economic growth and endanger economic stability. The high public deficit is indicative of the political constraints that still affect the performance of the Brazilian economy, particularly the weight of special interests within and outside the state and the unsolved issue of the balance of financial resources and spending responsibilities between the federal and state governments. Until the deficit is brought under control, the economy will remain fragile and vulnerable to external shocks. In the absence of fiscal consolidation, stop-go cycles – like the ones experienced in 1995, 1997–98 and 1999–2000 – will continue to hamper economic growth.[59]

How have the economic changes of the second half of the 1990s affected poverty and inequality in Brazil? Initially the massive fall in inflation which followed the implementation of the Plano Real contributed to a significant reduction in the number of poor. According to a study by Rocha, the percentage of people living under the poverty line declined from 42 per cent to 28 per cent between 1994 and 1996.[60] However, once the redistributive benefits of the permanent drop in inflation are discounted and the effects of the end of the century recession are taken into account the impact of the Cardoso governments economic policies on poverty and inequality has been extremely limited. The models' reliance on high rates of economic growth as the main tool for the reduction of poverty requires much higher growth rates than those registered in the second half of the 1990s to make a significant dent on the country's social deficit. Moreover, volatile economic growth and industrial restructuring have led to a steep growth in unemployment and informal employment, widening the gap between those who have access to social security and the large number of Brazilians who are excluded from the benefits of the country's considerable wealth and deprived of social rights. Volatile and insufficient economic growth since democratisation has not provided a strong enough springboard to tackle the country's massive problems of inequality. According to the World Bank, in

1994 51.3 per cent of total income was concentrated in the richest 10 per cent of the population, whereas the poorest 20 per cent saw their share restricted to 2.1 per cent. Life expectancy at birth is higher in some countries which have a fraction of Brazil's average per capita income.[61]

Poverty and inequality are deeply rooted in the country's history and politics. Even the post-war decades of high economic growth benefited the poor in a limited way. High concentration of landownership and the legacy of slavery still affect rural poverty and racial inequality.[62] The distribution of human capital, particularly in the field of education, has been a major contributing factor to the country's socio- economic disparities. Gross socio-economic inequalities divide the country regionally as well as socially. The North-east consistently has the worst performance for per capita income, life expectancy, literacy rate, infant mortality and absolute poverty, followed by the North and the Centre-West, while the South and the South-East compete for the highest position in social development.[63]

No government can be expected to reverse this state of affairs within the time limits of its mandate. The country's social problems require a concerted effort over a long period. However, the weight of long-term social factors on poverty and inequality has been compounded by the democratic governments' failure to take appropriate measures to significantly reverse this trend. Although international comparisons show that the magnitude of social expenditure in Brazil is comparable to those of other countries at similar levels of development, the consequences of social expenditure on the quality of life of the poor have been comparatively less effective. Poor targeting and inefficient allocation of resources are behind this failure. According to a 1988 study by the World Bank, while only 20 per cent of all public-sector social expenditure is allocated to the poorest 41 per cent of the population, 34 per cent is allocated to higher-income groups even though the latter group represents only 16 per cent of the total population.[64] Moreover, in the 1980s, the combination of erratic economic growth and high inflation led to an increase in both poverty and inequality, reversing the trend of the 1970s.[65]

By way of a conclusion

Brazil has been a late and reluctant convert to the free-market economic revolution that swept Latin America in the second half of the 1980s. While the economy improved in the second half of the 1990s, economic growth has trailed behind that of other major Latin American economies and is well below its post-war trend. To understand the reasons for the relatively slow pace of economic reform it is necessary to look beyond narrow economic indicators and set economic policy within the broader political and institutional framework in which democratic politics operate. This chapter has explored three broad clusters of factors which contribute to explain Brazil's economic performance under democracy. The first refers to the political, institutional and ideological legacy of the developmental state. For over forty years the country remained anchored to the legacy of the statist model of economic development first laid down by Getulio Vargas. This developmentalist legacy was not just politico-ideological but also institutional, as powerful political interests have remained entrenched in the very same state institutions in need of reform.

The second cluster of factors that have affected economic reform are related to the working of the political system. The return to democracy brought with it a deconcentration of power away from the federal state and the Executive towards a wider plurality of political actors both within an outside the state. As such, the deconcentration of power is a healthy aspect of democratic politics, but in the specific context of contemporary Brazilian politics, it left open some of the fault lines of the country's political system. The President is still the single most important actor, but the power of the Executive and the high bureaucracy that are at the core of the federal state are more conducive to the initiation of economic policy from the top than to its long-term sustainability. Governing the country requires the support of Parliament, state governors and other significant political actors. It also necessitates the building of strong state institutions able to establish a non-predatory relationship with civil society. But stable political support and consolidated institutions are not yet characteristics of Brazilian politics. In the absence of political reform, parties remain fragmented, regionally divided and vulnerable to the influence of special interests, making it extremely difficult for the Executive to form a stable parliamentary majority.

A third obstacle to economic reform in Brazil is the way traditional political practices of *fisiologismo*, personalism and patronage have survived under democracy. Cardoso's relative success in advancing economic reform has been the result of his government's ability to restore the authority and the relative unity of the state. Paradoxically, however, success has been achieved through the appeal to 'old politics' as a mean of gathering support for the reforms. The government's majority was grounded in a broad multi-party alliance, which incorporates, in a delicate balance, traditional regional political bosses with modern-minded politicians. The alliance was held together by the success of the *Plano Real* but also by the President's ability to operate within the system and allocate state resources in exchange for political support; the politics of *fisiologismo*. The piecemeal progress of economic reform shows that even governments with a strong parliamentary majority, such as the Cardoso administration, are subject to gridlock and permanent bargaining, a characteristic of a political system with weak political parties and strong regional, state and local interests.

Finally, it should be stressed that some of the key features that affect economic development are also constitutive of Brazil's democratic deficit. The coexistence of an active citizenship and a vigorous civil society with hierarchical, personalist and legally unaccountable forms of exercising political power is a symptom of the lack of universality of democratic concepts of citizenship, equality before the law and universal judicial accountability. This constitutes the weak link in the 'citizenship-creating chain' and is as central to the consolidation of democracy as to the requirements of a modern economy. When economic inequality reaches the extremes it has in Brazil, it unavoidably spills over to matters of equality before the law which are at the heart of democracy. Moreover, extreme levels of poverty and inequality are linked to high levels of urban violence in the country's main cities in which the culture of 'paralegality' thrives. This creates a climate of fear and demands for strong police action which is behind the widespread violations of human rights associated with the so-called police war against crime.[66] This is why putting an end to gross political and economic inequalities, in order for an inclusive society to become the foundation for stable economic development and a modern and fair democracy, is the task that Brazil faces on the eve of the twenty-first century.

Appendix: Main political parties

Partido do Movimento Democrático Brasileiro (PMDB, Brazilian Democratic Movement Party)

The PMDB was created in the early years of the military regime as a legal outlet of opposition to the government. The party played an important role in the process of transition to democracy and has been the largest party in Congress since Brazil's return to democracy. Situated at the centre of the political spectrum, the party is highly heterogeneous and has very little internal discipline or ideological coherence. In the 1998 parliamentary election the party obtained 82 seats in the Chamber of Deputies and 27 seats in the Senate. The PMDB was part of the Cardoso coalition government and had three representatives in the cabinet.

Partido da Frente Liberal (PFL, Liberal Front Party)

The PFL stems from a split of the pro-military government Partido Democratico Social (PDS, Social Democratic Party) in 1984. It is a centre-right party. Its political stronghold is in the underdeveloped north-east of the country and it has been accused of appealing to traditional political practices like patronage to gather electoral support. The PFL had the largest number of seats in Congress: in the 1998 election it elected 106 deputies and 20 Senators. The party supported the presidential candidacy of Fernando Henrique Cardoso in 1994 and 1998 and was a key member of his coalition government. It had two representatives in the cabinet.

Partido da Social Democracia Brasileira (PSDB, Brazilian Social Democracy Party)

The PSDB was set up in 1988 by a group of dissidents from the PMDB. It was broadly modelled on the European social democratic tradition, although it has no organised working-class support. A moderate centrist party, the PSDB is strong in the state of São Paulo and other states of the South-East, as well as in the north-eastern state of Ceará. The victory of its Presidential candidate, Fernando Henrique Cardoso, in the 1994 and 1998 elections gave the party a considerable political boost. The PSDB was the second largest party in Congress (99 Deputies and 16 Senators in the 1998 election).

Partido Progresista Brasileiro (PPB, Progressive Brazilian Party)
The PPB is made up of the remnants of the party set up by the military as the political base of support for the military government. Since its origins, what is now the PPB has changed its name several times and has undergone multiple splits as well as mergers with other parties. The PPB is on the political right. Although not an original member of the coalition government, the PPB supported the government of President Cardoso. The PPB had 60 seats in the Chamber of Deputies and 5 in the Senate, making it the fourth largest party in Congress.

Partido dos Trabalhadores (PT, Workers' Party)
The PT was created in 1980 by trade union leaders, activists from the progressive branch of the Catholic Church and members of small left-wing groups. The PT is the most important left-wing party in Brazil. It is closely associated with the main trade-union umbrella organisation the Central Única de Trabalhadores (CUT, United Workers' Congress). Its main leader is a former metalworkers' union leader, Luiz Inácio Lula da Silva, who ran for president three times. The PT had 58 seats in the Chamber of Deputies and 7 in the Senate. It acted as the main opposition party to the Cardoso government.

Partido Democrático Trabalhista (PDT, Democratic Labour Party)
The PDT originated as the old Partido Trabalhista Brasileiro (PTB, Brazilian Workers' Party), set up by Getulio Vargas in the 1940s and disbanded by the military. Its main leader is the veteran former governor of Rio Grande do Sul and Rio de Janeiro, Leonel Brizola, one of the most prominent political figures in Brazil since the 1960s. The PDT is on the political left. In 1998 the party elected 25 Representatives and 2 Senators.

Notes

1 There is a vast literature on democratisation in Latin America. See, among others, G. O'Donnell, P. Schmitter and L. Whitehead (eds), *Transitions From Authoritarian Rule: Comparative Perspectives* (Baltimore, John Hopkins University Press, 1986) ; J. Malloy and M. Seligson (eds), *Authoritarians and Democrats: Regime Transition in Latin America* (Pittsburgh, Pittsburgh University Press, 1987); L. Diamond, J. Linz and S. Lipset (eds), *Democracy in Developing Countries: Latin America* (Boulder and London, Lynne Rienner, 1989); S. Mainwaring, G. O'Donnell and A. Valenzuela (eds), *Issues in Democratic Consolidation: The New South American Democracies in Cmparative Perspective* (South Bend, Notre Dame Press, 1992).
2 Donald Share and Scott Mainwaring consider 'transition through transaction': cases in which

the authoritarian regime initiates the transition, establishes some limits to political changes, and remains a relatively significant electoral force during the transition. More specifically, the term 'transaction' connotes an unequal negotiation between elites of the authoritarian regime and the democratic opposition in which the leaders of the outgoing authoritarian regime take the initiative in beginning liberalisation. During most of the process the outgoing elite remains in a position to significantly influence the course of political change. D. Share and S. Mainwaring, 'Transitions Through Transaction: Democratization in Brazil and Spain', in W. A. Selcher (ed.), *Political Liberalization in Brazil* (Boulder and London, Westview, 1986), p. 175.

3 Most notably the new civilian president, José Sarney, had been president of the *Partido Democrático Social*, (PDS), the party set up by the military to support their regime.

4 M. Chaui, 'A quand la démocratie au Brésil?', in Centre National de la Recherche Scientifique, *Quel avenir pour la démocratie en Amérique Latine?* (Paris, Editions du CNRS, 1989), p. 185.

5 P. Cammack, 'Resurgent Democracy: Threat and Promise', *New Left Review*, 157 (1986). Furthermore, as Daniel Levine reminds us, negotiations, balance and accommodation are the essence of liberal democracy, and the stress on pacts as antidemocratic manipulation ignores the many ties that bind the leaders who make the pacts to their followers, and thus obscures the reasons why the latter give them a grant of legitimacy. D. Levine, 'Paradigm Lost: Dependency to Democracy', *World Politics*, 40 (1987).

6 For an overview of the military period see T. Skidmore, *The Politics of Military Rule in Brazil, 1964–85* (New York, Oxford University Press, 1988).

7 See W. Selcher, 'Contradictions, Dilemmas and Actors in Brazil's *Abertura*, 1979–1985', in Selcher (ed.), *Political Liberalization*; and A. Stepan, *Democratizing Brazil: Problems of Transition and Consolidation* (New York and Oxford, Oxford University Press, 1989).

8 See R. Berins Collier and J. Mahoney, 'Adding Collective Actors to Collective Outcomes: Labor and Recent Democratization in South America and Southern Europe', *Comparative Politics*, 29 (1997); M. H. Moreira Alves, 'Trade Unions in Brazil: A Search for Autonomy and Organization', in E. Epstein (ed.), *Labor, Autonomy and the State in Latin America* (Boston, Unwin Hyman, 1989); M. Keck, *The Workers' Party and Democratization in Brazil* (New Haven, Yale University Press, 1989).

9 In São Paulo and Rio de Janeiro, the country's two largest cities, more than one million people participated in demonstrations requesting direct presidential elections.

10 For the persistence of traditional politics under the military see F. Hagopian, *Traditional Politics and Regime Change in Brazil* (Cambridge, Cambridge University Press, 1996).

11 Sarney was originally the vice-presidential candidate of the elected president Tancredo Neves. Neves fell seriously ill on the days before his inauguration as President. Sarney took office, initially as acting President, and was subsequently confirmed as President upon Neves's untimely death a few weeks later, on 21 April 1985.

12 The new democratic government's initiatives signified the culmination of a process of reinstitutionalisation of the democratic institutions, which began with the political amnesty and restoration of major civil liberties in 1979, and was followed by the political reform of 1980 and the direct congressional and gubernatorial elections of 1982.

13 Constitutional amendment no. 25 of 15 May 1985.

14 For a classical view of the Brazilian political system which stresses the centralising role of the federal government bureaucracy see R. Faoro, *Os donos do poder: formação do patronato político brasileiro* (São Paulo, Editora Globo, 1975). For an alternative view that stresses political and organisational fragmentation see K. Weyland, *Democracy Without Equity: Failures of Reform in Brazil* (Pittsburgh, Pittsburgh University Press, 1996).

15 Vargas ruled Brazil both as a dictator and as a democratically elected president in the periods 1930–45 and 1950–54 respectively.

16 See K. Weyland, 'The Rise and Fall of President Collor and its Impact on Brazilian Democracy', *Journal of Interamerican Studies and World Affairs*, 35:1 (1993).

17 The privatisation of state enterprises during the administration of Fernando Henrique Cardoso has significantly reduced although not completely eliminated the opportunities for patronage

within state enterprises. For the patrimonial aspects of the Brazilian state see R. Roett, *Brazil: Politics in a Patrimonial Society* (New York, Praeger, 1984).

18 The alliance between the military-controlled Executive and technocrats which is at the heart of Guillermo O'Donnell's 'bureaucratic authoritarian model' was inspired by the Brazilian military regime. However, a powerful state technocracy has been a characteristic not just of the military but of the entire post-war Brazilian state. See K. Sikkink, *Ideas and Institutions* (Ithaca, Cornell University Press, 1991); and G. O'Donnell, *Modernization and Bureaucratic Authoritarianism* (Berkeley, University of California Press, 1973).

19 For a study of the hegemony of the Finance and Planning ministries in economic decision-making see L. Sola, 'Heterodox Shock in Brazil: Técnicos, Politicians and Democracy', *Journal of Latin American Studies*, 23 (1991).

20 See L. Sola, 'The State, Structural Reform and Democratization in Brazil', in W. C. Smith, C. H. Acuña and E. Gamarra (eds), *Democracy, Markets and Structural Reform in Latin America* (Miami, North–South Center and Transaction, 1993).

21 Against those who argue that the 1988 Constitution has shifted power from the presidency in favour of Congress, Figueiredo and Limongy claim that the new Constitution has not substantially eroded the Executive's ascendancy over Congress. According to these scholars, the Executive's power over Congress is grounded in the Presidency's constitutional power to issue law-like presidential decrees *(medidas provisórias)* and on his/her political influence over the party leaders who, collectively, control the working of Congress. See A. C. Figueiredo and F. Limongi, 'Mudança constitucional, desempenho do Legislativo e consolidação institucional', *Revista de Ciências Sociais*, 29:10 (1995).

22 S. Mainwaring, 'Presidentialism, Multipartidism and Democracy: The Difficult Combination', *Comparative Political Studies*, 26 (1993).

23 For an overview of Brazil's party system see P. Cammack, 'Brazilian Party Politics, 1945–87: Continuities and Discontinuities', in V. Randall (ed.), *Political Parties in the Third World* (London, Sage, 1988); and S. Mainwaring, 'Brazil: Weak Parties, Feckless Democracy', in S. Mainwaring and T. Scully (eds), *Building Democratic Institutions: Party Systems in Latin America* (Stanford, Stanford University Press, 1995).

24 According to Brazil's electoral system, known as 'open-list proportional representation', parties do not rank candidates in closed lists. Voters choose individual candidates rather than parties. Votes are then added up to determine the number of seats won by each party. The election of a given candidate is dependent on the candidate's performance relative to other candidates of the same party. Thus the system promotes intra-party competition and individualism over party organisation and discipline. See T. Power, 'Why Brazil Slept: The Search for Political Institutions, 1985–1997', paper prepared for delivery at the meeting of the Latin American Studies Association, Guadalajara, Mexico, 1997; S. Mainwaring, 'Brazilian Party Underdevelopment in Comparative Perspective', *Political Science Quarterly*, 107:4 (1992); and M. D. G. Kinzo, 'Party Politics, Executive–Legislative Relations and the Constitutional Reforms in Brazil', paper presented at the conference on 'The Economic, Social and Political Consequences of the Stabilisation Plan in Brazil', London, Institute of Latin American Studies (ILAS), 1996.

25 Kinzo, 'Party Politics'.

26 S. H. Abranches, 'O dilema político-institucional brasileiro', in J. P. Dos Reis Velloso (ed.), *Modernização política e desenvolvimento* (Rio de Janeiro, José Olympio Editora, 1990).

27 The states have control over all matters which the Constitution does not specifically attribute to other branches of the state. State governors are powerful political figures both nationally and within their own states. The governors of the largest and richest states, like São Paulo, administer budgets larger than those of many small Latin American nations.

28 For an analysis of *fisiologismo* see C. Barreto, 'Physiologism: A Political Disease Undermining Democratic and Economic Developments in Brazil', M.Sc. dissertation, Department of Government, London School of Economics and Political Science, 1997; and W. G. Dos Santos, 'Modernização política: Algumas questões pós-Constituinte', in Dos Reis Velloso (ed.), *Modernização política*.

29 Between 1988 and 1993, the extra revenue given to state and local governments rose from 8 to 12 per cent of GDP. See J. Martínez-Lara, *Building Democracy in Brazil: The Politics of Constitutional Change, 1985–95* (London, Macmillan, 1996).

30 S. H. Abranches, 'O dilema político-institucional'.

31 A. Stepan, *Rethinking Military Politics: Brazil and the Southern Cone* (Princeton, Princeton University Press, 1988), p. 5.

32 See D. Lehman, 'Religious Revolutions', in F. Wilson and F. Stepputat (eds), *People in Politics: Debating Democracy in Latin America* (Copenhagen, Centre for Development Research, 1994).

33 Brazil's labour movement is divided into three competing umbrella organisations: the *Central Única dos Trabalhadores* (CUT, United Workers' Congress), the *Central General dos Trabajadores* (CGT, General Workers' Congress) and *Força Sindical*. The CUT is the largest and most important of the three. Its origins lay in the metalworkers of São Paulo state, who, in the late 1970s and early 1980s, managed to shut down the powerful automobile industry for several weeks, heralding the renaissance of the union movement after its suppression by the military governments. The metalworkers' leader, Luiz Inácio Lula da Silva, became the CUT's first president and, later, the leader of the PT, Brazil's largest left-wing party.

34 L. Payne, *Brazilian Industrialists and Democratic Change* (Baltimore, Johns Hopkins University Press, 1993).

35 Weyland, *Democracy Without Equity*.

36 R. Schneider, *Brazil: Culture and Politics in a New Industrial Powerhouse* (Boulder, Westview, 1996).

37 See Martínez Lara, *Building Democracy*. An example of the more institutional approach of the social movements in the 1990s was their contribution to the drafting of Brazil's first National Plan for the Protection of Human Rights (PNDH) in 1995 and 1996.

38 Personalist politics form networks based on particularistic exchange and affective ties. In any large-scale society, these networks tend to assume a pyramidal form. The most widespread variant of personalism is clientelism, defined as system of personal relations between individuals of different status that is based on the unequal but reciprocal exchange of particularistic benefits and protection for obedience and support (see Weyland, *Democracy without Equity*, p. 33). The term 'patrimonalism' refers to the creation and maintenance of a highly flexible and paternalistic public order, dedicated to its own preservation and the preservation of the unity of the state. The concept emphasises the qualities of centralisation and authority. The patrimonial state is first and foremost a bureaucratic state in that the authority of public order is maintained by the administrative apparatus of the central government. See Roett, *Brazil*, pp. 19–21.

39 Hagopian, *Traditional Politics*.

40 R. Roett and S. Kaufmann (eds), *Brazil Under Cardoso* (Boulder, Lynne Rienner, 1997), p. 31 .

41 Weyland, *Democracy Without Equity*, pp. 144–5.

42 F. Panizza and A. Barahona de Brito, 'The Politics of Human Rights in Democratic Brazil', *Democratization*, 5:4 (1998).

43 So, for instance, in order to gain parliamentary approval for administrative and social security amendments, key elements of the government's economic modernisation plan, the Executive has had to resort to pork-barrel allocation of budgetary funds in exchange for political support.

44 For an extensive analysis of this point see Panizza and Barahona de Brito, 'Politics of Human Rights'.

45 For an overview of Brazil's economic history see W. Baer, *The Brazilian Economy: Growth and Development* (Westport, Praeger, 1995).

46 P. Malan and R. Bonelli, 'The Success of Growth Policies in Brazil', in S. Teitel (ed.), *Toward a New Development Strategy for Latin America* (Washington, DC, Inter-American Development Bank (IABD), 1992).

47 For an overview of the Vargas era and the years leading to the 1964 military coup see T. Skidmore, *Politics in Brazil, 1930–1964: An Experiment in Democracy* (New York, Oxford University Press, 1967).

48 Sola: 'Heterodox Shock'; P. Rabello de Castro and M. Ronci, 'Sixty Years of Populism in Brazil',

in R. Dornbusch and S. Edwards (eds), *The Macroeconomics of Populism in Latin America* (Chicago and London, University of Chicago Press, 1991).

49 Sola, 'Heterodox Shock', p. 168.

50 A tendency to perpetuate inflation by the actions and beliefs of economic agents through the widespread adoption of formal and informal indexation of prices and contracts. See R. Macedo and F. Barbosa, 'Brazil: Instability and Macroeconomic Policies', in M. J. F. Willumsen and E. Gianetti da Fonseca (eds), *The Brazilian Economy: Structure and Performance in Recent Decades* (Miami, North–South Center, 1996), p. 8.

51 Sola, 'Heterodox Shock', p. 81.

52 Baer, *Brazilian Economy*, p. 182.

53 Macedo and Barbosa, 'Brazil: Instability and Macroeconomic Policies'.

54 Fernando Henrique Cardoso was one of the founder members of the left-of-centre PSDB which split from the PMDB. The PSDB founders were strongly critical of the personalism and clientelism which pervaded the PMDB. Before entering politics Cardoso was one of Latin America's leading social scientists, having written a celebrated book on dependency theory and other development issues.

55 UN Economic Commission for Latin America and the Caribbean (ECLAC), *Preliminary Overview of the Economy of Latin America and the Caribbean 1997 and 1998* (Santiago, ECLAC, 1997), p. 4.

56 *Folha de São Paulo*, 17 May 1998.

57 *Folha de São Paulo*, 17 May 1998 and ELLAC Preliminary overview 1998.

58 For the 1980s and 1990s, see ECLAC, *Preliminary Overview 1997*. For the 1970s, see IDB, *Economic and Social Progress in Latin America 1996* (Washington, DC, IDB, 1996).

59 The Brazilian economy's performance for 1997 was severely affected by the deepening of the crisis in Asian financial markets in late October. The sharp cutback in financial inflows from abroad and the outflow of large sums of capital drove down prices on the country's exchanges and eroded its international reserves. In response to this emergency situation, the government doubled real interest rates and launched a drastic fiscal austerity plan designed to cut the public sector's deficit by $18 billion (2.3 per cent of GDP). The measures aimed at cooling down the economy brought GDP growth from an early estimate of 3.5 per cent to 3 per cent in 1997 and around 0.5 per cent in 1998 (ECLAC, *Preliminary Overview 1997*).

60 G. Schönleitner, 'Poverty and Inequality in Brazil: Obstacles to Economic Development and Democratic Consolidation?', mimeo, London School of Economics, 1997.

61 Malan and Bonelli, 'Success of Growth Policies', p. 48.

62 Brazil has one of the most concentrated and stable land-tenure structures in the world. Census data reveal that only 1 per cent of all rural properties are made up of more than 1,000 hectares, yet these holdings make up about 45 per cent of the total area. Properties with less than 100 hectares represent 90 per cent of the total number of properties; yet constitute only 20 per cent of the total area. (M. C. Cacciamali, 'The Growing Inequality in Income Distribution in Brazil', in Willumsen and Gianetti da Fonseca (eds), *Brazilian Economy*, p. 228).

63 Regional differences have declined in the 1990s as the South-East's participation in total GDP has declined since its 1970s peak and that of the North and North-East rose in the 1990s. Nevertheless, the improved performance of the comparatively less developed regions does not make it likely that their absolute position will be altered significantly in the near future (Willumsen and Gianetti da Fonseca (eds), *Brazilian Economy*, pp. 234, 260).

64 World Bank, 1988, cited in Willumsen and Gianetti da Fonseca (eds), *Brazilian Economy*, p. 204).

65 F. Ferreira and J. Litchfield, 'Growing Apart: Inequality and Poverty Trends in Brazil in the 1980s', London School of Economics/Suntory Toyota Centre for Economics and Related Disciplines, *Discussion Paper 23*.

66 Panizza and Barahona de Brito, 'Politics of Human Rights'.

2

Argentina

COLIN M. LEWIS

For the last half-century, Argentinian economics have been characterised as a distributional conflict and Argentinian politics as a quest for hegemony. Powerful economic agents such as business, labour and the state have competed for resources. The political game, in which the political parties, the armed forces, organised labour, the economic elite and the Roman Catholic Church have struggled for ascendancy, reflected institutional stress. In both contests, players recognised the need for change but could not agree on what direction it should take. Thus Argentinian economics and politics became a zero-sum game of consumption versus accumulation and of power versus exclusion. 'Ownership' of political office was a mechanism to secure sectional objectives and deny resources to opponents. It was a game of 'winner takes all', but in the long run, all lost. No single actor was sufficiently powerful to impose a preferred sectoral project on others, nor to contemplate a meaningful accommodation with them. Politics was represented by a sequence of sharp lurches from civilian to military, pragmatic to ideological and business- to labour-dominated administrations, while the economy displayed a tendency to shortening, increasingly volatile cycles. It was a system that was spiralling out of control. Yet, since 1983 elections have occurred regularly and, since 1991, there has been macroeconomic stability. Has a virtuous circle of democracy and growth emerged from the vicious cycle of economic and political violence?

This chapter considers the extent to which – and why – circumstances have changed. Has the restructuring of Argentinian society and polity associated with the new economic policy introduced at the beginning of the decade changed the rules of the game? Does the sequence of elections, which have followed constitutional prescriptions since 1983, and the transition from a Unión Cívica Radical (UCR, Radical Party) to a Partido Justicialista (PJ, commonly known as the Peronist Party) administration in 1989 signal institutional stability and sustainability? Key political events have been the UCR electoral victory in 1983 (the first time since 1946 that the Peronists had been defeated in free elections), the electoral successes of President Carlos Saúl Menem in 1989 and 1995, the Olivos Pact between Menem and former President Raúl Alfonsín in 1994, which facilitated constitutional change that allowed Menem to stand for a second consecutive term in 1995, and the emergence of a third major party, the Frente para el País Solidario (Front for the Solidarity of the Country, FREPASO, originally the Frente Grande), formed to contest Constituent Assembly elections in 1994. Benchmark economic events include bouts of hyperinflation in 1989 and 1990, the introduction of the Convertibility Plan in 1991, the banking crunch and recession triggered by the Mexican 'Tequila' crisis, which began in December 1994, and the departure of Economy Minister Domingo Cavallo in mid-1996.

The chapter adopts a political economy approach: economic policy and the policy-making process will be analysed in terms of the principal actors and the ideologies that shaped them. In order to capture the scale of recent change, reference will be made to the issues that have dominated the policy-making environment over the last two decades and to the long-run growth record. The first section of the chapter presents economic trends that framed (and continue to frame) policy discussions and the behaviour of political actors. The second identifies the main political actors and considers the dynamics of inter- (and intra-) sectoral conflict. The third analyses the content and political outcome of major stabilisation packages essayed in 1976, 1985 and 1991. The final section speculates about future developments.

Background

The nature and significance of the 1991 Convertibility Plan cannot be comprehended without some reference to recent economic history, as is acknowledged by its architects. When the Plan was introduced, President Menem and Economy Minister Cavallo argued that the objective was to break with a discredited development model as well as with failed stabilisation expedients of the past. For Menem, referring to the buoyant performance of the economy in the early twentieth century, the new strategy would enable the country to 'recapture its history'.[1] These sentiments would have been shared by Cavallo, who has made several contributions to the academic discussion about economic performance in the *longue durée*.[2]

By the 1980s, economic volatility had inculcated in Argentinians a sense of policy failure and a fear of imminent institutional collapse. There was, too, an awareness of relative as well as absolute decline. The poor economic performance of the country was marked not only by reference to the historic growth record but also the achievements of other economies. At the beginning of the century, Argentinians had compared their country in positive terms with 'settler' economies such as the USA and Australia or with Western Europe: in the 1980s, unfavourable contrasts were being made with neighbouring republics.[3]

Table 2.1 suggests the extent of the crisis, not least in the 1970s and 1980s. Aggregated data however, mask the degree of structural dislocation and the long gestation of the problem. Averaging, and the periodisation adopted in Table 2.1, disguise the extent of volatility during the second half of the twentieth century, particularly after the 1960s. Annualised output indices register only one year of negative growth between 1900 and 1913. In the turbulent period from 1914 to 1946, inclusive, the economy failed to grow on only eight occasions. In the 1950s and 1960s there were two years of negative growth per decade: in the 1970s three, and in the 1980s five, including 1988, when economic activity contracted by about a quarter.[4]

Table 2.1 *Annual average growth rates, Argentina, 1875–1989 (%)*

(A) Aggregate output		(B) GDP per capita	
1875–1896	3.7	1870–1890	1.9
1896–1912	2.3	1890–1913	2.2
1912–1928	−0.1	1913–1950	0.7
1928–1948	2.3	1950–1973	2.1
1948–1961	0.3	1973–1989	−2.2
1961–1976	2.3		
1976–1987	−1.8		

Source: (A) R. Cortés Conde, 'El crecimiento económico de la Argentina en el largo plazo', unpublished paper presented at Carlos III University, Madrid, 26–27 May 1994. (B) A. Maddison, 'Long-run Economic Growth in the European Periphery', unpublished paper presented at the European Historical Economics Society Workshop, La Coruña, 1993. For slightly different published data, see 'A Comparison of Levels of GDP *Per Capita* in Developed and Developing Countries, 1700–1980', *Journal of Economic History*, 43:1 (1983), Table 1.

The relatively positive performance in the immediate post-Second World War period suggested by the above data can also be questioned. Services grew faster than productive-sector output and, as the approximate correspondence between aggregate (1961–76) and per capita (1950–73) data hints, sluggish population growth may have contributed more to the apparently positive per capita performance than productivity gains. This contrasts with the situation at the turn of the century when, despite dramatic rates of population growth, substantial per capita gains were registered. And there was the post-Second World War contrast with Brazil and Mexico captured in Table 2.2. As Argentinian growth per capita slipped against that of Brazil and Mexico, the Argentine was experiencing very low rates of demographic growth while the other countries were undergoing a population explosion. At this point Mexico and Brazil recorded some of the highest rates of population expansion in the Third World. Cortés Conde has observed that the Argentinian conundrum was not an inability to sustain high rates of growth in perpetuity but a failure to realise median levels of performance following a phase of particularly rapid growth. After a development spurt, most economies experience a fall-back in rates of growth. Hence, the critical question is not why very high rates of economic growth were not sustained throughout the twentieth century but why the Argentine proved unable to approximate the long-run growth trajectory of, for example, Canada or even the United Kingdom.[5]

Table 2.2   *Comparative world economic performance: annual average growth rates of GDP per capita (%)*

Period	Argentina	Brazil	Mexico	Australia	Canada	United Kingdom	United States
1900–1913	2.5	1.4	1.8	1.1	3.3	0.7	2.0
1913–1950	0.7	2.0	1.0	0.7	1.5	0.8	1.6
1900–1950	1.2	1.8	1.2	0.8	2.0	0.8	1.7
1950–1973	2.1	3.8	3.1	2.5	2.9	2.5	2.2
1973–1987	–0.8	2.2	0.9	1.5	2.2	1.5	1.5
1950–1987	1.0	3.2	2.3	2.1	2.0	2.2	1.9
1900–1987	1.1	2.4	1.6	1.4	2.3	1.4	1.8

Source: A. Maddison, *The World Economy in the Twentieth Century* (Paris, Organization for Economic Cooperation and Development, 1989) pp. 15, 35.

Table 2.2 captures the slippage of which many Argentinians were only too painfully aware by the 1980s. Ranked second at the beginning of the century, the Argentine came last by the 1980s. Particularly poor performance in the inter-war period and the 1970s and 1980s offset the impact of the growth surge at the beginning of the century to deliver the lowest average in the set for the 1900–87 period as a whole. Argentinian growth per capita was around 76 per cent of the Canadian figure for 1900–13, some 360 per cent of the British and about 165 per cent of the Brazilian. Yet, for 1900–87, cumulative rates were only 48, 79 and 42 per cent respectively of the Canadian, British and Brazilian. Argentinian ranking and the trend in per capita data for each of the substantive sub-periods are equally telling. The consistency with which the Argentine filled the lowest position indicates that difficulties revealed in the 1970s and 1980s may have been deep-seated. Low rates of growth per capita suggest that the country was unable to sustain productivity gains once the impact of a development surge driven by massive factor imports around the turn of the century began to fade. This lends weight to the argument that the problem was structural rather than conjunctural and that it was deep-seated.

The trends in aggregate and per capita data indicate that the country was experiencing a 'productivity crisis', a problem exacerbated during the period of

ISI, when forced transfers of resources into manufacturing constrained production and reduced efficiency in other sectors while contributing little to industrial competitiveness. As indicated, the result was sluggish growth and increasing volatility, and a widening productivity gap with the rest of the world. The extent of this problem is captured by investment rates and difficulties encountered by the Argentine in terms of the level and efficiency of savings. As Table 2.3 shows, levels of investment were highly volatile between 1970 and 1990. Sharp upward swings were registered in the second half of the 1970s: marked downward shifts characterised the mid- and late 1980s. Indeed, rates of capital formation were low for much of the decade. Equally problematic was the return on investment. Long-gestation state projects absorbed a large share of investment and substantial sums were allocated to social infrastructure, which also yielded a low return in the short term. In addition, much capital was squandered. For example, imports of consumption goods and massive arms purchases during the late 1970s (when the dispute with Chile over the Beagle Channel threatened to end in war) had no positive impact on productivity. Relatively high savings rates in the early 1980s underwrote capital flight. Moreover, the above data disguise two significant changes in post-Second World War investment trends. First, the increasing weight of the state as supplier of capital. Second, a growing reliance on foreign savings. The collapse of investment in the 1980s is explained by these factors: namely, the inability of the state to generate savings in the face of economic contraction, capital flight and the drying-up of new foreign investment.

Table 2.3 *Gross domestic investment as a percentage of GDP, Argentina, 1970–90*

1970	21.6	1977	27.2	1984	11.3
1971	21.1	1978	24.4	1985	8.5
1972	20.9	1979	22.7	1986	8.8
1973	18.1	1980	22.2	1987	13.7
1974	19.4	1981	18.8	1988	12.4
1975	25.8	1982	15.9	1989	9.0
1976	26.8	1983	17.3	1990	8.4

Source: IBRD World Tables (various dates). Data differ from issue to issue.

If academic commentators and policy makers focused on savings rates and comparative economic performance, for most Argentinians the principal indicators were inflation (and the impact that price changes had on real incomes and income differentials) and the exchange rate. Inflation and accompanying exchange depreciation were both symptoms and mechanisms of distortions. Above all, they symbolised the conflict between accumulation and consumption and sectoral competition for resources.[6] Between 1975 and 1991, the annual rate of inflation only fell below 100 per cent on two occasions, and was often substantially higher. The result was a demonetisation of the economy: in 1930, the amount of broad money was equivalent to 65 per cent of GDP; in 1990 to 6 per cent.[7] It was this, and the demonstrable failure of a semi-orthodox stabilisation package during the military dictatorship and the heterodox Austral Plan of the Alfonsín period, coupled with the bloodletting of the 1970s, that finally facilitated the introduction of the 1991 Convertibility Plan. There was no alternative: all other expedients had been exhausted and discredited. Distributional conflicts, most graphically manifest in political violence and regime crises, ensured at worst a grudging acceptance of the Cavallo medicine. When Menem came to power, the public-sector accounts had been in deficit for more than three decades.[8] Amongst most social groups and economic sectors there was a dawning recognition that quasi-autarchic interventionist strategies were no longer working and could not be sustained. There was an alliance for economic stability and a near-collective willingness to assume some of the burden of readjustment. Whether all sectors were aware of the full implications of fiscal rectitude, the rolling-back of the state and renewed international insertion are debatable. Arguably, the task of Menem and Cavallo was made somewhat easier because shock trade liberalisation under the military regime and hyperinflation during the Alfonsín government had decimated those sectors most wedded to statism, while at the same time provoking a society-wide anxiety for stability.

The politics of economic instability

For Guido Di Tella, the defining moments in twentieth-century Argentinian political history are the *relatively* peaceful incorporation of the middle classes into the political process during the early decades of the century and of the working class following the Second World War. According to Di Tella, this widening of the political system occurred in a much shorter space of time than in many countries and was accomplished with less disruption. Acknowledging that the process of political opening was neither unilinear nor problem-free, he argues that 'backsliding', such as the oligarchic reaction of the *década infame* (infamous decade, 1930–43), when rigged elections and the politics of proscription (on this occasion the Radical Party) were substituted for the open, democratic system in place after the electoral reforms of 1912, the proscription of Peronism for most of the period between 1955 and 1982 and the 'dirty war' against 'internal subversion' waged with such ferocity between 1975 and 1979 should be considered within an international context. Contrasted with twentieth-century examples of political experiments in Europe associated with fascism and Marxist–Leninism, or earlier challenges to the political status quo such as the French Revolution or American Civil War, Argentinian political institutional adjustment in the twentieth century appears less turbulent and bloody.[9] This is an interesting perspective, though the political reference point for most Argentinians is their recent past rather than world political history since 1789. Perhaps it is a paradox of contemporary Argentinian history that economic comparisons are usually made domestically *and* internationally while political comparisons are almost invariably made internally.

As indicated, there have been three major attempts at stabilisation over the past two decades: first, the programme applied during the last period of military rule (1976–82), the so-called Proceso de Reorganización Nacional (Process of National Reorganisation, commonly known as the *Proceso*); second, the Austral Plan introduced in June 1985 during the Alfonsín presidency; and third, the Convertibility Plan, officially launched on 1 April 1991. By common consensus, the Convertibility Plan marked a profound departure from measures essayed in the 1980s and 1970s, and even earlier, to correct structural economic imbalance. The 1991 Plan could only have been effected in a new political reality. An examination of the content and implementation of these reform projects illuminates the nature of sectional and sectoral tensions in Argentinian politics. As in other societies, moments of economic crisis are associated with political distress.[10] Yet Di Tella and Dornbush caution against a crude association of civilian and populist governments with economic expansion and consumptionism, and military regimes with 'economic correction' and accumulation.[11] This suggests that, although a powerful influence, inter-sectoral conflict does not wholly explain the politics of instability.

The post-Second World War power constellation consisted of the party-political establishments (the political class), business and finance, labour, the military and the Roman Catholic Church.[12] Clearly, these groupings are not mutually exclusive: individuals may be located in more than one of them. These corporations, however, are far from homogeneous. Potash and others have demonstrated the extent of inter-service rivalry and disunity within individual branches of the armed forces. There have been sharp differences on issues such as the necessity or otherwise of military intervention. Some sections of the forces have argued for action in defence of the constitutional order at the same moment as others have viewed a coup as the means of dismantling liberal-democratic institutions. Legalists and constitutionalists clashed with corporatists and pragmatists.[13] Military regimes, like those headed by Generals Pedro Eugenio Aramburu (1955) and Alejandro A. Lanusse (1971–73), saw their function in terms of house-cleaning and the preparation of institutions for a restoration of civilian government. Others, notably the administration headed by General Reynaldo Benito Antonio Bignone (1982), and possibly also that of Lanusse, were charged by colleagues with the task of facilitating an orderly (if not an honourable) return to the barracks. Yet other juntas, particularly those presided over by Generals Juan Carlos Onganía (1966–70), Jorge Rafael Videla (1976–81) and Leopoldo Fortunato Galtieri (1981–82), envisaged a lengthy period of rule by the military in order to effect a profound transformation of economy and society.

Moreover, if important sectors of the army high command were committed to constitutionalism, the preference of their navy colleagues generally appeared to be in favour of the technocratic and the authoritarian. There have been several moments of spectacular inter- (and intra-)service rivalry and a general collapse of military cohesion. During the civilian presidency of Arturo Frondizi (1958–62), different factions of the Army, allied with elements of the Navy and Air Force, engaged in open warfare: at the height of the crisis of the Revolución Argentina ('Argentine Revolution') in 1970/71, three different army generals held the presidency in a nine-month period. Following defeat in the Falklands war (1982), the navy and the air force withdrew from the ruling military junta, leaving the army to soldier on alone in search of an accommodation with civilian politicians. Military budget cuts under Alfonsín, which fell disproportionately on the army, and fiscal discipline and privatisation under Menem, have further weakened and divided the armed forces.[14] Only two issues now unite the military: first, anxiety to draw a line under the events of the 'dirty war'; and second, a defence of the military budget (and military honour) against further savaging by civilians.

Business, too, was fragmented with fault-lines changing over time. Conflicts of interest associated with scale and sector were reinforced by the fairly consistent application of ISI policies (though with differing degrees of intensity) from the 1940s to the 1970s. Divisions were epitomised and exacerbated by the proliferation of organisations representing business. Sub-sector unity proved illusive even for the powerful pastoral group, particularly as prices were squeezed and access to markets threatened during the inter-war period. As Smith and others indicate, after the 1930s tensions grew between fatteners and breeders (and between very large-scale cattlemen and those with more modest, though by no means small, estates). Hence, the authority and leadership role of the Sociedad Rural Argentina (SRA, Argentine Rural Society), dominated by *bonaerense estancieros* (Buenos Aires landowners), was challenged by the Confederación de Asociaciones Rurales de Buenos Aires y La Pampa (CARBAP, Confederation of Rural Associations of Buenos Aires and La Pampa), a federation of autonomous local agencies that drew membership from medium-sized landowners and tenants engaged in ranching and farming across more diverse regions of the *pampa húmeda* (wet pampa) and the *pampa seca* (dry pampa).[15] Later, the Confederación Rural Argentina (CRA, Argentine Rural Confederation) was formed to represent small farmers. Market changes in the late 1960s and 1970s further confounded cooperation: crisis in the pastoral sector associated with the closure of foreign markets and conflict with meat-packing houses was offset by the growth of cereal exports.

While rural business organisations cooperated from time to time, particularly to protest against tax measures that were viewed as penal by all sections of the community, their interests were as often as not distinct. These divisions were sustained and many times exploited by government. But it was forced industrialisation that intensified divisions within the agricultural sector and between agriculturalists and other segments of business. Large agricultural capitalists were not congenitally opposed to manufacturing. On the contrary, economic instability in the inter-war period fostered broad support for pro-industry policies.[16] Forced industrialisation, on the other hand, antagonised agriculturalists because the profits of agro-exporters were squeezed to deliver savings and foreign exchange essential to sustain manufacturing. Most agriculturalists were also more firmly opposed to interventionism than their manufacturing counterparts, a difference of opinion that limited business sector cooperation until the 1990s. The agricultural sector was most alarmed by pressure on profits and access to foreign exchange during the early years of the first Perón administration. Yet, from the 1950s to the 1990s, rural producers continued to complain at what they regarded as unfair and excessive taxation levied by administrations of all complexions – military and civilian, supposedly free-market and interventionist. Another perennial protest involved unfavourable credit regimes and a combination of exchange and tariff regulations which limited capital imports. Forced industrialisation inculcated scepticism and perverse behaviour in rural producers. From the 1940s to the 1970s, farmers and ranchers came to accept that all administrations were over-committed to industrialisation and that even those regimes which espoused market economics were unlikely to refrain from rigging domestic terms of trade against the rural sector. The result was under-investment and apparently illogical responses to price changes. On those occasions when real prices rose, producers were inclined to withhold supplies, assuming that prices could be pushed up further. When prices fell, products were dumped on the market on the assumption that prices would fall further. The consequences were erratic supply responses in the long term and repeated production bottlenecks and discord.[17]

Industrialists were only marginally more united, as suggested by a growth in the number of organisations formed to represent their interests. As late as the 1950s, the industrial entrepreneuriat could still be divided into three distinct groups: penny capitalists of immigrant origin; manufacturers firmly embedded in the dominant business elite (many closely connected with agro-export interests); and managers of foreign firms. These distinctions were furthered by differences of firm size and area of operations. Penny capitalists tended to operate smaller firms manufacturing basic-wages goods: 'national' and foreign capital were concentrated in large-scale establishments processing rural products for export and domestic consumption, in commerce and, after the 1920s, in the manufacture of durables.[18] Until the 1940s, industrialists of immigrant origin were distinctly the junior partner in this firmament of manufacturers.[19] This was reflected in the composition of the Unión Industrial Argentina (UIA, Argentine Industrial Union). Until the 1950s, membership was dominated by foreign-owned enterprises and business associated with the rural sector.[20] This membership configuration limited the effectiveness of the UIA as an industrial lobby. In time the Confederación General Económica (CGE, General Economic Confederation), formed with government support in 1952, came to represent the interests of small businesses. As a Peronist creation, it was used to counter the influence of the UIA and was regarded with suspicion by subsequent regimes and by other business sectors.[21] There was intense rivalry between the UIA and the CGE (when not prescribed) and its industrial wing, the Confederación de Industria (CI, Confederation of Industry), which claimed to represent the 'national industrial bourgeoisie'. By the 1970s, lack of sectoral coherence was reflected in organisational diversity as a multiplicity of entities competed for the allegiance of firms. More free-market-orientated (largely anti-Peronist) associations formed an action group, ACIEL, or the Co-ordinated Action of Free Entrepreneurial Associations, which included the UIA, commercial associations, and entities representing the rural sector. The CGE, continuing to project a more 'national' image, campaigned for government intervention and was more inclined to seek an accommodation with organised labour. Competition to represent business fostered factionalism and instability and firms moved from association to association, while associations splintered and re-formed.

At the beginning of the turbulent 1970s, the UIA broke with the ACIEL and merged with the CGE to form the Confederación Industrial Nacional Argentina (CINA, Argentine National Industrial Confederation), only for the new entity to suffer a haemorrhage of members. Following the military coup in 1976, the CGE/CINA was proscribed while dissident members of the former UIA, mainly large firms based in Buenos Aires, forged the Movimiento Industrial Argentina (MIA, Argentine Industrial Movement).[22] As a corporate body, however, the business lobby never recovered from the trauma of the *Proceso*. Membership was severely reduced as a result of the sudden opening-up of the economy in the late 1970s and economic instability in the 1980s. The magnitude of the industrial crisis is captured in Table 2.4. The onslaught was partly intentional – the competitive shock resulting from the opening-up of the economy during the early years of the *Proceso* – and partly unanticipated, such as the banking crisis of the early 1980s and turmoil associated with the disintegration of Radical stabilisation efforts at the end of the decade.

Table 2.4   *Average annual growth rates of industrial added value,*
Argentina, 1950–94 (%)

1950–74	4.9
1974–80	−0.6
1980–90	−1.4
1990–94	6.9

Source: Elaborated from J. M. Benavente, G. Crespi, J. Katz and G. Stumpo, 'Changes in the Industrial Development of Latin America', *CEPAL Review*, 40 (1996), p. 57.

Few economies have experienced such a lengthy period of contraction in manufacturing output as that sustained in the Argentine from the mid-1970s to 1990. Between 1975 and 1982 the share of manufacturing in GDP fell by five percentage points, output declined by 20 per cent and the workforce by 35 per cent.[23] Privatisation in the 1990s has generated new opportunity for private business in sectors previously dominated by the state but the new, post-1991 programme has hardly resulted in the opportunities for corporate influence on economic policy-making to which manufacturers of the 1920s aspired.[24]

For most of the second half of the twentieth century, the cross that organised labour has had to bear is the myth that the movement was created by Perón. Sometime Secretary of Labour in the 1943–46 military regime, Perón cultivated trade-union leaders and promoted the formation of unions to represent unorganised workers. During the latter part of the 1940s, trade-union membership grew exponentially and government intervention ensured that wages and working conditions improved massively. This earned Perón the gratitude (and the votes) of workers and the enduring loyalty of many union bosses. Nevertheless, trade-union history pre-dates Perón and, despite his efforts to the contrary, important sections of the labour movement vigorously resisted co-option.[25] The powerful railway locomotive and footplate men's union, La Fraternidad, proved particularly recalcitrant: its independence was not broken until 1951. Arguably, it was the attitude and action of early post-1955 regimes that welded most unions to Perón. Yet by the 1960s some sections of organised labour were beginning to think the unthinkable (Peronism without Perón), and were willing to contemplate an accommodation with regimes, both civilian and military, of the period.[26] Thus, in addition to the 'democratic' anti-Peronist segment of organised labour that had been carefully nurtured by the 'normalising regime' of General Aramburu, a further split occurred in the mid-1960s between those union leaders who remained loyal to the exiled Perón and others who, espousing their continuing support for Peronism, sought to pursue an independent course, arguing that the interests of workers would be best served by opening a dialogue with government. As a result, besides 'non-political' unions, the greater part of the union movement was divided in three hostile camps: anti-Peronists, neo-Peronists and Peronists.[27] These distinctions cut across the skilled/unskilled divide, though anti-Peronist unions tended to represent those sections of the labour movement that had been organised before 1943 and were most influenced by reformist socialism and classist ideologies.

Administrations of the 1960s and early 1970s encouraged these divisions through a policy of selective repression. However, union corruption and the politically charged atmosphere of the time did most to frustrate attempts to reintegrate the labour movement. Yet, as a wave of factory occupations and wildcat strikes in the late 1960s and early 1970s testified, relations between rank-and-file members and the union leadership were deteriorating. In short, there was a breakdown of union discipline. As the larger unions became increasingly bureaucratised and responsible for the administration of a range of welfare services and social facilities, possibilities for corruption, and the resentment of ordinary members, increased.[28] Corruption, cronyism and the use of violence in defence of their empires by union bosses came to a head between 1973 and 1976, a period when the union leadership also found itself in conflict

with other sectors of the Peronist Party. Fragile unity was hardly restored during the early years of the *Proceso*. Discredited by its association with the chaos
of 1975/76 and confronted by employers seeking to recapture control of workplace discipline, the labour leadership and membership was cowed by state terrorism and a coordinated attack on wages. Recovery of confidence was slow:
labour bosses were shocked by the Radical electoral victory in 1983, a victory
in part explained by exposure by the UCR of links between sections of the
labour bureaucracy and elements of the military during the dark days of the
Proceso. Nevertheless, efforts by the Alfonsín regime to democratise the trade
unions and weaken links between organised-labour Peronism were largely
unsuccessful.[29]

Since the 1940s organised labour has been a major political actor and sections of the labour movement constituted the most effective element of the Peronist Party from the 1940s to the 1990s. But, as suggested above, organised
labour was not a monolithic bloc and was rarely able to advance a clear, consistent project. Post-1955 regimes could not ignore organised labour, but divisions within the movement facilitated phases of co-option and marginalisation.
Macroeconomic changes since the 1970s have further weakened the power of
labour and intensified inter-union feuds. And, as ever, there is the distinction
between organised and non-organised labour. In relative, and perhaps absolute
terms, trade-unions membership expressed as a proportion of the economically
active population probably peaked in the early 1950s, following a massive
recruitment drive during the first Perón administration. Yet it is doubtful if
union members ever represented 60 per cent of the workforce.[30] For much of
the last quarter of the twentieth century, the relative importance of organised
labour slipped. Changes in the labour market triggered by deindustrialisation
in the 1970s and de-statisation in the 1990s have an adverse impact on trade-
union membership.

It might be expected that the political parties would be most committed to
democratic institutions. Certainly, the parties and prominent politicians were
among the first victims of military rule. The closure of Congress, the banning
of parties and the ousting of democratically elected regimes signalled a loss of
office and employment, if not imprisonment, for politicians and officials. The
parties were certainly firm advocates of constitutionalism. Yet support for the
niceties of open political contest was often conditional. The history of Argentinian political parties in the twentieth century is one of proscription (or self-
exclusion), dogmatism and factionalism. Long periods of single-party
ascendancy and the political longevity of key party figures – possibly indicat-
ing a structural deficit in terms of a capacity for generational renewal – are
other prominent features of modern Argentinian party-political history. It is a
commonplace of Argentinian politics that Perón and Peronism have been the
defining influences of the last half-century. Perón was *the* political figure from
the mid-1940s until his death in 1974. His memory casts a long shadow and
his name was repeatedly invoked in presidential and congressional election

campaigns in 1983 and 1989, and continues to provide a reference point for the Menem administration.[31] Yet, if half of the electorate was for Perón, the other half was not. (The highest share of votes captured by the PJ was in the second presidential election of 1973: the Perón-Perón ticket obtained 62 per cent of votes cast. In the first 1973 presidential and congressional elections, the Peronist Party and its allies obtained 49 per cent of the votes.) From 1946 until 1983, the view was widely held that the PJ could not be defeated in fair and free elections. It was also acknowledged that Peronism was a movement, rather than a formal party. It was a 'verticalist', highly factionalised organisation with little internal accountability. This was its strength during periods of proscription and its weakness when in office.[32] Peronism experienced some structural change in the 1960s and more effective 'renovation' after 1983, notably in the mid-1980s, when efforts were made to give the PJ a more open, formal structure. For the first time in the history of the movement/party, supporters had a say in the selection of the presidential slate in 1988.[33] Yet there is still an 'accountability gap', as events of the 1990s indicate. For Peronism, its apparent electoral strength and proscription were different sides of the same coin. The consequences were a freeze on institutional modernisation and, paradoxically, multi-layer contacts with elements of the military and other political actors, which underscored internal divisions and often discredited the PJ in the eyes of its supporters and voters.

Although banned for much of the period between 1955 and 1973 and between 1976 and 1982, in the 1950s and 1960s sections of the army contemplated building a new political alignment on the basis of the Peronist labour movement. (This was hardly surprising, since organised labour and elements of the military had constituted the main props of the 1946–55 Peronist administrations.) Similarly, between 1955 and 1966 factions of the Radical Party depended on the votes of Peronists to secure electoral victories. From 1955 to 1973 Perón was engaged in semi-clandestine negotiations with political opponents and the generals to establish conditions for his return. These negotiations, however, did not indicate a willingness to share power, rather they were a strategy to recapture it. Hence, if Perón and Peronism were the dominant features of Argentinian politics during this period, the substance and style of politics were informality, subterfuge and increasing distance between those in control of the levers of power within Peronism and the rank-and-file membership.

The UCR was no stranger to prohibition. With the promise of electoral reform at the beginning of the twentieth century, the Radicals abandoned abstentionism and triumphed in 1916. In spite of internal rivalry deriving from a heterogeneous constituency – the party comprised dissident sectors of the landed elite, urban professionals and 'national' capitalists – the UCR went on to take the presidency again in 1922 and 1928. In a trend that prefigured Peronism, the style of Radicalism became increasingly personalistic. Three consecutive presidential victories and congressional gains, coupled with a willingness to manipulate the electoral process, induced complacency amongst Radicals and despair amongst their opponents.[34] A number of explanations have been advanced to account for the 'fall of democracy' in the Argentine in 1930, when a military coup enjoying widespread civilian support overturned the administration of President Hipólito Yrigoyen (1916–22, 1928–30). In addition to economic dislocation provoked by the world crisis, liberal and conservative critics of Yrigoyen accused him of a demagogic 'abuse of power' (not least the use of the military to curb opponents), corruption, political favouritism and what would later be described as fiscal populism.[35] These charges are not dissimilar to those later levied against Peronism. Others saw the failing regime as mired in cronyism, unwilling to strengthen democratic institutions and unable to take prompt action in the face of a deepening economic crisis. After 1930, electoral fraud and the exclusion of the UCR (later the Radicals would abstain) ensured victories at the polls for parties of the Left and Right excluded from office during the Radical ascendancy. As democracy and democratic institutions became marginalised, or appeared increasingly irrelevant, nationalism and socialism became the principal ideological forces.

Nonetheless, when the military regime that brought to an end the *década infame* of 'patriotic fraud' in 1943 promised to hold elections, the Radicals were confident of victory. With other parties, notably the Communists and Socialists (but also including some Conservatives), the Radicals assembled the Democratic Union to oppose Perón in the 1946 presidential and congressional elections. Perón was supported by organised labour, dissident Radicals, various nationalist groups and provincial interests and the Roman Catholic Church. To the surprise of many, Perón won, and another decade of 'political exclusion' began for the UCR as Peronists enjoyed electoral successes to rival those of the Radicals between 1916 and 1928. Arguably, it was this double 'exclusion' – after 1930 and between 1946 and 1955 – that encouraged Radical factions to compromise with both the military and Peronism in the 1950s.[36] Unable to guarantee electoral success, Radicals were obliged to deal with forces they depicted as anti-democratic. The issue of how to deal with Peronism and the military split the party. Yet, when the UCR obtained its own surprise electoral victory in 1983, despite some conciliatory language, unmindful of past experience, triumphalist Radicals were consumed with a vision of a new hegemony – after *yrigoyenismo* and *peronismo*, an *alfonsinista* ascendancy had dawned.[37] Prefiguring sentiments expressed by Peronists in 1989, sections of the UCR envisaged constitutional change to allow Alfonsín to serve a second consecutive term.

Until 1989 Argentinian democracy had not witnessed an electoral succession involving an outgoing democratically elected regime transferring power to a democratically elected administration of a different political party. As illustrated by the language of victorious party activists in 1983 and 1989, and expressed in projects for constitutional reform, electoral politics was viewed as another route to hegemony, not so different from appeals to extra-democratic forces. Until the 1990s, this had been the principal institutional deficit in the

Argentinian political structure – a quest for hegemony which, in denying others access to power by electoral means, encourages recourse to the extra-democratic. Thus, for political parties as much as other actors, democracy was not so much a means of resolving conflict but of secure access to, and retaining control of, power. In a system characterised by a quest for dominance, groups unable to obtain an electoral majority were hardly encouraged to participate. Until the popular conservative coalition assembled by Menem after 1989, the actor most conspicuously absent from the democratic game had been business.[38] Ghettoised in the federal capital, the Unión del Centro Democrático (UCéDé, Union of the Democratic Centre), the party of Buenos Aires business, depended on the military or direct action as a means of influencing policy in a political system in which the PJ was considered the party of labour and the UCR increasingly the organ of middle-class professionals, suspicious of big business and foreign capital. In this respect, the agreement between Menem and Alfonsín which paved the way for constitutional reform in 1994 (and cost Radicals dear), the switch of the business vote to Menem in 1995 and the 1998 electoral pact between the UCR and the FREPASO suggest institutional change and a realignment of political forces in favour of democratic contest.

Perhaps the Roman Catholic Church is the organisation that has been least subject to internal, fissiparous pressure. It is also the organisation that has changed least in the last half-century and, with the possible exception of the military, that has lost most influence. It is a moot point whether Perón co-opted the hierarchy in 1945, or the hierarchy assumed that it could 'capture' Perón to implement long-cherished projects. The 1853 Constitution which provided for the separation of Church and state nevertheless required that the President of the Republic should be a Roman Catholic, a provision not overturned until the new constitution was sworn in 1994. For the Roman Catholic hierarchy, the principal issues determining Church–state relations have been divorce and religious education in state schools. From time to time, principally since the 1930s, other issues such as family and labour legislation commanded attention.[39] Senior churchmen have been closely associated with a number of military regimes, for example General José Félix Uriburu (1930–32), General Eduardo Lonardi (1955) and Juan Onganía (1966–70).

Reminding voters that Communists were represented in the UD, the hierarchy endorsed Perón in 1946 as he promised to retain religious instruction in state schools (introduced in 1943). Moreover, as the 1945/46 election campaign developed it was clear that Peronist welfare projects were substantially indebted to ideas floated by Catholic Social Action in the 1930s. There was also suspicion of the traditional anticlericalism of many Radicals.[40] The break with Perón came around 1954, with the suppression of religious instruction in state schools and an end to state subsidies for private (mainly Roman Catholic) schools. There was, too, the threat of a renewed separation of Church and State. This loss of support was an essential ingredient in the 1955 coup. Yet, of all regimes, it was the Videla government (1976–81) which appeared closest to the Roman Catholic hierarchy. It was an association that allowed critics of the clerical establishment to maintain that it sanctified (if it did not sanction) the excesses of the *Proceso*. While important sections of the Roman Catholic Church in Brazil protested against state terrorism in the late 1960s, and in post-1973 Chile the Church became the only effective – certainly the only tolerated – critic of the Pinochet regime, the Argentinian Church was largely silent in the face of state terror. Was this further evidence of the conditional approach of the Church establishment, one of the most conservative in Latin America, to democracy? This (in)action and the diffusion of anti–hierarchy opinion account for the loss of political influence. Accustomed to exercising informal leverage over public policies, the hierarchy was uneasy at its inability to put a break on the re-establishment of freedom of expression and innovation in education under Alfonsín. In the teeth of virulent opposition from Roman Catholic bishops, divorce was finally legalised in 1986, a reform that attracted wide support. While continuing to voice opinion on social matters, there is little evidence that the Roman Catholic episcopate has re-established its former influence, notwithstanding the open religiosity of President Menem.

The years since 1970 have seen significant changes in the behaviour of – and interaction amongst – Argentinian political actors. As already suggested, these changes are captured in responses to three major efforts to stabilise the economy. The first of these was applied by authoritarian military regimes of the 1976–82 period. The second was introduced in the middle period of the UCR government – the 1985 Plan Austral. The most recent is the Convertibility Plan of 1991.

The politics of stabilisation and macroeconomic restructuring

Stabilisation packages associated with Economy Ministers José Martínez de Hoz (1976–81), Juan V. Sourrouille (1985–8) and Domingo Cavallo (1991–96) derived from a similar set of assumptions: namely, that the ISI model had failed and that the state sector was too large. And there was a subtext, explicitly articulated during the *Proceso*, that forced industrialisation had produced a dangerous social transformation, and that national security and traditional values were being challenged by popular sectors and elements of the middle class. Hence, while stabilisation was the immediate objective, increasing competitiveness of the productive sectors was the underlying purpose. All regimes came to view economic efficiency and greater macroeconomic stability as an essential prerequisite for the re-establishment of political order. The definition of what constituted political order, however, varied considerably. The extent to which economic policy-makers were able to deliver depended, in part, on their ability to ignore the clamour of powerful lobbies.

Serving a regime that had eliminated all forms of political and union activity, it might appear that Martínez de Hoz was well placed to effect the project of macroeconomic restructuring based upon neoliberal precepts with which his name would later be associated. A member of a traditional, landowning family, he appeared to personify the policy of international reinsertion and agro-export revival. He was also president of the largest private steel producer. Did this further reflect his capacity to represent the national business elite? Much has been written about the ideology and the ideas that shaped the strategy of the 1976–82 period.[41] It is possible that contemporary comment, over-influenced by the rhetoric of the regime, was inclined to see economic measures introduced after 1976 as part of a grand design. Most commentators now observe different phases in economic strategy. There is disagreement, however, as to the number of phases and the degree of policy coherence between them. The first phase, variously depicted as running from 1976 to 1977 or 1978, sought to address balance-of-payments disequilibrium, and inflation, which was regarded as driven by excess demand. Tariffs were liberalised and the financial sector deregulated, though deposits would continue to be guaranteed by the Central Bank. Above all, this was the period of wage compression, a by-product of which was reduced government expenditure. By 1978 assumptions about the cause of inflation had changed: did this mark the onset of the second or third phase and a change of policy? Inertial factors were now held to be primarily responsible. It was at this point that the *tablita* was launched, a set of pre-announced adjustments in the exchange rate and public-sector charges. At the same time a programme of further downward revisions of the tariff was posted and de-indexation continued. But as foreign capital flowed in, the exchange rate became progressively overvalued. By 1981 the final phase was already under way, featuring capital flight, the bankruptcy of businesses in the productive sector and bank failure. While the onset of the international loan/debt crisis hardly assisted, the programme was largely brought down by inherent flaws and the power of vested lobbies.

The initial strategy – to correct inflation and promote exports – seemed to be based on a policy of adjustment through recession. It might have been expected that wage compression and sharp tariff reductions would curb domestic consumer demand, lower production costs and facilitate investment and production for export. As already stated, wage reduction also reduced government expenditure. But there were limits to government expenditure curbs. The military refused to countenance cuts in public investment. Hence, government demands for domestic credit (notwithstanding extensive foreign borrowing) meant that interest rates remained high. Further fiscal pressure resulted from the border dispute with Chile. Meanwhile, business protested at the extent of the recession and the cost of borrowing. As the crisis began to unfold, although Martínez de Hoz was more inclined to support the financial rather than the productive sector, the military was not prepared to see what were regarded as strategic firms go out of business. For the junta national security took precedence over the Economy Minister's drive for efficiency. Hence, in the wake of bank failure and business collapse, the state sector grew. Private firms were absorbed by associated military-administered companies and the private foreign debt was nationalised. Stabilisation failed due to military opposition to the sale of public-sector firms and military and business pressure on the banking sector, which was probably the principal beneficiary of policies initially devised to foster investment in manufacturing and agriculture.

When the Austral Plan was introduced in June 1985, it was launched as a 'surprise' package by an economic team that had consciously isolated itself from the influence of lobbies. However, unlike its predecessors of the *Proceso*, the team, headed by Sourrouille, was aware that its strategy was required to deliver immediate positive economic and political results. Stabilisation through recession was not an option. Nor was it required. Instability was diagnosed as deriving from inflationary expectations. Hence the combination of 'shock' therapy (and a proscription of indexation) to excise inertial factors and a heterodox emphasis on stabilisation through growth. Democratic consolidation also required growth within the context of macroeconomic stability. Consequently, while orthodox stabilisation strategies of the past, not least that of 1976, had involved a wage freeze, the 1985 plan was based on a wages and prices freeze with wages being frozen at a level that partly took account of residual inflation. One other lesson had been learnt from the Martínez de Hoz failure – the need for fiscal discipline. Taxes and utility rates were raised and the Central Bank would not monetise the public-sector deficit. Privatisation was also mentioned.[42]

Initially, the results were auspicious. The rate of inflation fell dramatically, virtually every consumer was enrolled in the 'price police', production picked up and confidence returned. The external environment, however, was not propitious: export price falls increased the burden of external debt service. Alfonsín had expected a 'democratic dividend' (a debt write-off) from the international financial community. What he got – from the World Bank – was excessive tolerance in meeting agreed targets, the turning of a blind eye to an undeclared moratorium and lax terms for new borrowing. This was cruelty dressed up as kindness. The economic team had anticipated that with confidence returning, domestic savings would grow, thereby reducing the cost of borrowing. The contrary occurred. Confidence triggered a consumer boom which squeezed domestic productive capacity while constraining the supply of funds necessary for investment. There were insufficient reserves to take the strain. In addition, the gradual easing of price and wage controls – never an easy task – to facilitate an orderly return to a market mechanism was delayed. The regime failed to deliver in several crucial areas. Controls on public spending were not applied with the promised rigour, and privatisation, which would have yielded substantial savings, was quietly shelved. But the Plan was also compromised by the action of key domestic actors.

The shock of electoral defeat in 1983 engendered amongst Peronists a retreat into vociferous, obstructionist opposition. For the UCR, this constituted irresponsible opposition which, given the parliamentary arithmetic, derailed the legislative programme required to carry forward essential reform. Moreover, in control of most of the provinces, the Peronists refused to heed calls by the federal government for fiscal responsibility. In short, there was no party-political consensus and no coalition in favour of democratic institutional renovation. Equally critical was opposition by vested interests in the form of organised labour and business, who reneged on undertakings given to the government.[43] Peronist trade unions mounted a guerrilla war against the project, partly in response to earlier attempts to democratise the labour movement and due to the threat to jobs posed by fiscal rectitude. Initially, chastened by the ideology and the experience of the *Proceso*, namely the novelty of a military regime that sought to marginalise it in the decision-making process, the business community had given the UCR regime a cautious welcome, notwithstanding the traditional antipathy of Radicals to 'big business'. The early success of the Plan also reduced business scepticism. Conflict, however, occurred over the dismantling of the social pact and government subsidies to business. As the stabilisation package unravelled, the government accused the business community of engineering a 'strike': a tax strike – non-payment of taxes became critical as the administration had foresworn printing money to cover expenditure; an investment strike – new investment was required if demand was to be sustained without provoking price increases; a production strike – exporters, in particular, withheld commodities from the market, denying the treasury access to much-needed foreign exchange. It may also have been the case that too much official effort had been absorbed by stabilisation, and insufficient emphasis had been given to structural reform.

The political arithmetic of the Convertibility Plan was more favourable. In 1989, the Peronists carried both houses of Congress and most provinces and increased their share of the vote in every mid-term and full-term election held after the Plan was formally introduced up to, and including, 1995. Indeed, the success of stabilisation after 1991 contributed massively to the electoral performance of the government. Post-1991 reforms may be divided into three phases. The characteristics of the first phase were high, sustained growth, a sharp decline in the rate of inflation, substantial inflows of capital and large balance-of-trade surpluses. Stability was predicated on monetary order, fiscal reform (mainly cutting expenditure), the beginning of the reform of the state and the opening-up of the economy. This phase came to a close with the swearing of the new Constitution in 1994, which paved the way for the re-election of President Menem, which promised policy continuity, and with the onset of a recession. The 'Tequila effect' – provoked by the ill-managed devaluation of the Mexican peso in December 1994 – produced a run on the Argentinian peso and the banks in 1995. Anxious savers withdrew deposits, pesos were converted into dollars, interest rates rose and the recession began. The principal policy features of the second phase were deepening fiscal reform, notably the imposition of discipline on the provinces in the face of pre-election pressure to relax control, the reorganisation of the banking sector and the virtual completion of the process of federal privatisation. Possibly the main achievement of the period, besides policy continuity (no mean feat, given previous history), was the growth in international competitiveness. Politically, the period witnessed the electoral triumph of Menem in May 1995, in the face of a sharp rise in unemployment driven as much by productivity changes resulting from privatisation and investment as by the recession. The third and present phase may be dated with the return of economic growth in the second quarter of 1996, a decline in rates of unemployment and the run-up to the mid-term congressional elections in October 1997, which saw the government lose its majority in the lower Chamber of Deputies. In policy terms, the most positive feature of the period is the broadening of political support for the main features of the Convertibility Plan: in October 1997, all the mainstream political parties were pledged to maintain macroeconomic stability. In addition, the government has sought to advance the process of institutional reform, particularly of the social security system and labour code, in the face of considerable internal opposition within the Peronist Party.

Survival – policy continuity – is the most remarkable feature of the Convertibility Plan. How is this to be explained? First, the failure (and the consequences of failure) of previous stabilisation projects induced not scepticism but an almost desperate alliance in favour of change. This derived from the political and economic violence of the 1970s and 1980s. It is doubtful if many sectors of society fully comprehended the technical logic of the economic policy launched in 1991. There was, however, general agreement about what the electorate did not want. And, notwithstanding many early doubts, the phenomenon of rapid, sustained growth without inflation from 1991 to 1994 reinforced the consensus in favour of stability. Second, the events of the 1970s and 1980s undermined the position of sectors that might have challenged key ingredients of the new economic policy. If sections of the military remained incorrigibly wedded to autarchy, the ability of the armed forces to shape policy was virtually extirpated by the military institutional crisis that followed defeat in the Falklands and the unrelenting exposure of the horrors of the 'dirty war'. Many aspects of civilian–military relations remain unresolved, but in the field of foreign relations, policy continuity since 1983 has eroded conventional strategic arguments for economic interventionism. UCR and PJ administrations have effected dramatic improvements in relations with Chile while the growing economic importance of the Mercosur/Mercosul (the South American Common Market, composed of the Argentine, Brazil, Paraguay and Uruguay, with Bolivia and Chile as 'associate members') further weakens the ideological underpinning of – and economic justification for – 'strategic autarchy'.[44] Business resistance to structural adjustment has also been constrained by the economics and sectoral institutional crisis of earlier failed stabilisation. The triple shock of abrupt economic opening-up in the late 1970s, bank failure in the earlier 1980s and economic contraction associated with the hyperinflation of 1989–90 excised whole sections of manufacturing, probably those firms most committed to statism. These processes also weakened the influence of organised labour whose room for manoeuvre has been further limited by privatisation and state shrinkage. Moreover, only a PJ administration could have pursued the 'reform of the state' with such ruthlessness. Closely associated with the Peronist Party, where else could old union bosses go if they rejected Menem? Third, the external environment has been more favourable to economic restructuring. There was much greater global stability in the 1990s and greater trade openness. Foreign savings became available on increasingly positive terms, while a gradual shift from portfolio to direct investment made for less volatility in capital flows. This contrasts with the 1982–90 period, when external transfer equivalent to 3 per cent of GDP occurred on average each year. Traditional export prices have been firmer and improving efficiency has ensured greater overseas market penetration across the board. Four, the economic team of 1991 benefited from the lessons of the failure of its predecessors. In 1991, the fiscal and foreign reserve position was much stronger than in 1976 or 1985. Economic growth, privatisation and a favourable external environment reinforced rather undermined this position in the years immediately following 1991. And, with growth, it was relatively easier to sustain the momentum of reform, ensuring greater coherence in the transition from stabilisation to macroeconomic restructuring.

Looking ahead: problems yet to be resolved

Despite initial doubts, the macroeconomic strategy introduced in April 1991 continues. It has survived major shocks such as the devaluation of the Mexican peso in 1994, a run on the banking system in 1995 and the dismissal/resignation of Cavallo in 1996. The strategy has also continued in the face of often acute domestic opposition, a steady deterioration in the external accounts in the early to mid-1990s and fiscal difficulties, financial belt-tightening and a recession in 1995/96. To date critics have been confounded and broad-based political support for the economic policy of the Menem administrations has been sustained.

Yet questions remain. These may be identified as technical doubts about the profundity of the institutional transformation, residual socio-economic problems, and global issues. There are also continuing doubts about 'regime politics'. Notwithstanding improvements since 1995 and the gradual expansion of private pension funds, the capital market remains small and relatively shallow. The level of financial intermediation is low by continental and international standards: prior to the 1995 Tequila crisis, the ratio of bank deposits to GDP was around 1:7, compared with around 3:10 in Mexico and 3:7 in Chile.[45] In part this may account for the relatively low domestic savings rate. Although there has been a substantial increase in investment, from mid-1993 to early 1997 the rate of gross investment to GDP fluctuated between 20 and 25 per cent (usually closer to the upper limit[46]) – external capital inflows represent a significant proportion of the total. While direct investment may be less footloose than short-term portfolio lending, global, rather than domestic factors can constrain the flow of new funds. Corruption and rent-seeking pose problems in terms of micro- and macro-level efficiency and carry fiscal implications. In many cases, the process of privatisation fostered the growth of quasi-private monopolies in sectors of the economy less exposed to foreign competition.[47] One of the principal flaws of the privatisation process was the failure to install effective regulatory agencies. However, even had they been set in place, given the level of corruption, it is doubtful that they could have functioned effectively as agencies of price control and efficiency-raising. In general, there can be little doubt that the level of corruption in several branches of government increases transaction costs, arguably creating both opportunities for, and the necessity of, rent-seeking. While the government is anxious to deregulate the labour market in order to remove barriers to mobility and competitiveness, efficiency in other areas may result from regulation. Effective regulation, if transparent, is not incompatible with the neoliberal model. On the contrary, agencies can complement market mechanisms.

Unemployment and poverty present a social and an economic challenge. Indeed, unemployment is one of the principal causes of poverty.[48] As Table 2.5 indicates, unemployment rose markedly in the mid-1990s.

Table 2.5   *Unemployment rates, Argentina, 1989–91 (%)*

May 1989	8.4	May 1992	6.9	May 1995	18.4
Oct. 1989	7.1	Oct. 1992	7.0	Oct. 1995	16.4
May 1990	8.6	May 1993	9.9	May 1996	17.1
Oct. 1990	6.3	Oct. 1993	9.3	Oct. 1996	17.3
June 1991	6.9	May 1994	10.7	May 1997	16.1
Oct. 1991	6.0	Oct. 1994	10.1	Oct. 1997	13.8

Source: República Argentina, Instituto Nacional de Estadísticas y Censos (Buenos Aires INE, 1997).

The rate of open unemployment increased during the turmoil of the late 1980s to stand at around three times the 'historic' level of 2–3 per cent. Economic stability, and returning confidence, saw the rate decline during the early years of Convertibility before rising again as privatisation and the contraction of state employment took hold. As Table 2.5 shows, the sharpest increase occurred between October 1994 and May 1995. Some of this increase may have been cyclical, triggered by the 1995/96 recession. But a greater part of unemployment growth was structural, resulting from recapitalisation in the productive sectors. The Tequila recession simply masked these effects. Consequently, although beginning to fall in the last quarter of 1996 and the first quarter of 1997 and with a further fall of two percentage points between May and October 1997, it is clear that even a return to early 1990s levels of economic growth will not bring the rate of unemployment back to pre-recession levels.

The government may be correct in stating that greater flexibility and social security reform (making it easier for employers to hire and fire workers and make other reductions in labour costs) will have a positive impact upon employment without reducing workers' living standards. But aspects of the existing Labour Code relating to social security and redundancy payments are not the only factors contributing to rigidities in the labour market. Recent evidence, notably very high variations in provincial rates of job growth and unemployment, point to skill shortages and location factors. The labour market is becoming socially and regionally fragmented. Market mechanisms alone will not solve these problems and only the naive or the disingenuous would fail to accept that high levels of unemployment have already introduced a great deal of 'flexibility' into labour relations.

Global insertion and the new political and economic internationalism have been much vaunted by the Menem government and are an undoubted success. The process, however, is not without cost, as the structure and volatility in international capital movements in the 1990s have demonstrated. Economic openness and macroeconomic stability have contributed to domestic and overseas investor confidence. Flight capital has returned and direct foreign investment increased. Nevertheless, the initial benefits – largely due to privatisation – were observed more in the fiscal and external accounts than in the productive sectors. Since 1993/94 this has changed and years of under-investment in plant and equipment are being corrected – the productivity time-bomb is being defused. But foreign investors and international agencies require constant reassurance. The fact that Convertibility has stood the test of the 1995 crisis and that all the main opposition parties have now embraced the current economic model does not mean that there will be no future shocks, nor that adverse movements in overseas financial and stock markets will not have a negative impact upon the Argentine, even if the real economy is demonstrably sound. While neighbouring economies, particularly Brazil, which now accounts for around one-third of Argentinian overseas trade, struggle to accomplish their own adjustment, the Argentine will continue to be plagued by doubters at home and abroad. Official analyses of a worst-case scenario of turmoil in Brazil assert that this would produce a contraction of no more than 5 percentage points in Argentinian GDP. Hence its impact can be discounted, as this would be of more or less the same order as the 1995/96 recession – a crisis that was handled efficaciously.[49] But how would the electorate respond to another sequence of demands for belt-tightening? Finally, underpinning official rhetoric about the long-term consequences of macroeconomic stability and adjustment is the assumption that the trickle-down effects of growth will generate absolute improvements in living standards and substantive industrialisation. Growth may, indeed, ultimately raise living standards across the board (not least if accompanied by social programmes that target the needy), but the market may push the economy more towards primary production than manufacturing. Would this be a politically acceptable outcome?

Many pressing political questions remain unaddressed. Like several of its predecessors, the current administration has sought to validate its position by reference to economic success. However, unlike many previous regimes engaged in orthodox (or neo-orthodox) adjustment programmes, the Menem government has had to submit itself to electoral appraisal. It has done so, and has gained and (until very recently) retained popular approval. Nevertheless, a 'political reform gap' remains. Politics have changed less than economics: growing confidence in and acceptance of economic restructuring have produced demands for a parallel political restructuring. This produces tensions because increasing transparency in the economic market place has not been matched by a similar growth in transparency in the political market place. Corruption, abuse of power and opaque rules of the political game remain. Is the Argentinian political system organically democratic or best described as plebiscitary, a victim of populist monetarism that has strengthened, not weakened, a tendency towards the authoritarian?[50] Within the party structure, a democratic deficit continues. During and after the 1980s, the UCR struggled to achieve greater internal democracy and to institutionalise rather than personalise decision-making. The recently constituted FREPASO has promised a similar degree of intra-party democracy and transparency in the policy-making process. Possibly, given the heterogeneous nature of the FREPASO, there was no other course. Despite organisational modernisation in the 1980s, the PJ has found it more difficult to formalise and depersonalise internal structures. This has resulted in a haemorrhage of talent, notably individuals such as Octavio Bordón (who has since rejoined the party), and Gustavo Béliz and Domingo Cavallo, who have established rival political organisations. Personalism and recourse to executive decree (a device employed by both recent Radical and Peronist administrations, particularly the latter) continue to limit democratic accountability.[51]

Judicial independence and the balance of power between the federal government and other jurisdictions – the provinces and municipalities – are equally pressing problems that must be confronted. Some progress has been made under these headings, notably a new fiscal pact which provides for a more equitable distribution of tax revenue between the federal government and the provinces. Fiscal reform has also entailed the devolution of areas of administrative responsibility from federal to provincial administrations, although funds have not always been devolved to the same degree. Provincial administrations are pressing for greater correspondence between the devolution of responsibilities and resources but have reacted with suspicion to the latest round of devolution – to the municipalities. Opposition and Peronist dominated provincial governments view the move as likely to limit their outreach while strengthening that of the federal government. These issues would be less problematic were there more confidence in the administration of justice.

Conclusions

Decades of low or declining productivity and increasing international uncompetitiveness produced an economic time-bomb. The principal manifestations were distributional conflict as fairly evenly matched sectors contended for resources, and alternative cycles of civilian military rule punctuated by increasing violence. Do the return to constitutionalism in 1983, the uninterrupted sequence of elections held since then and the economic stability enjoyed since 1991 indicate that democratic institutions and a strong civil society are being constructed?

Discounting the 1995/96 recession, since 1990 the Argentinian economy has registered rates of growth per capita last recorded at the beginning of the century. The country has also experienced some of the highest rates of investment and productivity growth witnessed amongst the so-called emerging market economies. Mindful of their economic history, Argentinians are aware of the symbolism, as well as the substance, of this achievement. The changing behaviour of key actors since the 1970s evidences a grudging consensus, perhaps a consensus of exhaustion, in favour of reform. Groups which undermined stabilisation in the 1970s and 1980s have not done so in the 1990s, possibly because they lacked the ability to do so or because costs are seen to be outweighed by actual and potential gains. This 'alliance for change' has included most sectors of society, from the most powerful to the weakest, including the very poor, who have voted consistently for stability. While many corporate groups gained during the period of forced industrialisation, or were able to minimise the costs of the process, the unorganised benefited least and paid most.

Economic reform has underpinned macroeconomic stability, which has in turn fostered demands for political reform. The lessons of the recent past are that economic instability focuses attention on the economic. When inflation or coping with inflation is no longer an issue, politics is back on the agenda. In the past, authoritarian regimes were accepted because they promised stability. During the early years of the Convertibility Plan, the government of President Menem received largely uncritical support from the electorate. However, by 1994, when stability appeared to be secure, demands for political accountability increased and the electorate penalised organisations perceived as unable or unwilling to deliver. If there is a clear trend in voting patterns for the 1994 Constituent Assembly and for presidential and congressional elections between 1995 and 1997, it is that the electorate wants 'clean economics' *and* 'clean politics'. In 1994 the PJ and UCR (particularly the Radicals) paid the price for what was regarded as a lack of democratic transparency. In 1995, the electorate would not support parties which did not promise economic stability. In 1997 the majority of votes went to parties promising stability and transparency. Greater sectional coherence may also facilitate institutional consolidation and accountability. If democracy requires debate and if debate is best articulated through organised entities with clearly defined internal structures, intra-sectoral consolidation could foster meaningful inter-sectoral dialogue.

Notes

1 See, for example, C. Menem and M. Baizán, *Conversaciones con Carlos Menem: Como consolidar el modelo* (Buenos Aires, Editorial Fraterna, 1993) and *Desde el poder: Carlos Menem responde* (Buenos Aires, Corregidor, 1994); C. S. Menem and R. Dromi, *El estado hoy: Integración, participación, solidaridad* (Buenos Aires, Ediciones Ciudad Argentina, 1996).

2 D. Cavallo and R. Domenech, 'Las políticas macroeconómicas y el tipo de cambio real: Argentina, 1913–84', *Desarrollo Económico*, 28:3 (1988); and Y. Mundlak, D. Cavallo and R. Domenech, *Agriculture and Economic Growth in Argentina, 1913–84* (Washington, DC, International Food Policy Research Institute, 1989).

3 The literature is vast. See, for example J. Fogarty, E. Gallo and H. Diéguez (eds), *Argentina y Australia* (Buenos Aires, Instituto Torcuato Di Tella, 1979); T. Duncan and J. Fogarty, *Australia and Argentina: On Parallel Paths* (Melbourne, Melbourne University Press, 1986); D. Platt and G. Di Tella (eds), *Argentina, Canada and Australia: Studies in Comparative Development, 1870–1965* (London, Macmillan, 1985); C. Solberg, *The Prairies and the Pampas: Agrarian Policy in Canada and Argentina, 1880–1930* (Stanford, Stanford University Press, 1987); D. Platt (ed.), *Social Welfare, 1850–1950: Australia, Argentina and Canada Compared* (London, Macmillan, 1989); C. B. Schedvin, 'Staples and Regions of Pax Britannica', *Economic History Review*, 43:4 (1990); D. Díaz Fuentes, *Las políticas fiscales latinoamericanas frente a la gran depresión: Argentina, Brasil y México, 1920–1940* (Madrid, Instituto de Estudios Fiscales, 1993), and *Crisis y cambios estructurales en América Latina: Argentina, Brasil y México durante el período de entreguerras* (Mexico, Fondo de Cultura Económica, 1994); J. Adelman, *Frontier Development: Land, Labour and Capital on the Wheatlands of Argentina and Canada, 1890–1914* (Oxford, Oxford University Press, 1994); and I. Ortíz Donat, 'Economic Transitions: State and Industry in Argentina and Spain, 1975–1990', Ph.D. thesis, University of London, 1993.

4 *Statistical Abstract of Latin America* and *The Americas and Australasia* (various issues).

5 R. Cortés Conde, *La economía argentina en el largo plazo (siglos XIX y XX)* (Buenos Aires, Sudamericana, 1997), pp. 15–43.

6 R. Mallon and J. Sourrouille, *Economic Policy-making in a Conflictive Society: the Argentine case* (Cambridge, MA, Harvard University Press, 1975); G. Wynia, *Argentina in the Postwar Era: Politics and Economic Policy Making in a Divided Society* (Albuquerque, University of New Mexico Press, 1978); P. Lewis, *The Crisis of Argentine Capitalism* (Chapel Hill, Unversity of North Carolina Press, 1989); and M. Peralta Ramos, *The Political Economy of Argentina: Power and Class Since 1930* (Boulder, Lynne Rienner, 1992).

7 J. Machinea, *Stabilization Under Alfonsin's Government: A Frustrated Attempt* (Buenos Aires, CEDES, 1990).

8 International Bank for Reconstruction and Development (IBRD), *Argentina: From Insolvency to Growth* (Washington, DC, IBRD, 1993), p. 6.

9 G. Di Tella, *Perón-Perón, 1973–1976* (Buenos Aires, Sudamericana, 1983).

10 M. Mamalakis, 'The Theory of Sectoral Clashes', *Latin American Research Review*, 4:3 (1969). See also Mamalakis, 'The Theory of Sectoral Clashes Revisited', *Latin American Research Review*, 6:3 (1971). G. Merks, 'Sectoral Clashes and Political Change: The Argentine Case', *Latin American Research Review*, 4:3 (1969).

11 G. Di Tella and R. Dornbusch (eds), *The Political Economy of Argentina, 1946–1983* (Pittsburgh, Pittsburgh University Press, 1989), pp. 2–8.

12 Although somewhat dated, the classic categorisation of Argentinian political organisations remains J. L. de Imaz, *Los Que Mandan (Those Who Rule)* (Albany, State University of New York Press, 1970). More recent refinements are provided by Lewis, *Crisis of Argentine Capitalism*

and Peralta Ramos, *Political Economy of Argentina*. See also A. Ciría, *Parties and Power in Modern Argentina, 1930–1946* (Albany, State University of New York Press, 1974).

13 The best work on the military (notwithstanding the title) is the multi-volume series of R. Potash: *The Army and Politics in Argentina, 1928–1945* (Stanford, Stanford University Press, 1969), *The Army and Politics in Argentina, 1945–1962* (Stanford, Stanford University Press, 1980) and *The Army and Politics in Argentina, 1962–1973* (Stanford, Stanford University Press, 1992). Potash offers the most informed account, particularly for the critical 1949–76 period, of conflicts between 'legalists' (*azules*) and 'interventionists' (*colorados*), between anti-Peronists and pragmatists. He also identifies different approaches to economic policy – 'liberal' and 'nationalists' – and details distinct attitudes to organised labour within the military. See also Wynia, *Argentina in the Postwar Era*, Part III; D. Rock, *Argentina, 1516–1982: from Spanish conquest to the Falklands War* (Berkeley, University of California Press, 1985), chapters VII, VIII; and J. C. Torre and L. de Riz, 'Argentina since 1946', in L. Bethell (ed.), *The Cambridge History of Latin America. Volume VIII: 1930 to the Present* (Cambridge, Cambridge University Press, 1991).

14 R. Potash, 'The Military Under Alfonsín and Menem: The Search for a New Role', in C. M. Lewis and N. Torrents (eds), *Argentina in the Crisis Years (1983–1990): From Alfonsín to Menem* (London: Institute of Latin American Studies (ILAS), 1993); Peralta Ramos, *Political Economy of Argentina*, pp. 122–4.

15 P. Smith, *Politics and Beef in Argentina: Patterns of Conflict and Change* (New York, Columbia University Press, 1969); and H. C. Giberti, *El desarrollo agrario argentino* (Buenos Aires, Eudeba, 1964).

16 M. Murmis and J. C. Portantiero, 'Crecimiento industrial y alianza de clases en la Argentina, 1930–40', in M. Murmis and J. C. Portantiero (eds), *Estudios sobre los orígenes del peronismo* (Buenos Aires, Siglo XXI, 1971), p. 55; J. Schvarzer, *La industria que supimos conseguir: una historia política-social de la industria argentina* (Buenos Aires, Planeta, 1996); and J. Llach, 'El Plan Pinedo de 1940: Su significado histórico y los orígenes de la economía política del peronismo', *Desarrollo Económico*, 92 (1984).

17 Mallon and Sourrouille, *Economic Policy-making*; Wynia, *Argentina in the Postwar Era*, pp. 240–3.

18 A. Dorfman, *Cincuenta años de la industrialización argentina, 1930–1980* (Buenos Aires, Solar/Hachette, 1983); and Lewis, *Crisis of Argentine Capitalism*, chapters III, XIII.

19 O. Cornblit, 'Inmigrantes y empresarios en la política argentina', *Desarrollo Económico*, 6:24 (1967).

20 J. Schvarzer, *Empresarios del pasado: La Unión Industrial Argentina* (Buenos Aires, Planeta, 1991); and Ciría, *Parties and Power*, pp. 247–53; Peralta Ramos, *Political Economy of Argentina*, pp. 22–3.

21 Lewis, *Crisis of Argentine Capitalism*, pp. 164, 168–9, 340, 542 (n. 20).

22 Lewis, *Crisis of Argentine Capitalism*, pp. 343, 424–5, 458–60.

23 D. Azpiazu and B. Kosacoff, *La industria argentina: Desarrollo y cambios estructurales* (Buenos Aires, Centro Editor de América Latina, 1989). See also B. Kosacoff, *La industria argentina: Un proceso de reestructuración desarticulada* (Buenos Aires, Comisión Económica para América Latina and Centro Editor de América Latina, 1994).

24 D. Azpiazu, E. Basualdo and M. Kavisse, *El nuevo poder económico en la Argentina de los años 80* (Buenos Aires, Editorial Legasa, 1986); and Kosacoff, *La industria argentina*.

25 J. Adelman, 'The Political Economy of Labour in Argentina, 1870–1930', in J. Adelman (ed.), *Essays in Argentine Labour History, 1870 to 1930* (London, Macmillan, 1992), pp. 1–3; D. James, *Resistance and Integration: Peronism and the Argentine Working Class, 1946–1976* (Cambridge, Cambridge University Press, 1988); J. Horowitz, *Argentine Unions, the State and the Rise of Perón, 1930–1945* (Berkeley, University of California Press, 1990); and J. C. Torre, *La vieja guardia sindical y Perón: sobre los orígenes del peronismo* (Buenos Aires, Sudamericana and Instituto Torcuato Di Tella, 1990).

26 James, *Resistance and Integration*, pp. 161–6.

27 Lewis, *Crisis of Argentine Capitalism*, pp. 389–90; James, *Resistance and Integration*; and J. P. Brennan, *The Labor Wars in Córdoba, 1955–1976: Ideology, Work and Labor Politics in an Argentine Industrial City* (Cambridge, MA, Harvard University Press, 1994), pp. 10–2.

28 Lewis, *Crisis of Argentine Capitalism*, pp. 406–9, 423–4, 437–41; and James, *Resistance and Integration*.

29 Torre and de Riz, 'Argentina since 1946', p. 176; and Peralta Ramos, *Political Economy of Argentina*, pp. 113–14.

30 Lewis, *Crisis of Argentine Capitalism*, pp. 388–9; Peralta Ramos, *Political Economy of Argentina*, p. 31; and Rock, *Argentina, 1516–1982*, pp. 254–6, 283.

31 P. Waldman, 'The Peronism of Perón and Menem: From Justicialism to Liberalism', in Lewis and Torrents (eds), *Argentina in the Crisis Years*, p. 91.

32 P. Waldmann, *El Peronismo, 1943–1955* (Buenos Aires, Sudamericana, 1981); and C. H. Waisman, *The Reversal of Development in Argentina: Post-War Counterrevolutionary Policies and Their Structural Consequences* (Princeton, Princeton University Press, 1987).

33 Torre and de Riz, 'Argentina since 1946', p. 187.

34 D. Rock, *Politics in Argentina, 1890–1930: The Rise and Fall of Radicalism* (Cambridge, Cambridge University Press, 1975).

35 K. Sikkink, *Ideas and Institutions: Development in Brazil and Argentina* (Ithaca, Cornell University Press, 1991).

36 C. Szusterman, *Frondizi and the Politics of Developmentalism in Argentina, 1955–1962* (London, Macmillan, 1993).

37 Torre and de Riz, 'Argentina since 1946', p. 181.

38 R. Fraga, 'The Menemist Movement: Sustaining a Popular Conservative Coalition' mimeo, Buenos Aires, 1996.

39 M. Dodson, 'The Catholic Church in Contemporary Argentina', in A. Ciría (ed.), *New Perspectives on Modern Argentina* (Bloomington, Latin American Studies Program, Indiana University, 1972). See also Ciría, *Parties and Power*, p. 161.

40 J. M. Ghio, 'The Argentine Church and the Limits of Democracy', in A. Stuart-Gambino and E. Cleary (eds), *The Latin American Church and the Limits of Politics* (Boulder, Lynne Rienner, 1991).

41 See, for example, J. Schvarzer, *Martínez de Hoz: La lógica política de la política económica* (Buenos Aires, Centro de Investigaciones Sociales sobre el Estado y la Administración, 1983); A. Canitrot, 'Teoría y práctica del liberalismo: Política anti-inflacionaria y apertura económica en la Argentina', *Desarrollo Económico*, 21: 82 (1981); R. B. Fernández and C. A. Rodríguez (eds), *Inflación y estabilidad* (Buenos Aires, Macchi, 1982); and J. Ramos, *Neoconservative Economics in the Southern Cone of Latin America, 1973–1983* (Baltimore, Johns Hopkins University Press, 1986).

42 R. Frenkel and J. M. Fanelli, *Políticas de estabilización e hiperinflación en Argentina* (Buenos Aires, Tesis, 1990); and J. L. Machinea, 'Stabilisation under Alfonsín', in Lewis and Torrents (eds), *Argentina in the Crisis Years*.

43 J. C. Torre, 'Conflict and Co-operation in Governing the Economic Emergency'; and J. L. Machinea, 'Stabilisation under Alfonsín', in Lewis and Torrents (eds), *Argentina in the Crisis Years*.

44 See N. Phillips, 'Global and Regional Linkages', in J. Buxton and N. Phillips (eds), *Developments in Latin American Political Economy: States, Markets and Actors* (Manchester, Manchester University Press, 1999).

45 Economist Intelligence Unit, *Argentina; 1996/7* (London, EIU, 1996), p. 31.

46 República Argentina, Ministerio de Economía y Obras y Servicios Públicos, Secretaría de Política Económica, *Economic Report: First Quarter, 1997* (Buenos Aires, MEOSP, 1997), p. 40.

47 D. Azpiazu and A. Vispo, 'Some Lessons of the Argentine Privatization Process', *CEPAL Review*, 54 (1994), pp. 129–47.

48 Economic Commission for Latin America and the Caribbean (ECLAC), *Social Panorama of*

Latin America, 1994 (New York, ECLAC; 1994).

49 República Argentina, Ministerio de Economía y Obras y Servicios Públicos, Secretaría de Programación Económica, *Economic Report, 1995* (Buenos Aires, MEOSP, 1996), p. 7.

50 A. Mustapic, 'Problems of Democratic Institutionalisation: relations between the Executive and Congress', mimeo Buenos Aires, 1996; Fraga, 'Menemist Movement'.

51 See A. M. Mustapic and N. Ferretti, 'El veto presidencial bajo Alfonsín y Menem (1983–1995)', mimeo, Buenos Aires, 1997; D. Ferreira Rubio and M. Goretti, 'Cuando el presidente gobierna solo: Menem y los decretos de necesidad y urgencia hasta la reforma constitucional (julio 1989–agosto 1994)', *Desarrollo Económico*, 36:141 (April–June 1996); M. P. Jones, 'Evaluating Argentina's Presidential Democracy, 1983–1995', in S. Mainwaring and M. Soberg Shugart (eds), *Presidentialism and Democracy in Latin America* (Cambridge, Cambridge University Press, 1997); and G. Molinelli, 'Las relaciones presidente-congreso en Argentina, '83–'89', *Post Data*, 2 (November 1996).

3

Chile

JONATHAN R. BARTON

The end of transition?

Since 1970 there have been three delineated phases in Chile's political economy: the socialist experiment of Salvador Allende (1970–73); General Pinochet's military authoritarianism and accompanying neoliberal economic model (1973–89); and the democratic transition (1990–99). There is a strong likelihood that the presidential elections of 1999 will establish a new phase in this development process, ending the decade of transition from authoritarianism.

In October 1988 the Chilean population voted in arguably the most important ballot since independence: 'Yes' for continued military authoritarianism, 'No' for a democratic election the following year. The 'No' vote won by 54.7 per cent to 43 per cent and the transition to democracy began. Whilst the Yes/No referendum led to elections which were won by an anti-military coalition in December 1989, the years of dictatorship were not swept away overnight. The transitions from authoritarianism to democracy in Latin America have been long and difficult, requiring social reconciliation, a reorganisation of power relations, and political compromises.[1] In the Chilean case, the former dictator Augusto Pinochet remained as Commander-in-Chief of the armed forces to shadow the transition process and frustrate the attempts of the coalition to move beyond the militarism of the past. This is one reason why, over a decade after the referendum, the transition has still not run its course and democracy remains unconsolidated.

The transition in Chile has been discussed extensively: to what extent is it democratic? When does the period of transition end?[2] There are some comparisons to be drawn with the transitions in Eastern and Central Europe and South Africa, but the Chilean case is riddled with particularities such as the continuing influence of Pinochet on the transition process and the persistence of the neoliberal economic model. The end of transition is embedded in these two issues: the balance of political power, and the role and operation of the economy. Since the transition process is one from authoritarianism to democracy, the key issues are political and are determined by the civil–military balance of power. These include a reconfiguration of the power relations within the state, a reorganisation of the electoral system (which currently favours the right-wing minority) and a shift towards competitive rather than consensual politics.

In 1988, a coalition of 17 parties was established to oust the military from power. However, it remains largely intact and in government over ten years later. More than a decade of coalition politics has masked differences and divisions across the political spectrum. The simple binary division between parties to the right – *Renovación Nacional* (RN, National Renovation) and the *Unión Democrática Independiente* (UDI, Independent Democratic Union) – and the parties to the left and centre, including the *Partido Demócrata Cristiano* (PDC, Christian Democratic Party), the *Partido Social Demócrata* (PSD, Social Democratic Party), the *Partido Socialista* (PS, Socialist Party) and the *Partido por la Democracia* (PPD, Party for Democracy) – does not reflect the traditional three-way split in the Chilean electorate: left, centre and right (see Table 3.1). The 1999 presidential elections may well lead to a change in this situation, with the collapse or reorganisation of the coalition and the opportunity for a new era of post-transitional politics.

'Mission accomplished': civil–military relations and constitutional change

General Pinochet came to power following the military coup of September 1973 which ended the socialist government of Salvador Allende (1970–73). During the 17 years of dictatorship that followed, thousands of Chileans fled into exile, more were imprisoned, 3,000 were killed or 'disappeared', and a large percentage of the population lived in perpetual fear of the military and its declared internal war against the 'Marxist cancer'. Throughout these years the military established itself as the sole arbiter of political control. A central feature of the transition period has been the struggle to overhaul the conflictive civil–military relations that were constructed and to democratise the Constitution put in place by the junta in 1980 to consolidate the regime; it was in order to comply with his own Constitution that Pinochet organised the plebiscite eight years later and sought public support for his policies and methods. The main opposition to the changes put forward to consolidate the transition to democracy has come from General Pinochet, now over 80 years old, and his supporters.

Following Pinochet's 1988 plebiscite defeat and the electoral loss of his political surrogate Hernán Büchi in 1989, Pinochet has shadowed the two presidencies and continued to destabilise the relationship between civil society, the state and the armed forces.[3] This process began immediately after the plebiscite defeat, when the military and the civil opposition leaders negotiated a number of constitutional and legislative changes that were passed by an 85.7 per cent

Table 3.1 *Parliament and presidency in Chile, 1989 and 1993*

Parliament	1989		1993	
	Senators	*Deputies*	*Senators*	*Deputies*
Centre-left coalition				
Coalition of Parties for Democracy (CDP)				
Principally:				
Christian Democratic Party	37	13	39	13
Socialist Party	15	5	18	4
Party for Democracy	15	2	7	1
Radical Party	2	1	6	3
Subtotal (all coalition parties)	70	21	70	22
Right coalitions and allies				
Principally:				
National Renovation	29	11	32	13
Independent Democratic Union	15	3	14	2
'Designated'	–	8	–	8
Subtotal (all parties to the right)	50	25	48	24
Total (all parties and independent candidates)	120	46	120	46

Presidency	1989 *(% of vote)*		1993 *(% of vote)*	
CPD (Coalition of Parties for Democracy)				
P. Aylwin	55.17	E. Frei		58.01
		Other left candidates		
		M. Max-Neef		5.55
		J. Pizarro		4.69
		C. Reitze		1.17
Right parties				
H. Büchi	29.40	A. Alessandri		24.39
Independent Right				
F. Errázuriz	15.43	J. Piñera		6.18

Source: El Mercurio, 13 December 1993.

majority in a plebiscite in July 1989. While these included an enlarged Senate, a change in the composition of the National Security Council and easier constitutional amendments, the armed forces were resolute on maintaining the existing electoral system (which favours their supporters) and 'binding' laws were passed to restrict the options of the future government, such as the continuation of the privatisation process, job security for civil servants placed by the military and security of position for existing Commanders-in-Chief. These were the military's conditions for transition.

General Pinochet ended his term as Commander-in-Chief of the armed forces to enter the Senate as an Honorary Senator in March 1998, as prescribed in the 1980 Constitution. In his retirement speech he announced that he felt that his mission had been accomplished. From the coup in 1973 the missions of Pinochet were numerous: the subordination of the political system; the imposition of a far-reaching economic model; the orchestration of constitutional change; the maintenance of the armed forces' autonomy; and recently, the supervision of the transition. These goals were achieved by human rights abuses, intimidation and violence, and also a range of constitutional, legislative and economic changes. For instance, the 1980 Constitution provided an ideal tool to legitimise the state of siege and emergency powers employed against the left-wing 'terrorist' groups.[4]

The issue of human rights abuses has been a critical factor in the military's desire to oversee the transition and ensure impunity. The armed forces have been protected by the General Law of Amnesty of 1978 which declared that military personnel would not be indicted for violations of human rights during the 1973–78 period. With such an important piece of legislation to defend acts of barbarism supposedly in defence of the state, the military has remained free from blame.[5] In 1991, the Rettig Commission on Truth and Reconciliation set up by President Aylwin announced the findings of its investigations into human rights cases during the dictatorship. It identified abuses, deaths and disappearances, but the Commission did not target individuals and the outcome of the report did not lead to convictions of military personnel, only criticisms of the judiciary.[6] Despite the Rettig report and in many cases because of it, the human rights issue continues to divide Chilean society and promotes military intransigence.[7] As well as avoiding criminal prosecution, the military has also been successful in protecting its budget, which is guaranteed at a certain level by law and is also linked to 10 per cent of the revenue of Codelco, the state copper company.

The military's role in the transition has been so influential that the two post-dictatorship administrations of Patricio Aylwin (1990–94) and Eduardo Frei (1994–99)[8] have been described as little more than 'tutelary' democracies supervised by the armed forces.[9] Other terms employed to define this political situation include 'electoralism', whereby there are elections but the military has given up its position, not its power, and *democradura* – a mix of democracy and dictatorship.[10] All these references fit with Pinochet's own desire for a 'protected' democracy. Within this supervised transition the military and right-wing parties have remained embedded within the political system via two mechanisms: the electoral system and the provision for *designados*, or 'designated' Senators.[11] The Chilean binomial electoral system favours minority parties in terms of the distribution of seats in the Chamber of Deputies and Senate, while the 1980 Constitution facilitates the selection of nine 'designated',

unelected Senators. This bias has made constitutional reform difficult, especially since the reforms have targeted the military's 'authoritarian enclaves'
such as the *designados*, presidential selection of high-ranking military officers,
and Ministry of Interior rather than military control of the police.

President Aylwin made initial advances in constitutional change in 1992 but
his policies reflected the delicate relationship with the military and the priority
of national reconciliation rather than confrontation.[12] If Aylwin's democratic
administration was a 'founding' one, the Frei administration was expected to
be a 'consolidating' one, with an emphasis on constitutional change and a
reversal of the trend in social polarisation.[13] Despite military intransigence,
President Frei has challenged the authoritarian enclaves, including the 1997
restructuring of the constitutional tribunal. With the President able to replace
two of the four replaceable members of the eight-member tribunal, and also
being able to replace some of the designated Senators and military Chiefs of
Staff, presidential authority has been gradually strengthened during the 1990s.

So far the process of change has been slow, and it will not be facilitated by
Pinochet's own transition from General to Senator, where he will consolidate
the Senate's intransigence and opposition to the political and constitutional
reforms of the President and Chamber of Deputies. In spite of national elections
to change the composition of the Senate in December 1997 (with the coalition
gaining 51 per cent of the vote), there has been little effect on the right-wing balance of the Upper House (eight of the nine right-wing UDI candidates were
elected, to be added to the 'designated' Senators and Pinochet).[14] A key consolidating factor for the right wing, which is supported for the most part by the
coalition government, is the direction of economic policy. For over twenty years,
Chile has followed an economic model that was initially promoted by the dictatorship and is now pursued with equal vigour by the regime's opponents.

The Janus face of the economic 'miracle'

Privatisation and exportation

Within a five-year period (1970–75), the Chilean economy shifted from a command economy to neoliberalism. With little economic experience, the junta
sought the advice of an economic team trained at the University of Chicago –
the so-called 'Chicago Boys'.[15] The economic model instituted as a 'shock treatment' from 1975 dominated Chilean development strategy throughout the dictatorship years, leading some observers to declare it to be miraculous. Chile was
Latin America's 'jaguar' competing with the Asian 'tigers'. Rather than free-
market economics, the major similarity with the 'tigers' was the underlying
state involvement in the orientation of the economy, supporting shifts in production, subsidising privatisation, intervening on a grand scale during periods
of market failure, and maintaining strict labour controls and weak environmental regulations. Martínez and Díaz note that: 'paradoxically, the radical
nature of the neoliberal subsidiary state required an increase in public inter-

vention',[16] citing five areas in which the state was highly interventionist: high levels of public spending (see Table 3.2); political pressures on state agencies; continued public ownership of the copper industry; strategic control over relative prices, labour markets and wages; and fiscal support and subsidies to the poorest sectors of Chilean society. The experience was far removed from the more theoretical liberalism claimed by some commentators.

Table 3.2   *Basic economic indicators, Chile, 1974–1995*

Indicator	1974	1977	1980	1983	1986	1989	1992	1995
A								
Population (1974 = 100)	100.0	104.7	109.5	114.7	120.4	126.5	133.1	139.6
Total GDP (1974 = 100)	100.0	99.9	126.2	113.6	131.8	165.5	203.7	244.0
Per capita GDP(1974 = 100)	100.0	95.4	115.2	99.1	109.5	130.8	153.0	174.7
Investment (% of GDP)	17.4	13.3	16.6	12.0	18.9	26.0	28.2	30.7
Public expenditure (% of GDP)	32.4	24.9	23.1	28.4	30.0	29.5	23.5	22.5
Annual inflation rate (%)	375.9	63.4	31.2	23.1	17.4	21.4	12.7	8.2
B								
Exports as % of GDP	20.4	20.6	22.8	24.0	30.6	32.0	35.9	37.3
Foreign debt ratio to exports	1.9	2.4	2.3	4.5	4.8	2.0	1.8	1.3
C								
Unemployment rate (% of labour force)	10.8	11.8	10.4	19.1	8.8	5.3	4.4	4.7
Average real wage (1974 = 100)	100.0	113.9	138.2	135.1	143.2	155.1	173.1	195.0
Average minimum wage (1974 = 100)	100.0	93.4	110.4	97.1	83.6	106.3	127.0	91.2

Source: Central Bank of Chile; Instituto Nacional de Estadistica, in J. Martínez and A. Díaz *Chile: The Great Transformation* (Geneva, UNRISD and Brookings Institution, 1996).

The declared central tenets of the model were strict monetary policy, opening of the market place to international trade, liberalisation of capital markets, privatisation of state assets, and the orientation of the economy towards increased exports rather than the promotion of domestic industrialisation. The Chicago Boys, confidently operating within the military–technocratic alliance, set a trend towards technocratic approaches to political economy issues that would be adopted in many other Latin American republics during the 1980s, notably Mexico and Argentina.

An important argument embedded in the neoliberal philosophy was that economic liberty was more fundamental than political liberty.[17] Facilitated by excessive labour controls such as the banning of trade unions, greater flexibilisation of labour and low wages, the model was successful and passed through two distinct phases. The first phase, from 1975 to 1982, was a 'naive' stage of liberalisation ending in financial crisis and deep recession, followed by the 'pragmatic' stage from 1983, focusing on greater diversity in export-led development and improved financial controls.[18] Juan Fontaine maintains that this second phase was directed by more of a 'pragmatic orthodoxy', providing greater flexibility to meet the same objectives.[19] Throughout these two stages, the private sector was favoured as the engine of economic development within a 'pragmatic neoliberal coalition' with landowners and the regime.[20] In their desire not to jeopardise economic stability, the transition governments supplanted the military in this coalition, neither extending it nor transforming it, and even giving rise to criticisms regarding rent-seeking and corruption.[21] As a result they have been censured for continuing the socio-economic legacy of the regime.

From the mid-1970s, entrepreneurialism and a culture of 'popular capitalism' were promoted, the entry of multinationals was encouraged, and assistance was offered to domestic economic groups, particularly within the privatisation programme.[22] Apart from Codelco, almost all of the state companies of the Allende period had been privatised by 1988; only 45 of the 400 public-sector banks and firms that existed in 1973 remained in state hands by 1980.[23] The strength of the economic model into the 1990s under the coalition administrations can be witnessed in the continuation of the privatisation programme into areas such as energy and public utilities. The business-friendliness of the Chilean economy model has given rise to a mix of powerful Chilean economic groups and foreign multinationals. Many Chilean economic groups benefited from the neoliberal model, borrowing heavily on international capital markets to invest in diverse financial and production activities, revelling in the underpricing of the nationalised companies going under the privatisation hammer in a 'speculator's paradise'; the treasury lost \$2 billion due to the privatisations between 1985 and 1989.[24] By 1979, 130 of the 250 largest private enterprises were controlled by ten economic conglomerates.[25]

Whilst the 1982–83 economic crisis led to the exposure of the indebtedness of many economic groups – with the two leading groups, Vial (BHC) and Cruzat-Larraín, forced into bankruptcy – the remainder were assisted by the government's support of the banking sector and took advantage of the structural adjustment and the promotion of export-led growth that followed.[26] Ironically for a regime dedicated to neoliberalism, in the period 1983–85 the state controlled 14 of 26 Chilean banks and 8 of 17 financial institutions.[27] The 1982–83 crisis was a turning point. By replacing Sergio de Castro, the Finance Minister since 1975, Pinochet broke with the first phase of neoliberalism and ushered in the second, export-driven phase to reduce the burgeoning foreign debt. As a first step, the Chilean peso was floated and immediately depreciated 40 per cent against the dollar. Once again, as in 1975, growth would take place from a low starting point.

Despite difficulties, the benefits of the neoliberal model have been numerous (see Table 3.3). Chile is now recognised as being one of the most attractive havens for foreign capital amongst the developing economies, due to its political stability and limited restrictions on profit repatriation and company operations. Another benefit of the model has been the generation of a more diverse economic structure. Mining in Chile, particularly copper mining, has provided the backbone of the economy during the twentieth century but since the 1980s recession there has been a movement towards greater diversification in the non-traditional sectors of the economy.

Table 3.3   *Annual average export increases, Chile, 1960–94 (%)*

Period	Exports	GDP
1960–65	4.2	3.8
1965–70	3.0	4.7
1975–80	5.6	2.3
1980–85	15.3	6.8
1985–90	1.8	0.4
1985–90	10.8	6.5
1990–94	9.1	7.2

Source: Central Bank of Chile, in P. Meller and R. Sáez (eds), *Auge exportador Chileno: Lecciones y desafíos futuros* (Santiago, CIEPLAN/Dolmen, 1997).

The non-traditional sectors such as forestry, wood pulp, paper and cellulose, fruit and wine, and aquaculture (fish farming) have experienced rapid increases during the 1980s and 1990s, increasing the profile of Chile and its products in the international market place.[28] These new sectors have provided new employment opportunities, have stimulated multiplier economic activities (goods and services) in local and regional economies, and have led to increased infrastructural developments and also a reduction in the rate of outmigration from some of the poorest regions of the country. Despite these positive factors, a balanced assessment of export-led development must also consider the related issues such as tariff mechanisms, exchange-rate support and the stagnation in domestic industrialisation which have enabled this process.[29]

Export orientation has been the linchpin of the Chilean political economy of the 1990s. To enable the export model to function the state has maintained tight control over domestic economic factors. Soon after the transition to democracy the government was beset with an overheating economy, resulting from a high degree of liberalisation, with insufficient controls and inflationary tendencies. This overheating provided Chile with its most significant economic threat since the 1982 crisis. The response from the Central Bank was the activation of a tight-rein policy to curb the overexuberance of Chilean entrepreneurs and consumers in the face of large capital inflows. The Central Bank maintained an austere policy of interest-rate controls to keep inflation low and it remains vigilant despite a lowering of the rate, especially in view of rising consumer spending, much of it credit-based. By 1996, the economy had been stabilised and slowed to a sustainable growth rate, restrictions were lifted and legislation had been passed to reduce capital market controls. With fewer restrictions on capital transfers to match the limited tariff obstacles to trade, the Chilean government is setting up the country as a financial and commercial haven balanced between the traditional ties of Europe and North America, new opportunities in South America and the rising importance of the Pacific basin in the new millennium.

A global strategy

Chilean neoliberalism has dovetailed well with developments in the international political economy from the 1980s. The movement in the global arena towards greater regional integration and increased trade liberalisation has been ideally suited to Chilean export-led development. Whereas Chile was once considered as little more than a copper-supplying nation in a peripheral region of the world economy, it now has a different profile. During the 1980s and 1990s commercial policies have encouraged integration with North American trading partners, regional integration with its Southern Cone neighbours, and greater aspirations around the Pacific Rim.[30] Alongside the promotion of export-led development, Chile adopted a proactive commercial strategy inclusive of bilateral, regional and multilateral negotiations and agreements. This open trading policy gained considerable support from partners in East and South-East Asia, North America and Europe, who were already pushing towards greater liberalisation.[31] The strategy has proven to be highly beneficial to Chile, ensuring strong foreign-exchange earnings and raising the country's international status.

Since the Second World War, Chile's foreign and commercial policy has been interlinked with North America. The founding of the North American Free-Trade Agreement (NAFTA) in 1993 provided a fillip to the Mexican economy by being linked with its powerful neighbours to the north – the United States and Canada. For Chile, the Mexican model was an attractive one since the NAFTA members provided large potential markets and new sources of foreign direct investment and intermediate and capital goods imports; prior to the NAFTA, Mexico and Chile signed a bilateral agreement which stimulated trade and investment between the two countries. Although the United States made it clear that if the NAFTA were to enlarge Chile was the leading contender for entry, it is Mexico and Canada which have been more proactive in establishing commercial agreements with Chile, whilst the United States has prevaricated. The lack of certainty regarding its northern neighbours has been a factor in Chile's push for greater integration with its regional neighbours.[32]

In 1996 Chile entered the Mercosur[33] (within a free-trade zone Economic Complementarity Agreement rather than as a full member) as the next step in its strategy. Since the 1980s, the Mercosur (the Southern Cone trade bloc) has been dominated by Brazil and Argentina (other members include Uruguay and

Paraguay). Previous Latin American trade blocs have been largely unsuccessful, such as the Latin American Free-Trade Association (LAFTA) established in 1960, and the Andean Pact, which Chile withdrew from in 1977. However, integration in the Mercosur is a recognition of the need to maintain regional economic ties and to exploit its neighbours' larger markets and seek possibilities for investment. Discussions of links between the Andean Pact and the Mercosur by the year 2000 also provide increased opportunities.[34] The other Mercosur members regard Chile as a market for industrial goods, such as for Brazilian vehicles and chemicals, and also a regional gateway to the markets of Pacific Asia (a $160 million investment in ports and transandean communications outlined in the Chile–Mercosur agreement supports this strategy). As the tariff barriers within the trade bloc are slowly phased out – 90 per cent of products are expected to be traded at a zero tariff by 2004 – the competitive capacities of the Chilean economy will be tested. However. Chile's experience of export orientation over more than twenty years suggests that it has the ability to perform well in a regional context, especially if value can be added to its range of leading exports.[35]

For these same competitive reasons, Chile's geographical situation is increasingly being exploited. With the next century being hailed as the 'Pacific Century', Chile's links with Asian capital and markets is undoubtedly strengthening its position in this geo-economic region.[36] Chile's early involvement in the APEC (Asia-Pacific Economic Cooperation) is both an indicator of its strategy of seeking trading opportunities at every turn and also a realisation of the role of Asian demand for its non-traditional products, such as cellulose and farmed salmon. Although the APEC is not yet a trading bloc as such, it is indicative of the changing scale of regional integration. A further initiative on this scale is the trading bloc of the Americas (provisionally intended to operate from 2005), which has been discussed from the basis of the Organisation of the American States (OAS). In 1998, Santiago hosted the Summit of the Americas at which increased economic integration was discussed.

Growth with equity?

The economic miracle has a Janus face: macroeconomic success on the one side, social and environmental exploitation on the other. The Aylwin government arrived in office committed to linking economic growth with social equity, overcoming the social debt of the regime years and dedicating itself to a process of political learning, to take advantage of lessons from Chile's recent past and experiences across the continent.[37] However, progress has been slow. The flaws of the economic model include issues of social equity (the social costs) and environmental sustainability (the environmental costs).[38] The economic 'miracle' was linked to successes in the area of attraction of foreign capital and in the export-led model of foreign-exchange earnings.[39] In terms of GDP growth, balance of trade and incomes, there is indeed cause for celebration. However, once these figures are reviewed more critically in a socio-economic context and in terms of environmental and resource exploitation, the 'miracle' provides a more salutary lesson. Essentially, the Chilean 'miracle' failed to achieve basic macro-social and environmental balances.[40]

Under the military, social policy focused on the 30 per cent of the population in 'extreme poverty'. In several ways this policy was effective: infant mortality reduction; decentralised service provision; availability of household items for the poorest families.[41] However, there were also numerous flaws. It was top-down, technocentric and non-participatory and it left a vast number of people to fend for themselves within popular, community-based, self-help organisations. Other mechanisms were the scheme to restrict employmeht to the heads of households only (POJH) and the minimum employment (PEM) programme, which formed the basis of welfare for marginalised sectors of society. Social conditions were not improved by the 'seven modernisations' which led to major transformations in labour practices, agriculture, education, health, social security, justice and public administration.[42] Under the transition administrations there has been a reorganisation of social priorities but grave social problems remain.

Aylwin and Frei adopted a more inclusionary and consensual set of social policies, extending assistance to a wider range of the population via new mechanisms, for example, the Fund for Social Solidarity and Investment (FOSIS).[43] However, despite changes to policy, Chile retains a large social sector of marginalised urban and rural poor who have seen little or nothing of the fruits of the last quarter-century of development. It is apparent that the benefits of the model accrued to particular sectors of society to the exclusion of others. The scale of the problem of the *poblaciones* (shanty-towns), particularly in Santiago, which is home to over 40 per cent of the national population, the increased polarisation of society, and the health, education and housing security of many groups need to be questioned. In 1994, when President Frei assumed the presidency, his speech to the nation declared that his intention was to eradicate poverty in Chile. In 1999 his term of office will come to an end, yet there has been little change in the distribution of wealth, which favours the richer deciles of Chilean society (see Table 3.4).

In terms of the economy, the non-traditional activities have been the success story of the 1980s and 1990s, but operations are characterised by seasonal, low-wage labour which has provided the basis for the profitable returns of the non-traditional export firms.[44] In contrast to employment growth in these sectors, increased technological implementation in more traditional activities such as mining and capture fisheries have led to structural problems in terms of labour and employment. The closure of the largest coal mine in Chile at Lota in 1996 and the accompanying demonstrations and publicity were indicative of the type of changes that are taking place in the economy.

Collins and Lear and Sánchez emphasise the point that whilst capital, goods and services are freed up under neoliberalism, labour is not considered free and its costs are maintained at low levels, leading to 'neomarginality' and the growth of the informal economy.[45] Petras and Leiva describe the situation as one of economic deregulation coupled with state regulation of civil society.[46] In 1990, 44.4 per cent of Chileans lived in poverty compared with only 20 per cent in 1970.[47] Lack of employment security and the flexibilisation of labour date back to the labour reforms instituted under the military dictatorship. The banning of trade unions and the lack of ability of workers to organise themselves and oppose wage freezes and controls were crucial to the success of the model; to compound the problem, workers were also hard hit by the 1982 recession and real earnings did not recover until the late 1980s.[48] Despite reform by the Aylwin administration, labour is still characterised by a lack of organisation in the face of minimal state support for job security and improved working practices.

Table 3.4 *Distribution of total income by household deciles, Chile, 1990–96 (%)*

Decile	1990	1993	1996
I	2.2	2.2	2.0
II	3.3	3.4	3.3
III	4.1	4.3	4.2
IV	4.9	5.2	5.1
V	5.7	6.0	5.9
VI	6.6	6.9	6.7
VII	7.8	8.1	8.0
VIII	9.5	10.0	10.2
IX	13.7	13.8	13.9
X	42.4	40.2	40.7

Source: Intituto Nacional de Estadística, in H. Fazio, *Mapa actual de la extrema riqueza en Chile* (Santiago, LOM-ARSIS, 1997).

Non-traditional activities do little to change the country's perennial dependence on its natural resource base. Over 80 per cent of export earnings are derived from natural-resource products. Rather than reorientate and balance the economy, the military regime and subsequent governments have intensified export dependency and international vulnerability ('boom and bust' cycles), characteristics of Latin America's historical experience.[49] Until there is state policy to increase value-added products within these non-traditional activities and the mining sector (this would suggest a greater emphasis on manufacturing operations), it is unlikely that resource dependence (and thus resource exploitation and economic vulnerability to international pricing and market accessibility) will be reduced.

Dependence on the natural-resource base leads to questions about the sustainability of the activities involved. While a shift towards non-traditional activities has attempted to relieve environmental pressures such as over-fishing and degradation associated with mining, it has itself created new pressures such as the preservation of native forestry relative to introduced exotic species, and contamination associated with aquaculture and intensive chemical use in fruit cultivation. Although a state organisation (CONAMA) was established in the early 1990s to combat issues of environmental sustainability, it is a weak body with limited resources, working within a political and economic environment of industrial and commercial promotion in preference to environmental protection and sustainable economy–environment strategies. In many ways Chile's natural-resource dependence has not changed considerably, but rather merely shifted from mineral resources to the exploitation of other natural resources (marine and cultivated). This is a major structural obstacle to the current model, exposing Chile to issues of long-term economic insecurity and instability. In this respect, the lessons of 1929–32 and 1982–83 have not been heeded.

Towards a new model of consolidation

'Besides its ethical bases, the elimination of poverty, the attenuation of inequalities, the quest for equity and the opening up of an attractive horizon of opportunities are imperative requirements for the consolidation of democracy and the strengthening of a dynamic and modern economy.'[50]

Perspectives on the future of Chile's political economy fall into three broad and undefined schools. One school envisages a continuation and deepening of the current neoliberal model, eradicating elements of state intervention and market failure in order to maintain macroeconomic variables of growth with monetary stability. A second school desires a wholehearted revision of the neoliberal model with greater state intervention in order to distribute the benefits emanating from the successes of the export-led economy. These supporters advocate increased state control in the areas of health, education, social welfare and increased planning in the areas of transport, housing, energy and infrastructure. For these people the neoliberal model is a necessary evil in view of the need for integration in the global economy, although they consider the model to be insensitive to social needs, and therefore state involvement is required in certain areas in preference to market forces.

The third school is more radical in its alternatives and is highly fragmented. For example, the Communist Party, which provided armed opposition during the dictatorship and vocal opposition during the transition, attracted renewed support during the mid-1990s. In 1998 Gladys Marín, the party leader, publicly criticised General Pinochet and triggered a judicial investigation into his role in human rights abuses during the regime years. The Communist Party has also increased its share of the national vote in the parliamentary elections and established wide support in the universities. These recent events have been important in the revitalisation of the Left and their alternative views on the national political economy, although the extent to which their support amongst disaffected youth and student movements is reflected in wider society is debatable.[51]

This third school, more than merely a Communist approach to change, is also representative of different radical alternatives such as that offered by Manfred Max-Neef during the elections of 1993, advocating a humanistic and ecological approach to political and economic change. Ultimately the Chilean Left, as with the Latin American Left as a whole, is in itself in transition. Former Socialists and Communists who became involved in the transition process within the coalition have shifted their views towards the centre, becoming *renovados*, and there is confusion regarding ideology in political and economic policy-making.[52] Rather than offer radical alternatives to capitalism, Chile's 'new Left' appears to be as ready to run with the neoliberal model as Pinochet himself was in the mid-1970s.

The first school of growth 'as is' and secondary 'trickle-down' of the benefits to society is reaching the end of its ability to account for some of the social trends that have taken place in Chile since the 1970s. The second school of 'growth with more equity' looks towards the state for greater involvement in order to shape the pattern of the model, to account for its apparent social and environmental failings. The neostructuralists, who see the state as performing a modern role as 'effective' regulator of the economy and distributor of the benefits of growth, are moving towards centre stage to advocate a 'human' and 'green' face for neoliberalism. This will require a more interventionist state, but it has been weakened by 20 years of contraction and a process of 'selling-off' and 'farming-out' many of its undertakings from social welfare to economic activities, apart from the jewel in the crown, the national copper company.[53]

The medium-term future of Chile's political economy is in the hands of followers of the first two schools, although control of the political reins will be contested.[54] Until the social impacts, environmental impacts and questions regarding the sustainability of the existing model are questioned more critically, it is likely that the first school of thought will remain predominant. However, the 1999 presidential elections will be an important watershed, providing an opportunity for such discussions and also the possibility of an end to the existing centre-left coalition.[55]

The coalition is likely to fracture in response to pressures from within civil society. As economic development fails to engender real improvements in the lives of people in the lower-income sectors of society, the election campaign will provide an opportunity for these disaffected groups to register their opinions and to seek concessions from the politicians. There is little doubt that benefits of the model have accrued to a limited number of social groups whilst others have suffered from the greater flexibilisation of labour, rationalisation resulting from privatisations and reduced health and welfare security. The model's 'haves and have-nots' are likely to remain highly polarised, leading to social unrest. In 1996 and 1997 numerous demonstrations and strikes brought pressure to bear on the coalition. With teachers, civil servants, hospital staff, miners and fisheries workers all seeking improved salaries and job security, the government became aware of increased disaffection with the existing model and also the hopes that had been embodied in the concept of the democratic transition.

It is unlikely that social pressures for improved wages and reforms in various areas of the economy and polity will diminish. James Petras notes that mass popular protest, social mobilisations, general strikes, land occupations and provincial revolts have followed in the wake of neoliberal policies throughout Latin America.[56] The likelihood is that such discontent will force the diverse parties within the coalition to recognise their traditional support bases and ideologies, leading to fragmentation of the coalition. Since the coalition was established for one reason only, to end dictatorship, it is now long past its sell-by date and may well end with the millennium.

The transition from authoritarianism to democracy was not achieved during the 1990s. Pinochet controlled its pace and maintained authoritarian pillars of the past such as the central tenets of the 1980 Constitution and the economic model. His presence has limited the consolidation of democracy; Petras and Leiva make the apposite point that 'procedural changes in an authoritarian state framework do not define a democratic political system'.[57] As with other Latin American republics, personalism is not peripheral to political affairs but is central. Until Pinochet leaves the Senate, the ghost of the past will remain. As a result of the dictatorship years the military has developed into a powerful, highly autonomous institution with clear economic and political programmes that it seeks to promote. Despite the transition, the military remains more influential in political and economic affairs than it did in the 1960s and as such it has been unwilling to transform itself into a professional, unpoliticised institution operating on the instructions of the elected Executive.[58] Despite Pinochet and the military, however, there are genuine reasons for the return of competitive democratic politics within the country: the dissipation of the threat of a military return to power; the stretching of the 'coalition above party' cohesion; and the presidential elections of 1999.[59]

This shift in the political system will require a renegotiation of relations within the state: President – Senate; Senate – Chamber of Deputies; President – armed forces; President/Parliament – judiciary. As most of these relations are embedded within the Constitution, it is the Constitution and changes to it which will determine the establishment of the new rules. Further to the constitutional arrangements and power-sharing amongst the state institutions is the issue of how Chile can move towards a model of political development and economic growth that is both inclusionary, macroeconomically stable and with mechanisms for increases in productivity and savings alongside improvements in social distribution. The role of politicians in shaping this new model must not be underestimated. It is they who must establish a balance between the demands of business and the demands of lower-income groups.[60] These same politicians must decide on national priorities, such as the subtle but significant difference between growth with equity and equity through growth.

Lois Oppenheim points to four major challenges that have faced the transition administrations: reforming the political system to eliminate undemocratic features; to confront the human rights issue; to reformulate civil–military relations; and to maintain economic stability.[61] On these four counts, only the last has been dealt with effectively by the two transition administrations. In the other three areas, changes have been incremental rather than definitive, suggesting a continuity of the regime years. For example, President Frei emphasised poverty reduction, modernisation of the state and constitutional reform. In all three, his policies and legislation have fallen well short of the mark.

In the case of poverty, data reveal that the underclass in Chilean society is increasingly distant from the upper deciles of income earners. Geraldo Munck makes the relevant point that 'the fate of democracy appears closely tied to change favouring social cohesion'.[62] This cohesion will be derived from reducing the gaps between the political elites and social sectors and movements in civil society and building confidence in the effectiveness of participatory politics.[63] In the same way that entry into the NAFTA was discussed in terms of fast-track and slow-track, the same is true of Chilean society, where the beneficiaries of neoliberalism have fast-tracked into the affluent lifestyle and consumption patterns of contemporary Western European and North American cultures;[64] the slow-trackers have received little from the model. Debates regarding Chilean culture and identity have become more complex as a result. Many slow-trackers were made increasingly vulnerable during the dictatorship (others supported it), losing job security and welfare-support mechanisms, and they have been unable to recoup lost ground under the transition administrations. The influential Churches' National Commission on Justice and Peace noted that 'two Chiles are being constructed, one more prosperous and developed and another very poor and marginal', adding 'in terms of the process of overcoming poverty, the rhythm of this process is too slow'.[65] Chile has become a society of two halves separated not only by income, living conditions, opportunities and aspirations, but more importantly by confidence in the capacity of political and economic institutions and processes to bring about changes to the status quo *ex ante*. These are the priorities for the new President in the year 2000, and how they are tackled will indicate if the end of transition – consolidated democracy – has finally been reached.

Notes

1 See P. Schmitter, G. O'Donnell and L. Whitehead, *Transitions from Authoritarian Rule* (Baltimore, John Hopkins University Press, 1986).

2 P. Meller, *Un Siglo de Economía Política Chilena (1890–1990)* (Santiago, Editorial Andrés Bello, 1996), and J. Martínez and A. Díaz, *Chile: The Great Transformation* (Geneva, UNRISD and Brookings Institution, 1996) provide good overviews of the political economy to 1990. For recent literature on Chile's political economy, see G. Munck, 'Authoritarianism, Modernisation, and Democracy in Chile', *Latin American Research Review*, 29:2 (1994); and D. Richards, 'The Political Economy of the Chilean Miracle', *Latin American Research Review*, 32:1 (1997).

3 In December 1990 Pinochet ordered the army to barracks and declared a state of alert (in

response to pressure on Pinochet to resign), whilst in May 1993 the military surrounded its Santiago headquarters with combat-ready soldiers (in response to increasing human rights pressures on the military). The military also confronted the judiciary and the President after the prosecution of General Manuel Contreras; Contreras was given medical care in an armed forces hospital and the military was unwilling to let him be transferred to prison. As recently as September 1996 Pinochet made a speech suggesting that the possibility of another coup had not disappeared.

4 The fact that the Chilean electorate voted for the Constitution (67.7 per cent for, 31.1 per cent against) was more a matter of Chile's compulsory voting laws and the climate of fear within the country at this time rather than any popular desire to change the nature and function of the state and its officials.

5 In a highly publicised case in 1995, General Manuel Contreras, former Director of the DINA (military intelligence unit), and General Pablo Espinoza were found guilty of planning the murder of Orlando Letelier in New York. Amnesty was waived due to pressure from the US government.

6 Problems with the judiciary in terms of their connections continue. The judge investigating the terrorist murder of politician Jaime Guzmán (in 1991) resigned from the case in 1997 when avenues of inquiry leading to indictments of the Chief of Police Investigations and the Under-Secretary of Regional Development were closed to her by the Court of Appeal. Also in 1997, the right-wing UDI party accused the President of the Supreme Court of having links with drug trafficking.

7 The trauma of the regime years has subsided only gradually. A Centro de Estudios Públicos (Centre of Public Studies) survey prior to the 1989 election revealed that the principal preoccupation with the election of the right-wing candidate Hernán Büchi was the 'excessive influence of Augusto Pinochet' (42.8 per cent). Concerns with President Aylwin's candidature were 'eventual conflict with the armed forces' (38.8 per cent) and the potential influence of the Communist Party' (34.1 per cent). See O. Godoy, 'Algunas claves de la transición política en Chile', *Estudios Públicos*, 38 (1990).

8 Eduardo Frei continues the tradition of the political class in Chile. His father was President (1964–70); Aylwin's father was a Senator. In the 1993 election Frei was fighting against Arturo Alessandri, grandson and nephew of two former presidents. The persistence of family-based politics suggests that the transition is a redemocratisation, a return to the party system prior to Allende. In many ways the coup and the supervised transition have been responses by the military to the political 'class' which it regarded with disgust for letting the country end up with a socialist-led administration; these politicians were allowed to resume their activities within defined limits from 1989. Chilean society is apparently tired of contemporary politics. Voter apathy is registered in Chile, especially amongst young people, since voting is mandatory; in the December 1997 congressional elections, 19 per cent of votes were blank or nullified.

9 For discussions of changing interpretations of democracy relevant to Latin America, see B. Gills and J. Rocamora, 'Low Intensity Democracy', *Third World Quarterly*, 13:3 (1992); and A. Leftwich, 'Governance, Democracy and Development in the Third World', *Third World Quarterly*, 14:3 (1993).

10 See R. Rabkin, 'The Aylwin Government and "Tutelary" Democracy: A Concept in Search of a Case?', *Journal of Inter-American Studies and World Affairs*, 34:4 (1992).

11 The binomial electoral system guarantees one of two parliamentary seats in an electoral area to a party with 34 per cent of the vote, despite the fact that another party may have 66 per cent. The 'designated' Senators serve for eight-year terms: four are former high-ranking officers in each of the armed forces (including the police) selected by the military; three are former Supreme Court judges and controllers-general, selected by the Supreme Court; the President may select a former university rector and a former minister.

12 Rabkin, 'The Aylwin Government and "Tutelary" Democracy', in J. Petras and F. Leiva, *Democracy and Poverty in Chile: The Limits to Electoral Politics* (Boulder, Westview, 1994).

13 A. Angell and B. Pollack, 'The Chilean Elections of 1993: From Polarisation to Consensus',

Bulletin of Latin American Research, 9:1 (1995).

14 An example of Senate opposition to the President occurred in August 1996 when President Frei's choice of new Central Bank President (Carlos Massad) was turned down by the Senate. The right-wing President of the Senate, Sergio Diez, remarked that '(Frei) exercised his legal right to put forward a name, and the Senate exercised its right not to accept it.' Once the political point had been made, right-wing Senators walked out of the Chamber prior to a later vote and Massad was accepted.

15 Milton Friedman and Arnold Harberger, Professors of Economics at the University of Chicago, were the leading lights in the development of the school of liberal economic thinking that would be imported in its totality by the military leadership – Friedman visited Chile in 1975 to support the project. An academic link between the departments of economics in Chicago and Santiago's Catholic University had operated since the 1960s.

16 Martínez and Díaz, *Chile: The Great Transformation*.

17 See Latin America Bureau, *Chile: The Pinochet Decade* (London, Latin America Bureau, 1983).

18 O. Muñoz, 'Economy and Society in Chile: Frustration and Change in the Historical Process', *International Social Science Journal*, 134 (1992).

19 J. Fontaine, 'Transición económica y política en Chile: 1970–1990', *Estudios Públicos*, 50 (1993).

20 E. Silva, 'Capitalist Regime Loyalties and Redemocratization in Chile', *Journal of Inter-American Studies and World Affairs*, 34:4 (1992).

21 D. Hojman, 'Chile under Frei (Again): The First Latin American Tiger – or Just Another Cat?', *Bulletin of Latin American Research* 14:2 (1995).

22 Whilst privatisation was a key to the model, the desire to maintain control over Codelco revealed a particular Chilean approach to neoliberalism whereby the importance of copper to the balance of trade, foreign-exchange earnings, employment, regional development and the military budget meant that it remained in state hands. When the technocrats suggested privatisation in the 1970s, the military vetoed the idea.

23 Meller, *Un Siglo*.

24 Latin America Bureau, *Chile: The Pinochet Decade*; and J. Collins and J. Lear, 'Free Market Miracle or Myth: Chile's Neo-Liberal Experiment', *The Ecologist*, 26:4 (1996).

25 L. Oppenheim, *Politics in Chile: Democracy, Authoritarianism and the Search for Development* (Boulder, Westview, 1993).

26 The new business culture that the economy has promoted is also reflected in politics and in higher education: the electoral campaign of Javier Errázuriz (head of the Errázuriz economic group) for the presidency in 1993 is symptomatic of the confidence of the business elites, whilst the public and private universities have reorganised their curricula to respond to the demands of the business market. The emphasis has been placed on 'professional' courses such as information technology, business administration, accountancy, law and commerce.

27 Martínez and Díaz, *Chile: The Great Transformation*.

28 P. Meller and R. Sáez, 'Lecciones y desafíos futuros del auge exportador chileno', in P. Meller and R. Sáez (eds), *Auge exportador chileno: lecciones y desafíos futuros* (Santiago, CIEPLAN and Dolmen, 1997).

29 P. Meller, 'La apertura comercial chilena: lecciones de política', *Estudios CIEPLAN*, 35 (1992).

30 See A. Hurrell, 'Regionalism in the Americas', in A. Lowenthal and G. Treverton (eds), *Latin America in a New World* (Boulder, Westview, 1994), pp. 167–90; and R. Gwynne, 'Regional Integration in Latin America: The Revival of a Concept', in R. Gibb and W. Michalak (eds), *Continental Trading Blocs: The Growth of Regionalism in the World Economy* (New York, Wiley, 1994), pp. 189–208.

31 A. Velasco and M. Tokman, 'Opciones para la política comercial chilena en los 90', *Estudios Públicos*, 52 (1993).

32 See N. Phillips, 'Global and Regional Linkages', in J. Buxton and N. Phillips (eds), *Developments in Latin American Political Economy: States, Markets and Actors* (Manchester, Manchester University Press, 1999).

33 El Mercado Común del Sur. For a full discussion of the Mercosur see Phillips, 'Global and Regional Linkages'.

34 From the early 1990s, Chilean investment increased in the region. A large percentage of the $4.5 billion of investments outside the country is located in Argentina. Investment by Chilean firms has been notable following the entry of larger companies into the energy and finance sectors, such as Chilectra, Enersis, Energas and Endesa (55 per cent of Chilean investment in 1995 was in the privatised energy sector). Between 1993 and 1995, over a hundred companies crossed the Andes, including Chile's best-known firms such as Unimarc, Luchetti, Masisa and Madeco (involving the leading economic groups such as Luksic and Errázuriz). *Mercosul: Revista de Negocios*, 5:47 (May 1996); and 5:50 (August 1996).

35 This was a point made by the director of ProChile, Jean-Jacques Duhart, at the time of Chile's entry into the Mercosur: *Mercosul: Revista de Negocios*, 5:47 (May 1996).

36 M. Wilhelmy and R. Lazo, 'La política multilateral de Chile en Asia-Pacífico', *Estudios Internacionales*, 30:117 (1997).

37 See D. Hojman, 'Employment- and Earnings- generating Potentials of the Neo-liberal Model', in D. Hojman (ed.), *Neo-liberal Agriculture in Rural Chile* (Basingstoke, Macmillan, 1993), pp. 194–207; and K. Weyland, 'Growth with Equity in Chile's New Democracy', *Latin American Research Review*, 32:1 (1997).

38 See D. Green, 'The Impact of Neoliberalism', and J. Barton, 'The Environmental Agenda', in Buxton and Phillips (eds), *Developments*.

39 The institutions of Fundación Chile, a commercial development organisation, and ProChile, an export promotion organisation, have been important in driving this process of export-led development from the 1980s.

40 O. Sunkel, 'Consolidation of Chile's Democracy and Development: The Challenges and the Tasks', Institute of Development Studies (Sussex, UK) Discussion Paper 317 (1993); and Petras and Leiva, *Democracy and Poverty*.

41 E. De Kadt, 'Poverty-Focused Policies: The Experience of Chile', Institute of Development Studies (Sussex, UK) Discussion Paper 319 (1993).

42 See Oppenheim, *Politics in Chile*.

43 De Kadt, 'Poverty-Focused Policies'.

44 See D. Hojman, 'Chile after Pinochet: Aylwin's Christian Democrat Economic Policies for the 1990s', *Bulletin of Latin American Research*, 9:1 (1990).

45 Collins and Lear, 'Free Market Miracle or Myth', and G. Sánchez Otero, 'Neoliberalism and its Discontents, in F. Rosen and D. McFadyen (eds), *Free Trade and Economic Restructuring in Latin America* (New York, Monthly Review Press, 1995), pp. 120–6.

46 Petras and Leiva, *Democracy and Poverty*.

47 P. Oxhorn, 'Understanding Political Change after Authoritarian Rule: The Popular Sectors and Chile's New Democratic Regime', *Journal of Latin American Studies* 26:3 (1994).

48 Hojman, 'Chile After Pinochet'.

49 Collier and Sater make the important point that modern agribusiness, while more efficient and successful than the traditional agricultural systems prior to agrarian reform began under the Frei administration (1964–70; Frei is the father of Eduardo Frei, 1993–99) and intensified under Allende (1970–73), lacks any of the paternalism and job security of the latifundio system that it has replaced, making it arguably more responsible for the intensification of rural poverty. S. Collier and W. Sater, *A History of Chile, 1808–1994* (Cambridge, Cambridge University Press, 1997).

50 Sunkel, 'Consolidation of Chile's Democracy and Development', p. 11.

51 Since the end of the repressive, paramilitary state there has been a noted increase in social problems of drug-taking, delinquency, crime and suicide rates amongst young people. This sector of society has become recognised as deserving of special attention – the National Youth Institute was overhauled in 1997 to assist with the problem – but with continuing high employment and a lack of political-party response to the demands of young people in a rapidly evolving society (justifying voter apathy), the problems appear likely to remain.

52 Ricardo Lagos, a likely presidential candidate in 1999, was a vigorous opponent of the regime and a Socialist, yet he has instituted a range of market-related, private sector-oriented policies in his ministerial roles (education and public works). Most coalition Socialists have been termed 'renovated Socialists'. These *renovados* have promoted a social liberal agenda dependent on economic stabilisation and incremental income distribution rather than a social democratic agenda focused on popular mobilisation and effective public-welfare programmes (see J. Petras, 'Alternatives to Neoliberalism in Latin America', *Latin American Perspectives*, 92:24 (1997), pp. 80–91).

53 As with other Latin American economies, governments are finding it increasingly difficult to privatise remaining enterprises at suitable prices. In late 1996, Chile's state electricity company, *Colbun*, could not be sold at its planned price.

54 See Hojman, 'Chile under Frei (Again)'.

55 It is questionable whether the electoral system that has operated since 1989 has indeed been representative of popular socio-economic interests. It has continued as an 'authoritarian elitist institutional matrix' (see Petras, 'Alternatives to Neoliberalism', p. 82) which does little to represent wide-ranging social group interests since its focus is the political elite, the armed forces and the business sector. Until the Chilean government can turn its attention more to social affairs rather than having to pursue constitutional change against a recalcitrant military and right wing, and an economic policy dependent on an alliance with the business sector, it is unlikely that these criticisms of the current style of politics will be curtailed.

56 Petras, 'Alternatives to Neoliberalism'.

57 Petras and Leiva, *Democracy and Poverty*, p. 190.

58 Rabkin, 'The Aylwin Government and "Tutelary" Democracy'.

59 Divisions within the PDC emerged in 1997 over the election of a party leader and its share in the December elections suffered slightly (22 per cent – historically its lowest share), strengthening the position of Ricardo Lagos, representing the left of the coalition (PS–PPD).

60 See O. Muñoz and C. Celedón, 'Chile en transición: Estrategia económica y política', *Estudios CIEPLAN*, 37 (1993); and O. Godoy, 'Algunas claves'.

61 Oppenheim, *Politics in Chile*.

62 Munck, 'Authoritarianism, Modernisation', p. 208.

63 Oxhorn, 'Understanding Political Change'.

64 As Collier and Sater remark: 'The material marks of modernisation were manifold in the Chile of 1989 (shopping malls, supermarkets, consumer goods). A different and less friendly eye, however, also would have noticed that year, not only the obvious persistence of poverty, but also a certain social atomization, the American-style trivialization of the mass media, a tendency to rather mindless consumerism.' Collier and Sater, *A History of Chile*, p. 375.

65 *El Mercurio*, 23 July 1997.

4

Uruguay

HENRY FINCH

Predicting fundamental transformation in the functioning of a political system
is a hazardous enterprise, particularly in a country which is celebrated for its
reluctance to embrace change. There are nonetheless good reasons for suppos-
ing that the party system in Uruguay, which has survived with comparatively little modification through most of the twentieth century, is about to experience
a radical redefinition. The precipitating factor in this process is the increasing
electoral strength of left-wing forces, which in turn has required the traditional
parties, Blanco (Whites) and Colorado (Reds), to find ways of defending themselves. These developments open up questions concerning both the character
of the parties themselves and the way in which policy issues may be handled in
the future. The first section of this chapter provides a context for the analysis,
by outlining the changing balance of party forces since the restoration of
democracy in the mid-1980s and the particular nature of Uruguay's neoliberal
experience during this period. The second section reviews some of the policy
areas which are likely to form a central part of the agenda of the administration
which will take office in March 2000, whatever its complexion. The third section assesses the likelihood of a government of the Left, in terms of its evolution and present condition, and the reform of Uruguay's electoral law, which
was narrowly approved by a referendum in December 1996.

The experience of neoliberalism[1]

Although the restoration of democracy in Uruguay in the mid-1980s was
accompanied by a degree of continuity in party strengths compared with the
pre-coup situation, the necessity to reform and restructure the economy during
the years since Julio María Sanguinetti formed his first administration in 1985
has contributed to substantial changes in the situation of the parties, as well as
in the nature of politics and the policy debate. The principal features of the

changing party structure revealed in the three post-regime elections (Table 4.1) have been the growth of the left-wing Frente Amplio (FA, Broad Front) and Nuevo Espacio (NE, New Space) vote, the resulting squeeze on the Colorados and Blancos and the apparent volatility of support for the traditional parties. The latter resulted in the presidency alternating between the two parties, with Luis Alberto Lacalle's Blanco administration (1990–95) preceding Sanguinetti's return to office.

Table 4.1   *Shares of the vote in national elections, Uruguay, 1971–94 (%)*

Year	Colorado Party	Blanco Party	Frente Amplio	Nuevo Espacio
1971	41.0	40.2	18.3	–
1984	41.2	35.0	21.3	–
1989	29.2	37.7	20.6	8.6
1994	32.3	31.1	30.6	5.2

Note: In 1994 the FA allied itself with other leftist groups, and contested the elections as Encuentro Progresista (EP, Progressive Encounter). The FA contributed 92 per cent of EP's vote, and is therefore overwhelmingly dominant in this alliance (which is expected to run again in 1999).
Source: *Búsqueda*, 30 November 1989 and 1 December 1994.

The FA secured only a modest increase in 1984 compared with 1971, but many more of its supporters had been exiled or imprisoned during the dictatorship compared with the other parties, and its president Líber Seregni was excluded from the 1984 election. The Blanco party also suffered from the arrest and imprisonment of its outstanding leader (and most-voted candidate of any party in 1971), Wilson Ferreira Aldunate. Indeed, Sanguinetti was probably the preferred candidate of the outgoing military regime and may have represented the safest choice to an electorate reluctant to give the military any excuse to return. The 1984 election is therefore an inevitable but somewhat unsafe benchmark against which to measure voters' preferences in the subsequent period.

Sanguinetti's first administration (1985–90) faced enormous difficulties. The issue of lifting the economy out of the exceptionally severe crisis bequeathed by the dictatorship was addressed by economists of all parties as part of the Concertación Nacional Programática (CONAPRO, National Programmatic Convergence) initiative. Their agreement on objectives accepted the need to integrate the economy more closely with the international economy, but other proposals, including a 'selective and planned'[2] process of recovery, were always less likely to find favour with the new government. Its economic policy was by no means unsuccessful, with a strong growth performance during 1986–87 based on export demand from Brazil and Argentina, and a reduction in the central government deficit from 4.7 per cent of GDP in 1984 to 1.2 per cent in 1986. Unemployment fell sharply, from 13.9 per cent in Montevideo in 1984, to 9.3 per cent in 1987, and real wages during 1985–87 recovered some of the

losses incurred earlier. Nonetheless, there was little evidence of coherent policy-making, and the recovery by 1988 was proving unsustainable. Although
exports continued to grow up to 1990, GDP growth ceased in 1988 and inflation accelerated to peak at 129 per cent in 1990. Economic policy was largely
pragmatic. The restoration of Wages Councils and the improvement in real
wages were necessary steps to meet the strong social pressures which accompanied redemocratisation. Import tariffs were raised in 1985 for revenue purposes, but the process of opening up the economy was quickly resumed. In spite
of the CONAPRO call to reject neoliberalism, the liberalisation of the commercial and financial sectors initiated during the dictatorship was maintained,
and there were modest attempts to cut the size of the public sector. However,
the fiscal deficit widened as the 1989 elections approached, and by the end of
his term of office Sanguinetti had failed to define a set of policies which would
enable him to resist the (contradictory) charges of neoliberal or opportunist,
which were levelled at him by his opponents.

The period of the transitional government was marked by the confirmation
of many aspects of Uruguay's traditional political culture, in particular a preference for gradual and agreed change and a reluctance to abandon the protection
and social provision which a large public sector was believed to offer. The
restoration intact of the 1966 Constitution reinforced these characteristics, since
although Sanguinetti received 31 per cent of the total poll in 1984 (the highest
share to an elected president in five elections between 1966 and 1994), this fell
far short of a personal mandate, and votes cast for the other Colorado candidates were insufficient to give the Colorado party a congressional majority.
Hence Sanguinetti had to find support elsewhere. His administration included a
minority participation of members of other parties (though not the FA), acting
in a personal rather than representative capacity. In April 1986 an agreement,
the *acuerdo nacional*, was signed by leaders of all the main parties on economic,
social and institutional programmes, in the spirit of the CONAPRO of
1984–85.[3] But the results of the agreement were very limited. In particular, on
the key issue of crimes committed by members of the armed forces during the
dictatorship, the majority centre-left faction of the Blanco opposition resorted
to the notion of 'governability' to justify its support for the government's Ley de
Caducidad (expiry law) of December 1986, which granted immunity from prosecution to the military. Accompanied only by a few dissident Blanco legislators,
the FA was left isolated in its opposition to the granting of immunity, while
Lacalle, of the right-wing Herrerista Blanco faction, was able to propose (though
unsuccessfully) a full coalition government of Colorados and Blancos. However,
Article 79 of the 1966 Constitution allows for a referendum to be held for the
repeal of a law on presentation of a petition signed by 25 per cent of voters. In
the first use of this right, the immunity law was confirmed in April 1989 by just
58 per cent of those voting, but the mobilisation of the Left (which included elements of the traditional parties as well as the FA and the Tupamaros[4]) in the collection of signatures and in the campaign itself was highly significant.[5]

The elections of November 1989 resulted in the first presidency for the Blanco party in the twentieth century (excluding their victories under the 1952 collegial Constitution in 1958 and 1962). The unproblematic alternation of parties in the presidency helped to confirm the sense of the maturity of Uruguay's democracy. With Sanguinetti ineligible for a second term, the leading candidate of the Colorado Party was Jorge Batlle (of the Batllismo Radical group). In the event Lacalle was the most-voted candidate of the most-voted party, but with just 21.7 per cent of the total poll. Lacalle's electoral programme centred on reforms of the public sector, the social security, education and tax systems, lower import tariffs and regulation of labour's right to strike. Batlle, whose economic adviser in the campaign was Alejandro Végh Villegas, author of Colorado neoliberalism in the early 1970s and architect of the military regime's neoliberal policies from the Economics and Finance Ministry during 1974–76, proposed similar reforms. Thus, the most-voted candidates in the two largest parties were both committed to programmes of market-oriented economic reform, although their combined vote amounted to only 36 per cent of the electorate. The programmes were broadly in line with the electoral message of the principal private-sector interest groups.[6]

The 1989 elections might properly be regarded as the moment when the 'new economic model' arrived in Uruguay, but its implementation was constrained by the peculiarities of the political system. Lacalle faced the same difficulties as Sanguinetti in needing to construct an alliance of some or (preferably) all factions of his own party with sufficient sectors of the other traditional party that he could command a majority in the legislature. Unlike Sanguinetti, Lacalle secured the inclusion of members of the other party in his cabinet, on the basis of a Coincidencia Nacional (National Coincidence), but the agreement was fragile. The progressive faction of the Blancos, the Movimiento Nacional de Rocha, was unhappy with measures taken to deal with the deteriorating financial situation in 1990, but more serious was the withdrawal of support by Sanguinetti's faction in May 1991 and by Jorge Batlle, ideologically closest to Lacalle, in February 1992, less than two years into the five-year term. Almost irrespective of the pretext, such splits might be seen as inevitable, since each party faction has to prepare the ground for the next election by distancing itself from the others, especially those represented in the government.

Knowing this, Lacalle had to move quickly with his reform programme, but the problem of fiscal imbalance and inflation once more exceeding 100 per cent demanded immediate attention. The context was further complicated by the result of a referendum (held concurrently with the November 1989 elections), approved by 82 per cent of those voting, to index pensions to the average level of wages. The real value of pensions had fallen sharply during the dictatorship, and recovered little in the following years. Voters thus imposed the need for a greater degree of social equity above that of fiscal restraint. Nonetheless, the public-sector deficit was cut substantially during the course of 1990 (Table 4.2).

At the same time the government attempted to impose a tougher regime on wage adjustments, but after a period of confrontation with the trade unions, it backed away from use of an incomes policy to control prices. In its place, exchange-rate policy was quietly adopted as the principal weapon in the stabilisation effort, with a continuous devaluation of the dollar rate, a permitted band of fluctuation, and a lag between peso inflation and the rate of devaluation (especially in 1990–93).

Table 4.2   *Public-sector deficit, Uruguay, 1989–97 (year-end, current $m)*

Year	Central government	Reform expenditure	Public corporations	Official banks	Overall deficit	Deficit as % of GDP
1989	−281	–	33	−312	−560	−7.0
1990	16	–	75	−376	−285	−3.4
1991	85	–	137	−271	− 49	−0.5
1992	134	–	152	−232	54	0.5
1993	−164	–	83	−129	−210	−1.5
1994	−297	–	− 58	− 99	−453	−2.8
1995	−372	–	197	−110	−285	−1.6
1996	−227	−94	140	−131	−311	−1.6
1997[a]	− 54	−284	110	− 95	−323	−1.6

Note: a   January–October.
Source: Búsqueda, based on data from Banco Central del Uruguay.

With export growth restricted by the overvalued exchange rate during those years, the conclusion of a debt-reduction agreement with international creditors in January 1991 stimulated the return of flight capital and increased Uruguay's ability to borrow abroad. Such international support was basic to the success of the economy during 1990–94, with GDP growth averaging over 4 per cent and inflation cut to 44 per cent in the final year.

If Lacalle's administration can be credited with some success in its economic management, the same can scarcely be said of its reform programme. The need to reform the social security system was generally acknowledged, with contributions insufficient to finance benefits, which thus required an ever-increasing subsidy from general revenue. A system of personal pension accounts was proposed in a bill sent to the legislature in 1992, but it was quickly thrown out, as much as a result of political tensions as its own shortcomings. The previous year, Lacalle had secured the passage of a privatisation law authorising the policy in general terms and setting out specific terms for particular public-sector corporations. The FA and trade unions immediately announced their intention to campaign for a referendum to overturn certain parts of the law (in particular, the articles authorising privatisation in general and the partial privatisation of the telecommunications utility ANTEL), which, when held in December 1992, resulted in a victory for the Left by 72 per cent to 28 per cent. The result undoubtedly reflected disillusion with a government in the second half of its term, but the margin must also be seen as an expression of a widespread belief in the rightness of public provision of public services. Privatisation was not in fact halted: the operation of the port of Montevideo and the Gas Company were turned over to the private sector, the State Insurance Bank lost its motor-vehicle insurance monopoly in 1994, and a number of in-house services in public-sector operations have been contracted-out. But the only sales of public sector assets involved the airline PLUNA, the fishing enterprise ILPE, and ANCAP's sugar-cane operation, 'El Espinillar'.

Reform of the 1966 Constitution, especially the double simultaneous voting system (DSV), which enabled parties to present themselves with multiple candidates for the presidency, had been under discussion by elements in all parties for some time. In mid-1994 agreement was reached on a reform proposal to be submitted to a plebiscite. The proposal was in fact feeble, merely allowing voters to vote for one party list in national elections but voting differently in departmental elections (which were held simultaneously). In spite of support from all party leaders (except Tabaré Vázquez; see below) and the overwhelming majority of legislators in both Houses, the reform was decisively rejected by 71 per cent of voters. It seems likely that the reform was perceived as an irrelevance, and, for having endorsed the initiative, the judgement of the political elite was inevitably called into question.

Three months later ex-president Sanguinetti returned to office, but in circumstances far from triumphant. His election-campaign platform was 'social democrat' rather than neoliberal. He argued the need to secure the position of manufacturing industry and the rural sector against an over-dependence on the service sector, making specific reference to (if not endorsing) the protectionist policies of Luis Batlle in the 1950s. He attacked the over-valuation of the currency and the negotiation of inadequate safeguards within the Mercosur, which had jeopardised the position of producers and sources of employment. The danger of 'consumerism', to which cheap dollars and *apertura* had given rise, was the burden of expectation placed on the democratic process to ensure ever-increasing material satisfactions. He attempted to define the extended *batllista* state as part of Uruguay's national identity, which should give a continuing role for the state as monitor of the free market in the interests of social solidarity and tolerance.[7] But the election gave the Colorados only 32.3 per cent of the vote, the narrowest of margins over their two principal rivals (see Table 4.1), and only the FA, though disappointed not to have won, could look to the future with confidence. Sanguinetti dominated the other Colorado candidates, out-voting Jorge Batlle by nearly five to one, but evidently his administration even more than its two predecessors would need the support of other factions and parties. Moreover, Sanguinetti had been less than helpful to Lacalle, withdrawing his Foro Batllista representatives in Lacalle's cabinet after barely a year, opposing the social security reform and joining the referendum campaign against the privatisation law.[8] Lacalle had problems of his own, however, as a rejected candidate for the Herrerista presidential nomination, Alberto Volonté, outvoted Lacalle's nominee and took over the formal leadership (the presidency of the Directorio) of the Blanco party.

Volonté proceeded to play an important role in Sanguinetti's administration, which, uniquely in Uruguayan history, was constructed as a formal coalition with representation for all factions of the Colorado and Blanco parties. The leadership of the two traditional adversaries closed ranks – some, like Lacalle, with great reluctance, not only to secure agreement on a programme of government but also to isolate the FA, which consistently opposed the coalition. Compared with his pre-election rhetoric, as well as his own first administration, Sanguinetti's policy proposals for a formal coalition represented an important degree of continuity with the outgoing Blanco government. The *Bases for a Dialogue in Search of a National Government* spelled out a reform programme: electoral and political reform, the social security system, education, reform of the state ('to improve its management, decentralise its work and reduce its weight ... by privatisations, removal of monopolies and deregulation of the private sector'), law and order, economic reforms to secure 'sustained development with the greatest possible degree of equity', and an integration policy in which 'a policy of selective support will be developed and applied to those sectors which demonstrate their capacity to operate efficiently and competitively and adjust themselves to the conditions which will operate within the Mercosur from 2001 onwards'.[9] A further change compared with his 1985–90 government was the lower public profile kept by the President, avoiding, where possible, polemical issues and leaving ministers to justify their policies. This detachment was aided by Volonté, whose majority Blanco faction Manos a la Obra (Hands to Work) was strongly committed to the coalition and who operated in effect as a prime minister.

Although the coalition proved to be stable, in case it should break down the administration moved quickly to present its major reform proposals. By the end of 1996 three such measures had been enacted. The reform of the electoral system, approved by a plebiscite in December 1996, is certain to affect profoundly the functioning of the political system (see 'The electoral reform of 1996', below). Perhaps even more important was a reform of the social security system, with the creation of six competing Administrators of Pension Savings Funds (AFAPs), five of which are in the private sector.[10] Reform of the previous system which had a deficit in 1996 equivalent to 6 per cent of GDP was long overdue. The measure aroused opposition less from the leadership of the FA than from the trade unions and the pensioners' organisation, the Organización Nacional de Asocianciones de Jubilados y Pensionistar del Uruguay (ONAJPU) – National Organisation of Associations of Pensioners of Uruguay. An attempt to submit the law to a referendum in 1996 was disallowed by the Electoral Court. However, an alternative route to a plebiscite is by proposing a change in the Constitution to disallow the new system, to be voted on in November 1999, and the campaign to collect the required 233,000 signatures was under way in early 1998.

The administration's reform of the educational system also attracted strong criticism from the Opposition, though there was no move to reverse it. Education had already been the subject of a referendum, called by the FA and teachers' trade unions with backing from the Universidad de la República. Held alongside the November 1994 elections, it called for an amendment to the Constitution to require that a minimum of 27 per cent of public expenditure (or 4.5 per cent of GDP) be allocated annually to the public education system. However, only 29 per cent of the electorate backed the measure.[11] The reform which was enacted included an extension of pre-school provision and changes to teacher-training programmes and to the basic school syllabus. It was motivated by evidence of inadequate attainment levels and the need to produce school-leavers more fitted to the requirements of the labour market. The trade unions were not mollified by the intention of the reform to increase the professionalism of teachers, and their opposition was accompanied by the occupation of school buildings by students.

With pressure to reduce the tax burden on the private sector struggling to compete behind rapidly shrinking tariff barriers, and the need to contain the public-sector deficit, Sanguinetti included in his *Bases* document proposals for the reform of the state sector. Measures to improve efficiency and decentralisation of the bureaucracy were relatively uncontroversial. Reducing the numbers employed is harder to achieve, but a three-year moratorium on new appointments was announced in April 1995, and a programme to secure the early retirement of 11,500 employees (roughly half from central administration, the remainder from public-sector enterprises) at a cost of $200 million (part-funded by the Inter-American Development Bank, IDB) was announced in March 1997. The policy of reducing public employment had been initiated by Lacalle's government, and Correa Freitas claimed that on average 6,000 public-sector posts had been eliminated annually since 1993,[12] mostly from central administration.

In spite of Sanguinetti's invocation during the election campaign of the country's *batllista* inheritance of public sector provision, as well as his opposition to Lacalle's privatisation law in the 1992 referendum, his *Bases* accepted the principle of privatisation subject to certain conditions.[13] No doubt this reflected the logic of the new economic model as well as the need to secure Blanco participation in his government. But a few months later he felt obliged to explain his attitude to a less parochial audience: the 1992 referendum was fundamentally about the basic telephone monopoly, not the cellular, rural, long-distance and satellite systems, and it had in effect ratified the sale of PLUNA and the fishing enterprise ILPE; 'We are moving at a measured, deliberate, assured pace, with debates that the country has to handle with care, because in Uruguay, unlike other countries, state enterprises have not lost their good name. Now we want them to be efficient as well as prestigious.'[14]

Table 4.3   *Structure of public-sector employment, Uruguay, October 1997*

Central administration	95,557	
Civil service		37,313
Armed forces		33,277
Police		24,967
Judiciary, education, etc.	73,318	
Public education (ANEP)		52,304
Universidad de la República		11,490
Judiciary		3,816
Other		5,708
Official banks and public sector	40,195	
Departmental administration	37,063	
Parliament	1,545	
Total	247,678	
Total public-sector employees[a]	230,340	

Note: a   A discrepancy of 17,338 between the total number of posts and number of employees is due to the doubling-up of functions.
Source: Búsqueda, 12 February 1998, based on data supplied by Ruben Correa Freitas.

A particular characteristic of the privatisation programme has been the concession to the private sector of ancillary activities, joint ventures between private and public enterprise and removal of monopoly powers from public corporations. The rationale of the programme has therefore been to increase the level of competition in the public sector, rather than to secure the one-off revenue benefit of a sale. Much of this, for example ANCAP's loss of its monopoly position in the supply of alcohol in 1996, has been relatively uncontentious. But the 1997 measure, *ley de marco regulatorio del sector eléctrico (regulatory framework law for the electrical sector)*, designed to promote competition in electricity generation and allow the state corporation UTE to enter joint ventures in all aspects of electricity supply, was seen by the FA and trade unions as a move towards an eventual privatisation. Their campaign to secure a referendum on the law, requiring the assent of 25 per cent of the electorate, was supported by 22 per cent in June 1998 and therefore narrowly failed.

Seeking the new equilibrium

Whether or not a coalition of left-wing forces ends the electoral dominance of the traditional parties in 1999, it is clear that in the course of the 1990s the economic policy debate has changed substantially. It also seems likely that the new priorities will survive in their essentials to form the agenda of the new administration in 2000. Barring accidents, in 1998 Uruguay should experience single-figure inflation for the first time for over forty years, and this achievement provides a benchmark against which the competence of any future government will be assessed. The constraints within which policy is formed are not primarily internal, however. Financial and commercial liberalisation have opened up the economy to external scrutiny and strong competitive pressures. The benefits of that, in the form of sustained growth and a consumer boom, have required adjustment on the part of the public and private sectors; and whereas the 'global economy' imposes a discipline, membership of the Mercosur has focused attention strongly on the need to be competitive.[15]

The Mercosur has established itself as Uruguay's dominant economic project. Whatever the doubts about the terms of membership, or the extent of preparedness, there are none regarding the country's future within the sub-regional integration scheme. The decision to sign the Treaty of Asunción in 1991 was supported by the leadership of all political factions,[16] and the consensus in favour of the Mercosur has remained intact. The reception for the scheme may have been unanimous, yet it was far from wholehearted. Since the mid-1970s Uruguay had benefited from bilateral treaties with Brazil and Argentina, granting trade preferences in those markets, and their importance to Uruguayan exporters increased significantly. The revival of the economy in 1986–87 was based on demand from the sub-region, and by 1989–90 the two neighbouring countries absorbed one-third of Uruguay's exports. The news in July 1990 that Brazil and Argentina proposed to form a common market caused great alarm, since Uruguay would lose its exclusive preferences. The Mercosur was therefore an unlooked-for and, initially at least, an unwelcome development, which Uruguay had no option but to join.

Membership carries penalties and risks, as well as the benefit of continuing access to the sub-regional market on preferential terms. Measured by population, GDP, or the value of its sub-regional trade, Uruguay has little significance within Mercosur. On the other hand, for Brazil in particular, the Mercosur has no compelling commercial significance. Uruguay is therefore relatively powerless within an integration scheme whose success is fundamental to its economic strategy, but which is effectively dominated by one country for whom, in economic terms, the scheme is of marginal importance. Quite apart from the impact on Uruguayan exports (half of which are now directed to the Mercosur countries, 35 per cent to Brazil alone) that any disturbance in the neighbouring economies may have, Brazil has shown a propensity to modify the rules of the Mercosur game on a unilateral basis.[17] The Mercosur has undoubtedly underlined the need for firms to increase their competitiveness, but the evidence on the extent to which they have done so is mixed.[18] Earlier reductions in the import tariff had already imposed a reshaping on the manufacturing sector, but Uruguay entered the Mercosur in 1995 with 950 products benefiting from the *Régimen de Adecuación* (Adaptation Regime – which excluded them temporarily from sub-regional free trade) and 300 exceptions to the Common External Tariff. The remainder of these two transitional exemptions expire at the beginning, and end, of 2000 respectively, and at that stage the extent to which Uruguay's manufacturing and agro-industrial sectors have modernised will be put to the test.

The requirements of the Mercosur have inevitably had their impact on the central issue of the functions and dimensions of the state. The private sector has accepted the loss of protection and the need for greater efficiency, demanding public-sector reform in compensation. That should include a reduction in both the tax burden borne directly by the private sector and in the (high) level of public-sector tariffs, especially for energy. Reform has so far involved scaling down the level of employment in central administration, the reform of the social security system and the introduction of competitive pressures into the public sector. The first of these is likely to be a continuing process; the second has reduced the fiscal burden in the short term; the third is likely to continue, but there are problems to be confronted. Uruguay's chosen route to privatisation is principally via the granting of concessions (a further 140 services, most of them of an ancillary nature, have been identified for *tercerización* (tertiarisation) in 1998 and the withdrawal of public-sector monopolies. Efficiency gains passed on to the consumer have been claimed for the deregulated operations,[19] and the energy and communications utilities have entered joint-venture agreements with private capital. At the end of 1997 the intention was announced eventually to reform the legal status of public corporations, relieving them of the obligation to contribute their surpluses to central government, where they partially offset the deficits that government sustains under other headings (see Table 4.2). The calculation must be that the contribution in taxes of a deregulated public corporation would exceed the sums presently transferred as surpluses. However, according to a senior official charged with the implementation of the privatisation policy: 'the process carried out in Uruguay has not succeeded in bringing about a reduction of tariffs, has not required a quality of service, did not set up mechanisms for handling any complaints by consumers, and authorised the public corporations both to compete in the market and to act as regulators, at one and the same time'.[20] Barbieri's observations relate to a lack of the training and infrastructure which public-service regulators require and to the confusion generated in the public sector by its new role. He detected a new corporate sense among public-sector management, in which the consumer's interest was subordinated to that of the enterprise. There is confusion also in pricing policy, with government colluding with the public sector in its high tariffs (or even resisting proposals for price reductions[21]).

The challenge (or threat) of the Mercosur has also been a principal factor conditioning the evolution of industrial relations in the 1990s. Historically the trade-union movement drew strength from official recognition of its role in wage bargaining in the tripartite Wages Councils created in the 1940s, a position consolidated during the years of massive protection for manufacturing industry. Agreement between communist and non-communist unions followed, with the achievement of the first unified association, the Convención Nacional de Trabajadores (CNT, National Convention of Workers), in 1966. Since 1985, however, the movement has lost strength and significance. Membership of the Plenario Inter Union de Trabajadores – CNT (PIT–CNT, Inter Union Workers'

Plenary, successor to the CNT) fell from about 250,000 in 1985 to 198,000 in 1991, and perhaps 140,000 in 1997.[22] As tariff protection was progressively withdrawn from the manufacturing sector, the risk of job losses in the private sector (and to some extent in the public corporations) widened the gulf between unions prepared to seek an accommodation with employers, and those (particularly state and municipal employees, health workers and teachers) committed to a more radical militancy. The radicals initially consolidated their control of PIT-CNT, successfully resisting attempts to revise its statutes, but in the first-ever secret ballot for the board of delegates in July 1997 moderates effectively won control of the movement.

The thrust of government policy in the 1990s was to withdraw its own participation in Wages Councils, and to increase the flexibility of the labour market by reducing the extent to which wage and other agreements are negotiated centrally and then extended to all firms within an industry. The government's practice of publishing guidelines for pay settlements was also abandoned. An increasing number of agreements between unions and management have been registered with the Ministry of Labour and legislation is pending on the juridical status of voluntary collective negotiation. As well as pay, existing agreements have dealt with issues concerning investment plans and higher productivity, flexible roles in the workplace, tercerización and redundancies. The extent to which firms have been willing to involve labour in their planning, and the concessions made by labour (including pay cuts), imply a 'historic break' in the conduct of industrial relations which operated during the previous half-century.[23] No government in the foreseeable future is likely to attempt to reverse these changes.

The counterpart of 'modernised' industrial relations has been the question of the distribution of the benefits of sustained growth in the 1990s. Table 4.4 indicates a modest upward movement of the urban unemployment rate between 1989 and 1993, followed by a sharp rise persisting for three years to mid-1997. In addition, the proportion of the labour force underemployed showed an increase in 1994–96, though for reasons which are not clear, the proportion of the adult population in the labour-force declined during these years. There is abundant evidence that women have greatly increased their labour force participation in recent years, driven by the need to maintain household incomes. The underlying explanation for the trend in unemployment is essentially the adaptation process in manufacturing industry, which, between 1994 and 1997, shed over 12,000 jobs as a result of closures and redundancies (though the policy of tercerización should imply some compensating increase in the service sector). The indirect consequences of the Mexican financial crisis caused a sharp deterioration in 1995, but when economic recovery began in mid-1996 no improvement in employment levels was experienced for twelve months. In the short term, construction activity, agro-industry and non-financial services are the sectors best placed to absorb labour. A longer-run policy will emphasise education and training needs and the need for adaptability in the workplace.

Table 4.4   *Open unemployment, underemployment and labour supply,*
Montevideo and urban interior, 1987–97 (% of labour force)

	1987	1988	1989	1990	1991	1992	1993	1994	1995	1996	1997
Open	9.1	8.6	8.0	8.5	8.9	9.0	8.3	9.2	10.3	11.9	11.5
Underemployment[a]	n/a	n/a	n/a	n/a	4.7	3.5	3.1	3.7	5.1	6.0	na
Supply[b]	n/a	n/a	n/a	57.0	57.4	57.4	56.7	58.2	59.0	58.2	57.7

Notes: a   % of labour force under-employed; *b*   % of population aged 14+ employed or seeking work.
Source: Instituto Nacional de Estadística.

The variation in real incomes during the 1990s (Table 4.5) shows an improvement in the situation of low-income families (though not necessarily greater equality) during the early years of Lacalle's neoliberalism. Part of the explanation for this may be the significant increase in pensions as a result of the 1989 referendum.[24] However, wages and family incomes fell from 1995 onwards (earlier in the case of wages in manufacturing), as unemployment took hold. In spite of the modest improvement in incomes recorded in 1997, GDP growth in 1998 is unlikely to match the 5.1 per cent estimated for 1997. Employment creation is certain to be affected, and the issue of unemployment will inevitably remain at the forefront of future policy-making.[25]

Table 4.5   *Annual change in family incomes and real wages,*
Montevideo, 1991–97 (%)

	1991	1992	1993	1994	1995	1996	1997
Average family income,							
Montevideo	10.4	10.6	– 0.0	8.1	–3.4	– 0.6	0.5
20% poorest families	9.5	8.4	7.4	3.3	–4.5	– 3.3	3.2
20% richest families	7.7	12.5	–0.0	7.3	–2.6	– 1.1	– 0.5
Average pension	14.9	13.2	2.2	5.4	–0.6	2.6	2.1
Average real wage	5.0	4.3	7.5	4.6	–4.8	– 3.2	0.7
Private sector	6.1	4.0	3.3	1.1	–3.0	0.0	– 0.2
Manufacturing industry	4.5	1.5	5.3	– 0.7	–6.0	– 1.5	– 0.6
Public sector	0.3	– 0.7	7.4	0.6	–2.6	2.7	1.2

Source: Búsqueda, based on data from Instituto Nacional de Estadística, Banco de Previsión Social
and Banco Central del Uruguay.

Although the negotiated return to democracy in 1984 has not subsequently been seriously threatened, government relations with the armed forces continue to be extremely sensitive. Ratification of the Ley de Caducidad by referendum in 1989 effectively ended the possibility of initiating judicial proceedings against those members of the armed forces suspected of, or admitting to, criminal acts during the dictatorship. Following detailed disclosures in Argentina, and evidence of a reassessment by elements of the Argentine military of its conduct during the 1970s, Sanguinetti moved to reassure the armed forces in April 1995 that in Uruguay the matter was closed. That remained the position of the governing coalition. Nonetheless, pressure has intensified for the military to give some explanation of its human rights abuses during its regime and in particular to account for the 26 civilians who disappeared while in military custody. The campaign has been led by Rafael Michelini, leader of the left-wing NE group and son of the prominent FA figure Zelmar Michelini, who was assassinated in Buenos Aires in 1976, and by the FA and the PIT-CNT. Evidence has surfaced of an inconclusive inquiry conducted in 1989 (as required by the Ley de Caducidad) by military prosecutors into the disappearances; its work was obstructed by the refusal of the army to release information.[26]

It has also been alleged by a senior officer of the military regime that a secret lodge, the Tenientes de Artigas, was formed by right-wing officers within the army in 1965, and played a key role in the decision to stage the 1973 coup. A list of 133 presently serving or retired officers allegedly belonging to the group was published in the press in 1996. This shadowy faction within the army, predominantly Blanco in political affiliation and thought to be linked with military intelligence and counter-intelligence, has been associated with the Guardia de Artigas, which claimed responsibility for a series of bomb explosions in 1990–92.[27]

It is evident that the armed forces are not yet prepared to emerge from the bunker to which they retired in 1985 and confront the practices of the period after 1973. Their sense of grievance is enhanced by reduced salaries, smaller numbers and lower budget allocations that they have been forced to accept.[28] The mood was not lightened by Sanguinetti's decision in 1997 to restore the military status of 41 left-wing officers who were dismissed during 1972–76. There is every likelihood that demands for information about the fate of those who disappeared will intensify, and the military are no doubt correct to suppose that disclosure would not end the matter. If the issue has been difficult for the traditional parties, it must inevitably be more so for any future government of the FA. Attracting few headlines, there has in fact been cooperation between the municipal government of Montevideo (controlled by the FA) and technical branches of the armed forces in social and infrastructural projects. The FA has been content for Michelini to take the lead in demanding disclosure, and there was naked pragmatism in Tabaré Vázquez's commitment in November 1997 on behalf of the FA, not likely to win Michelini's support, to raise the salaries of the armed forces if the FA comes to power in 2000.

Towards left-wing government in 2000?

The electability of the FA

If the November 1999 elections were to be under the 1994 voting system, Uruguay would probably elect the candidate of the left-wing FA coalition, Tabaré Vázquez, as President. For the first time in its history, Uruguay would be governed by a president who belonged to neither of the two traditional parties which have monopolised political power since independence. The reasons for this prediction lie partly in an extrapolation of the voting trends in the last three elections, and in recent opinion-poll evidence. On the basis of 900 interviews in Montevideo and the urban interior in late 1997, it is clear that two years before the elections the FA has a commanding lead over the other parties, and that Tabaré Vázquez commands the support of his own party in a way that none of the other presidential hopefuls (apart from Michelini) can emulate. In addition, in the December 1996 referendum on changes to the electoral law, which was supported by all parties except the FA, Vázquez's opposition to the change won 46.2 per cent of the vote. However, there are two reasons why Uruguay may yet continue to elect a Colorado or Blanco leader: one is that the electoral reform was approved, the other concerns the limitations of the FA as a potential governing force.

Table 4.6   *Opinion-poll data on voting intentions, Uruguay, November–December 1997 (%)*

Frente Amplio	33	Tabaré Vázquez	73
		Danilo Astori	13
		Other/don't know	14
Colorado	21	Jorge Batlle	41
		Pablo Millor	12
		Other/don't know	47
Nacional	20	Luis A. Lacalle	29
		Juan Andrés Ramírez	24
		Alberto Volonté	22
		other / don't know	25
Nuevo Espacio	6	Rafael Michelini	100
Don't know/no response	20		
Total	100		

Source: Equipos Consultores, *El Observador*, 7 January 1998.

The FA came into formal existence in the early months of 1971, as a response by progressive political forces to the increasingly authoritarian regime of Jorge Pacheco Areco. The disturbed conditions of the period, especially the successes of the guerrilla organisation Movimiento de Liberación Nacional–Tupamaros (MLN-T, National Liberation Movement–Tupamaros) and the ineffectiveness of the institutions of politics and government in coping with growing civil disorder, led the parties and factions of the left to achieve a historic unity. It was not merely that the Partido Socialista (PS, Socialist Party) and the Partido Comunista Uruguayo (PCU, Uruguayan Communist Party) set aside their traditional differences. The essence of the FA was (and remains) that it should function as a coalition of Marxist and non-Marxist forces. The Partido Democrático Cristiano (PDC, Christian Democrat Party) played a prominent role from 1968 onwards in bringing together the radical Left and dissident progressive elements of both traditional parties. More than a dozen groups signed the FA into existence, including the former Colorado faction, Partido para el Gobierno Popular (PGP, 'For a Government of the People'), formed and led since 1962 by Zelmar Michelini. The programme of the FA included a rejection of the IMF, and the introduction of planning, agrarian reform, nationalisation of the banking system and foreign trade, and worker representation in policy making.[29] Probably the most significant decision taken by the new movement was to invite retired general Líber Seregni to become the FA's first president.

Until his sudden resignation on the 25th anniversary of the FA's foundation, Seregni dominated the history of the coalition. He was its presidential candidate in 1971, when the FA received 18.3 per cent of the vote, compared with a total of 10 per cent to the main left-wing parties standing independently in 1966. Analysis of polls taken in 1971 suggests that the FA was less successful than the traditional parties in securing support among manual workers and the unemployed, and more successful among the upper-middle-class and white-collar workers.[30] Intellectuals were particularly strongly represented in the coalition, which represented a reaction to corruption of public life and the inability of the traditional parties to formulate viable solutions to continuing economic decline. First imprisoned in 1973 following the military coup, Seregni was released in March 1984, 'anxious to integrate the Left into the mainstream of Uruguayan politics as a loyal democratic force, rather than the anti-system "popular tribune" it had been in 1971–3'.[31]

Seregni played a significant role in the negotiated transition to democracy, emphasising the need for peaceful reconciliation and participation in the CONAPRO talks to ensure that the FA made a constructive and stabilising contribution to the process.[32] Excluding himself from the presidential race in November 1984, Seregni nonetheless saw the FA vote increase to 21.3 per cent in spite of the absence of a major figure as candidate, and the severity of the repression visited on left-wing activists during the dictatorship. The coalition maintained its policy of a single presidential candidate, but the separate lists of congressional candidates revealed that the moderate non-Marxist PGP (now led by Hugo Batalla) contributed 40 per cent of the FA vote.

By November 1989, when Seregni was once again the FA's presidential candidate, many of the problems subsequently to afflict the FA were becoming evident. Seregni's conception of his task as its undisputed leader was to maintain the unity of the coalition, Marxist and non-Marxist, *históricos* (old guard) and

modernisers, while engaging in a dialogue of constructive opposition and criticism with the traditional parties. Thus in February 1986 the FA entered a
'national agreement' with them intended to promote the reactivation of the
economy, and his castigation in 1988 of the *blanquicolorado* 'party of government and governability', which he described as 'anti-national, anti-popular and
anti-democratic', caused a stir as much because of the personal respect which
he commanded amongst his political opponents as for its apparent intemper-
ance.[33] This attack on the other parties was intended to reinforce his main message: that the unity and mutual respect between members of the FA was in
decline, weakening its organisational efficiency and endangering its future. The
immediate problem was the attempt by the PGP and PDC to run their own
presidential candidate, an issue which led them to break with the FA in March
1989 and appear in the November elections (in alliance with the Unión Cívica,
or Civic Union) as Nuevo Espacio, NE.[34] The departure of the 'moderate Left'
opened the way for the Tupamaros and associated groups to join the coalition
in May 1989. The radical Left thus had greatly increased representation, chal-
lenging the ideological and organisational capacity of the Communist Party at
the head of the Marxist Left, on the eve of the break-up of the USSR. The financial strength of the PCU, and the role of its militants within the trade unions,
had provided Seregni with a core of support by which to control the coalition.
Now, the task of modernising the internal structure of the FA and its programme as a potential party of government was about to become even more difficult. The loss of the PGP robbed the FA of votes, but not of internal
divisions.[35]

The 1989 elections brought to prominence two figures who, along with
Seregni, dominated the history of the FA in the 1990s. Danilo Astori, Dean of
the Economics Faculty at the Universidad de la República in early 1989, was
chosen as vice-presidential candidate to accompany Seregni on the basis of radical proposals which won the support of the far Left. Astori was a *frenteam-
plista*, without strong ties to any party or group. Whereas Seregni proposed to
deal with the issue of privatisation on a pragmatic basis, Astori revived the idea
of a Latin American debtors' club to back the non-payment of the external debt.
The IMF, as the instrument of the capitalist world and the US government,
brought problems, not solutions, and Uruguay should deal directly with its
creditor banks. The underlying cause of the inflationary problem was not the
fiscal deficit, but the economic stagnation which gave rise to the deficit. Allied
to the more cautious declarations of Seregni, this radical global vision appealed
to the traditional revolutionary Left as well as to the radicals. Tabaré Vázquez
of the Socialist Party was nominated as candidate for mayor of Montevideo,
traditionally seen as a stepping-stone for the coalition to national government.
Vázquez emerged as a national figure, winning Montevideo in 1989, with a
much stronger identification as a medical practitioner than as a political
activist. Indeed, while continuing his career as head of the Radiotherapy Service of the National Cancer Institute, Vázquez perhaps deliberately cultivated

the image of an outsider unused to politicians' games.[36] There were nonetheless lessons to be learned. Criticised from the Left for admitting the principle of privatised municipal services, Vázquez had also to retreat from populist undertakings made in the election campaign regarding, for example, reduced bus fares, and a defence of street vendors.[37]

By 1993, both Astori and Vázquez were in contention for the FA candidacy in November 1994 left vacant by Seregni's decision to stand aside (though he continued as President of the FA). Following the split in the PCU in 1992 which left a rump of *históricos* in control of a greatly reduced force, the FA came together in the plebiscite on the privatisation law at the end of the year. But the struggle within the FA resumed in 1993, with the moderates in the PS, Vertiente Artiguista and Corriente Popular seeking a redistribution of power away from the parties of the radical Movimiento de Participación Popular (MPP, Popular Participation Movement) to reflect their greater popular support. The fact that all three leaders were in the moderate camp expressed a further division within the FA, between the 'triumvirate' on the one hand and the base committees and their delegates on the other. With no agreement on restructuring, but with no potential candidate from the radical camp, both Astori and Vázquez began to reshape their platforms. Astori effectively renounced his radical economics during 1993–94 and moved to a centre-left position: the debt should be paid, macroeconomic balance must be maintained, wage restraint implemented and lessons learned from the neoliberals. With support from ex-PCU members and other independents, Astori formed the Asamblea Uruguay (AU, Uruguayan Assembly), a group which essentially projected his own programme. Vázquez moved in the opposite direction. Fortified by a strong showing in opinion polls, in February 1994 Vázquez unexpectedly announced his opposition to the modest constitutional reform in the negotiation of which the FA had been indirectly involved (and which Seregni and Astori both supported). This was the crucial step which wrong-footed Astori and, more significantly, separated Vázquez from the rest of the political elite. In April 1994, confirmed as presidential candidate for the FA, Vázquez defined the essential choice in the election as being between neoliberalism and democracy, a dichotomy explicitly rejected by Astori.[38] But having thus endeared himself to the radical pole within the FA, Vázquez then temporarily freed himself from a radical embrace by making an electoral alliance with dissident progressive members of the Nacional Party and the PDC, creating Encuentro Progresista (EP, Progressive Encounter) and installing Rodolfo Nin Novoa, a Blanco, as his vice-presidential candidate.

The outcome of the November 1994 election, which saw Vázquez beaten into third place but a mere 35,000 votes (1.5 per cent of the poll) behind Sanguinetti, might have resolved the tensions within the FA, but it did not. Vázquez's own party, the PS, contributed 20 per cent of the total FA vote, but Astori's AU, with 43 per cent, emerged clearly dominant. Espacio Renovador (Space for Renewal), the non-FA element of EP, added 8 per cent to the FA vote. Both Vázquez, as President of EP, and Astori, with a commanding share of the

FA vote, now had a power base from which to develop their claims to lead the Left. Immediately following the election, Astori declared that the FA should enter negotiations with Sanguinetti in order not to be excluded from the political agreements necessary for the formation of a government; failure to do so would leave a future FA president vulnerable to the retaliatory combined opposition of the two other parties. However, Seregni designated Vázquez to meet with Sanguinetti, and no agreement resulted. While Astori proceeded to speak with increasing moderation,[39] Vázquez developed a discourse of outright opposition, identifying neoliberals as 'the enemy', and invoking 'a class struggle, comrades, with exploiters and exploited'.[40] Traditionally united and disciplined, FA legislators during 1995 were no longer able to vote as a single force.

Following attempts to achieve a semblance of unity in late 1995, crisis was reached when Seregni announced his resignation from the presidency of FA in February 1996, citing continued internal divisions, the inability of the decision-making bodies of the coalition to function adequately, and specifically their lack of support for the proposed constitutional reform, as reasons for his departure.[41] The strategy of relying on his personal authority to contain dissent, under strain since 1988, had ultimately failed. The radicals were critical of Seregni, believing that the resignation was a manoeuvre leading to an endorsement of Astori.[42] Certainly, on the need for dialogue, not confrontation, with the government, on the dangers of recourse to referendums, and on the need to reform the Constitution, Seregni and Astori were close. But even if this had been Seregni's intention, the outcome was very different. While Vázquez was never challenged in his bid to succeed Seregni at the end of 1996, Astori lost the confidence even of the AU,[43] and antagonised the FA by making clear his support for the constitutional reform which was narrowly approved in the referendum of December 1996. Vázquez called internal elections of delegates to the National Plenary of the FA in September 1997, which (compared with the national elections of 1994) saw support for his PS rise from 20 per cent to 32 per cent, while AU declined from 43 per cent to 10 per cent.[44]

The FA thus evolved from a united coalition, which, after 1984, offered constructive criticism of government and whose leadership won national respect, to a political force immersed in a culture of opposition and antagonism. *Vazquismo*, combining strong personal appeal, an oratorical identification with 'the people', and a discourse which has yet to address seriously the policy issues of national government, is a novel phenomenon in Uruguayan politics. The transformation of the FA has been accompanied by a change in its support base. The axis of intellectuals and trade-union activists has been dispersed by the disillusion of the one (to the benefit principally of NE) and the decline (along with the PCU) of the other. In its place, the radical parties have been particularly successful in securing the support of the young (noticeable in the militant opposition of students to Sanguinetti's educational reform), and in the poorest districts, which previously were attracted to the right-wing authoritarianism of the Colorado ex-president Pacheco Areco.[45] Astori remains an important figure within the coalition, with national political ambitions of his own. Assuming that he does not win the FA candidacy, his pragmatic moderation might yet prove crucial to Vázquez as a counterweight to the demands of the radicals. Remarkably, and perhaps as a portent of future problems to be faced, Vázquez resigned as president of the FA in September 1997, following the refusal of a (radical) MPP member of the FA-controlled city council of Montevideo to accept the privatisation of a municipal hotel agreed by the other FA councillors.

The electoral reform of 1996

The reform approved by plebiscite in December 1996 to take effect in the 1999 elections brings to an end Uruguay's system of DSV. Instead of presenting multiple candidates, the parties will each choose a single candidate in internal elections held simultaneously in April. To secure the nomination, a candidate must have an absolute majority (i.e. 50 per cent + 1) of the votes, or at least 40 per cent and a margin of at least 10 per cent over the closest rival. Failing that, a party convention will decide. On the last Sunday in October national elections will be held for President and Parliament. A further innovation is that if no presidential candidate secures an absolute majority, there will be a second-round vote (*ballottage*) between the two leading candidates on the last Sunday in November. Municipal elections, with candidates for mayor restricted to two per party, will now take place the following May. Finally, the system of 'electoral cooperatives' in departments of the interior, by which votes for candidates for the House of Representatives on separate lists have been accumulated, is to end.

These changes will affect profoundly the way the political system works. Uruguay currently has three major parties – strictly speaking, two traditional parties and an alliance of left-wing parties, none of which could expect to secure an absolute majority in the first round, but all of which could reasonably hope to win in the second. To do so, each must be able to pick up votes from the party placed third (plus NE and any other group which enters the first-round contest). The internal elections are therefore crucial. Each party must be aware that it needs to choose a candidate who, by dint of programme, personality or political record, is capable not only of uniting the party and therefore doing well enough in the first round, but also of attracting support from outside the party in the second round. The logic of the new system seems to imply that each party will maximise its chances of being elected by choosing a centrist candidate of broad appeal internally and to one other party.

How will these new rules play in Uruguay in 1999? For the EP/FA, the choice of candidate seems to be made, given Tabaré Vázquez's dominant position internally and the strength of the FA in opinion polls. However, Vázquez's conduct in declining to negotiate with the traditional parties makes him something of a liability in the second round. Only the small NE is a potential source of support at that stage, and NE voters, who left the FA in 1988 and showed no signs of wishing to return, are likely to be ambivalent. From its foundation

the FA has presented a single presidential candidate, consistent with its argument for the abolition of DSV. It would be ironic therefore to hold an internal
election for the presidential candidate, as Danilo Astori has proposed.[46]
Nonetheless, since the loss of a President who was not linked with any constituent party, and the emergence in the 1990s of deep splits on policy and
strategy, the FA has come to resemble a traditional party. Astori, who has
remained loyal to the FA throughout his career, consistently argued the need to
enter a dialogue with the traditional parties, and offers 'responsible' economic
policies, might reasonably suppose that he would make a better second-round
candidate than Vázquez.

For Blancos and Colorados, the situation is very different. Second-round
voting was for them the most important feature of the reform precisely because
they envisaged that it would prevent an FA victory. They believe, or hope, that
their historic differences are paradoxically what bind them together as authen-
tic expressions of Uruguayan nationality and distinctiveness, and that enough
supporters of one party would vote for the other in the second round to frustrate the Left. Administrations since 1985 have all required cross-party support
so that at the party hierarchy level cooperation has increased. Nonetheless, it
remains to be seen whether deals and endorsements will carry the voters.[47]
Most traditional party votes are now recorded in the interior of the country,
where traditional party identifications are likely to be stronger. Moreover,
although there was a small majority of interior votes in favour of the reform,
43 per cent rejected the wishes of the traditional party leaderships and voted
against, only a proportion of whom would be FA voters following Vázquez in
opposition to it.[48] If doubts about the behaviour of voters may be one source of
concern, the choice of candidates in the internal elections must be crucial. The
issues are both ideological and personal. Both parties have leaders who are
avowedly 'neoliberal' (including Lacalle and Batlle); others who are centrist or
reformist. Some, especially among the Blancos, have shown extended loyalty to
administrations headed by the other party (Volonté in particular); others might
for personal or historical reasons find it difficult to receive cross-party support.
A 'new' candidate without strong party-political antecedents or factional identification might have advantages similar to those which enabled Volonté, passed
over for the Herrerista Blanco nomination, to found his own faction, declare
his candidacy only five months before the 1994 election, and still be the most-
voted Blanco candidate.

Electoral reform has been the subject of political and academic debate in
Uruguay for many years.[49] DSV, which implies the transfer of votes between
candidates of the same party but very different politics, was difficult to
defend.[50] The 1966 Constitution resulted in the election of presidents receiving
a mere 21 per cent to 31 per cent of the total vote as a personal mandate, and
who had then to construct a majority in Congress to be able to govern. The
relationship between President and Parliament has been central to the debate,
but the outcome of the reform in these terms is difficult to predict. The expec-

tation of those in favour of *ballottage* is that the capacity of the Executive to secure support would be enhanced because an absolute majority of voters would have cast votes for the President, even though his/her party still had a minority of seats in the two Houses. But if the FA should win in the second round, such an outcome looks to be fanciful, given its antagonistic posture to the other parties. If either of the traditional parties should win, the increasing closeness of the two and experience of coalition should ease the process of forming an administration, irrespective of an inflated vote in the second round. Indeed, the importance of inter-party negotiation immediately following the 1989 and 1994 elections has been one factor in a tendency to diminish the significance of the legislature in the 1990s. The business of government has been increasingly agreed between party and fraction leaders, few of whom sit in either House. The role of Congress, with its built-in majority of members supporting the Executive, has become subsidiary, and effective opposition has moved outside, to the collection of signatures on the streets and the holding of plebiscites. Nor does experience in the legislature often figure in the careers of those aiming at political eminence.[51]

Commenting on the electoral-reform referendum, Líber Seregni viewed the FA's strategy of opposition and confrontation as 'a historic error, a political error which the FA will have to pay for in due course'.[52] Given that the traditional parties believe that second-round voting will enable them to defeat the FA, it is perhaps puzzling that the FA leadership should collectively have accepted its inclusion in the reform in November 1995, and only Vázquez joined with the coalition's activists in seeking to overturn it. The explanation is fundamental to the split which divides the FA. It was spelled out by Astori at the time and effectively repeated by Seregni a year later: 'The second round, comrades, is what will enable us to become the government in 1999', allowing us 'to make the agreements necessary for a coalition of transformation for Uruguay'; 'the government of the year 2000 has to be a government of agreement and coalition'.[53] The radical groups of the FA want a government of the Left which will not compromise with the enemy, and in Tabaré Vázquez they believe they have an electoral asset who can deliver it. Less clear is whether Vázquez himself shares that vision.

Notes

1 The information in this section is taken from H. Finch, 'Towards the New Economic Model: Uruguay 1973–1997', University of Liverpool, Institute of Latin American Studies, Research Paper 22 (1998).

2 *Búsqueda*, 21 February 1985.

3 The text of the *acuerdo nacional* was published in *Búsqueda*, 4 April 1986.

4 The Movimiento de Liberación Nacional–Tupamaros (MLN-T, National Liberation Movement–Tupamaros), whose leaders were granted an amnesty and released from detention in April 1985, committed itself to political activity within the framework of parliamentary democracy in 1985. It was not, however, admitted into the FA until 1989.

5 The provision for referendums was altered during 1989, as a result of difficulties in validating such a large number of signatures. To repeal a law, 12,000 signatures must be presented initially; at least 25 per cent of the electorate (approximately 600,000) must then vote in favour of a referendum, which may then be held. To reform the Constitution, a plebiscite may be called either by a petition from 10 per cent of the electorate, or by the vote of two-fifths of the Senate and House of Representatives meeting together as the Asamblea General. According to D. Butler and A. Ranney: 'Uruguay holds the Western Hemisphere record for referendums'; five have been held in the nine years since the Ley de Caducidad was confirmed, and in early 1998 campaigns were in process for two more. D. Butler and A. Ranney, *Referendums Around the World: The Growing Use of Direct Democracy* (London, Macmillan, 1994).

6 Comisión Intercameral Empresarial (1989). The groups sponsoring the report were the Asociación Rural (the Rural Association), the Cámara de Industrias (the Chamber of Industry), the Cámara Mercantil de Productos del País Hacia un Uruguay Con futuro: Analisis y Propuestas del sector empresarial privado (Commercial Chamber for National Products) and the Cámara Nacional de Comercio (the National Chamber of Commerce).

7 See the speech delivered on 20 May 1994 reported in *Búsqueda*, 25 May 1994. On the stump, philosophical social democracy could decline into neopopulism. Sanguinetti (16 April 1994) made the same apparent promise of protection to sugar-cane producers as did Tabaré Vázquez, the FA presidential candidate (13 May 1994), who criticised Sanguinetti for stealing these and other clothes: *Búsqueda*, 14 July 1994.

8 Lacalle's Herrerista faction placed most of the blame on Sanguinetti for the reverses the Blanco government experienced: E. Balcarcel, A. Mercader and R. Loza Aguerrebere, *60 meses que cambiaron al país* (Montevideo, Instituto Manuel Oribe, 1996), reviewed in *Búsqueda*, 6 June 1996.

9 The text of the *Bases* document was published in *Búsqueda*, 26 January 1995.

10 For a critique of the reform, see G. Márquez Mosconi, *An Assessment of Pension System Reform in Uruguay in 1995* (Washington, DC, Social Programs Division, Inter-American Development Bank (IDB), 1997).

11 Both Líber Seregni, then President of the FA, and Danilo Astori, vice-presidential candidate in 1994, made clear that their support for the referendum campaign was reluctant (*Búsqueda*, 16 September and 28 July 1994). Seregni also expressed his misgivings over the referendum mechanism, especially when used to reform the Constitution with reference to a specific sector.

12 Ruben Correa Freitas, Director, Oficina Nacional de Servicio Civil (Nation Office of the Civil Service) and member of the Comité Ejecutivo Para la Reforma del Estado (Executive Committee for the Reform of the State), quoted in *El Observador*, 3 March 1997.

13 Essentially, privatisations should not extend to activities which affect national sovereignty or security, and should not convert a public monopoly into a private monopoly, except where private capital is necessary for investment purposes. A further criterion was added subsequently: my government 'does not accept that all privatisations are good, and therefore a number of undertakings will remain in the state sector which represent important income for the maintenance of fiscal balance' (annual report to Parliament, *El estado de la República*, 1 March 1998). This latter principle tends to confirm the complaint made by a director of ANCAP (see note 21). Note also the remarkable similarity between the Sanguinetti criteria for privatisation and those set out by the FA leader Danilo Astori: they would exclude activities of a strategic character; those which can function only as monopolies; and those which because of their 'good profitability ... it would be a bad business to sell, above all in a country which needs fiscal resources amongst other things to balance the budget' (*Búsqueda*, 2 October 1997).

14 *Búsqueda*, 22 June 1995. Sanguinetti was speaking at the World Economic Forum, São Paulo, 20 June 1995.

15 For a full discussion of the Mercosur, see N. Phillips, 'Global and Regional Linkages', in J. Buxton and N. Phillips (eds), *Developments in Latin American Political Economy: States, Markets and Actors* (Manchester, Manchester University Press, 1999).

16 On 31 August 1990 Lacalle met with seven party leaders (including Líber Seregni) who gave

unanimous support: S. Abreu Bonilla, *Mercosur e integración* (Montevideo, Fundación de Cultura Universitaria, 1991), p. 120.

17 For example, in March 1997 Brazil imposed restrictions on the financing of imports into Brazil, and in November 1997 it increased by 3 per cent the level of the Mercosur's Common External Tariff. Both moves were the subject of protest by partner countries, and subsequent negotiation.

18 See the comments of exporters and industrialists in *Búsqueda*, 2 October 1997. Simón Berkowitz, former president of the Cámara Mercantil de Productos del País, is pessimistic, believing that the partner countries react more quickly to opportunity, while the Uruguayan labour market is still inflexible.

19 Significant price or tariff reductions were reported in port services, insurance, and alcohol and cement production: *Búsqueda*, 5 June 1997.

20 Eduardo Barbieri, Director of the Grupo Asesor sobre Reforma del Estado (Advisory Group on Reform of the State), speaking in a personal capacity, Department of Economics, Faculty of Social Sciences, Universidad de la República, 24 July 1997: *Búsqueda*, 31 July 1997.

21 A member of the directorate of ANCAP attributed government reluctance to authorise a reduction in the price of fuel to 'the greater weight given to the fiscal accounts than to the economic circumstances of the enterprise': *El País*, 16 February 1998.

22 *Búsqueda*, 19 September 1991, 4 December 1997.

23 The judgement was made by members of the Modernisation of Industrial Relations Programme of UCUDAL, reported in Julio Scavino, 'Empresarios y trabajadores dibujan un nuevo tipo de relaciones obligados por la globalización', *Búsqueda*, 2 October 1997. See also O. Díaz, *Relaciones laborales y convenios en el Uruguay: Los sindicatos ante la reestructura productiva* (Montevideo, Centro Uruguay Independiente, 1995) for a detailed account by union officials of ways in which industrial restructuring has affected industrial relations in five private-sector firms and one public corporation.

24 Other possible explanations for this outcome, not generally associated with the neoliberal project, are discussed in Finch, 'Towards the New Economic Model'.

25 The second meeting of the Círculo de Montevideo, Sanguinetti's international study group, was devoted to 'Employment, Labour Flexibility and Social Protection' in 1997.

26 *Búsqueda*, 12 February 1998.

27 *Búsqueda*, 1 and 8 February 1996. General Alberto Ballestrino, Chief of Police in Montevideo and Director of the Escuela Militar (military college) during periods of the dictatorship, described the Tenientes de Artigas during the *golpe* period as mostly supporters of the Nacional (Blanco) Party. 'They were people of the Right. They were much inspired by the career of General Francisco Franco; and other European leaders of that time, Mussolini, Hitler … . There were many of them, that's the truth.'

28 Numbers of the armed forces fell from 33,500 in 1985 to 26,000 in 1997 (*Búsqueda*, 2 October 1997). The practice of taking second jobs has become well-established among army officers. However, according to the International Institute of Strategic Studies, Uruguay devoted 2.6 per cent of GDP to defence in 1995, the fourth highest in the region.

29 Documents relating to the foundation of the FA are reproduced in *Cuadernos de Marcha*, nos 46, 47 and 53 (February, March and September 1971).

30 J. Ures, 'La relación clase–voto en Montevideo', *Revista Uruguaya de Ciencias Sociales*, 1:1 (1972), p. 12.

31 C. Gillespie, *Negotiating Democracy: Politicians and Generals in Uruguay* (Cambridge, Cambridge University Press, 1991), p. 143.

32 This contrasted with the part played by the Blancos, whose principal leader, Wilson Ferreira Aldunate, had been in exile during the dictatorship and was imprisoned on his return in mid-1984.

33 Speech reported in *Búsqueda*, 21 April 1988.

34 Until Seregni's April 1988 speech, Hugo Batalla's personal rating in opinion polls had been higher than Seregni's (*Búsqueda*, 5 May 1989). In 1994 he took the PGP out of NE when San-

guinetti shocked the Colorado faithful by choosing him as vice-presidential running mate. In 1997 he took the PGP back into the Colorado Party, from which it had separated in 1970.

35 The MLN-T condemned the FA strategy of prioritising agreements with the traditional parties, instead of frontal opposition and mobilisation: *Búsqueda*, 3 August 1989.

36 Relatively young (born 1940), Vázquez has 'the face of an angel' and is a skilled television performer.

37 'From inside one sees things in a different way, through a different lens, and that leads to a different style of action': Ariel Bergamino, Vázquez's political secretary, quoted in *Búsqueda*, 13 September 1990.

38 *Búsqueda*, 5 May 1994.

39 'I hold the view that Uruguayan neoliberalism was the most prudent and gradual in the whole of Latin America. It was neoliberalism Uruguay-style. A conservative neoliberalism, in the sense of risking little': seminar, Instituto Fernando Otorgués, reported in *Búsqueda*, 26 October 1995. Astori also affirmed the importance of fiscal and monetary discipline.

40 Speech to the Partido por la Victoria del Pueblo (PVP, Party for the Victory of the People), reported in *Búsqueda*, 3 August 1995. The PVP is a radical party within the FA coalition, and it is said of Vázquez that he sometimes finds it difficult to avoid saying what his audience wants to hear.

41 At the age of 79, Seregni had also suffered illness in late 1995.

42 It was noticeable that Vázquez did not attend the 25th anniversary celebration of the FA, at which the resignation was announced.

43 By February 1997, 6 of the AU's 17 members of the Cámara de Representantes (Chamber of Deputies) had left the group.

44 Provisional figures: *Búsqueda*, 2 October 1997.

45 Líber Seregni cited the loss of input from intellectuals as one reason for the creation of his 'think tank', the Centro de Estudios Estratégicos 1815 (Centre of Strategic Studies 1815), which in October 1997 published 'Algunas ideas sobre un proyecto nacional alternativo': *Búsqueda*, 13 February and 23 October 1997.

46 *Búsqueda*, 4 December 1997.

47 Traditional clientelist politics would have established a link between the two. Now that television has largely displaced the political clubs of the *barrios* (slums), and favours are no longer the currency of loyalty, voters may behave more autonomously. The alternation of the parties in power, and the growth of the FA, certainly suggest so.

48 There is speculation that because the reform ended the 'electoral cooperative' arrangement and thus reduced the power of interior party bosses, a rift may have developed between the party structures nationally and departmentally.

49 See, for example, D. Nohlen and J. Rial (eds), *Reforma electoral: Posible? Deseable?* (Montevideo, Ediciones de la Banda Oriental, 1986); and A. Cocchi (ed.), *Reforma electoral y voluntad política* (Montevideo, Ediciones de la Banda Oriental, 1988).

50 For an attempt to do so see C. Pareja and P. Romeo, 'Hacia otra reforma política', *Cuadernos del CLAEH*, 71, 1994.

51 Appointment to the directorate of a state corporation seems to be more popular: Alberto Volonté had been president of the electricity utility UTE before his presidential candidacy. Ricardo Lombardo, president of the communications utility ANTEL, announced his candidacy for the Colorado nomination in 1997, and Ruben Díaz, President of the port authority ANP, has expressed an intention to return to political life.

52 *Clarín* (Buenos Aires), 10 December 1996.

53 *Búsqueda*, 23 November 1995; *Clarín*, 10 December 1996.

5

Peru

JOHN CRABTREE

State, society and politics under Fujimori: introduction

Few countries in Latin America have undergone such rapid economic and political change in the 1990s as Peru.[1] In the economic sphere, in imposing the neoliberal order the Fujimori government elected in 1990 eschewed gradualism in favour of a radical programme of deregulation and privatisation. Having overcome hyperinflation by means of a drastic stabilisation programme, the government managed to achieve price stability and reactivate the productive economy, reorienting it towards the export sector. Politically, Fujimori engineered a palace coup, the *autogolpe*, in 1992, to remove his opponents from Congress and to reformulate the Constitution so as to permit his own re-election. The period of constitutional rule (1980–92) thus gave way to a 'controlled democracy', involving the concentration of political power in the hands of the President and a small ruling group. The Peruvian experience thus challenged the widely held notion that economic liberalisation and political liberalisation were complementary forces, suggesting rather that a rapid liberalisation of the economy required an authoritarian state structure to make it viable.

The political system that has evolved in Peru since 1990 is essentially a hybrid, combining democratic and autocratic features. Despite the rupture to the constitutional order in 1992, there is a functioning Congress and Supreme Court, elections take place regularly and reasonably fairly, there is little by way of overt censorship and political parties are free to operate. Nevertheless, despite the existence of democratic forms, the 'quality' of Peruvian democracy is questionable: the Executive exerts considerable sway over the other powers of the state, political parties and other representative institutions have little influence, municipal government is subordinate to fiscal control from the centre, the media holds back from criticising the government, the military and intelligence community have accumulated great influence and formal systems of government accountability are weak.

The prime objective of this chapter is to evaluate the nature of this political system and to hazard some guesses as to how it could evolve in the last years of the 1990s and beyond. The central preoccupation is with the question of political representation – or the lack of it – and how this affects the nature of the political system. The chapter concentrates attention on the 'public space', or the area that separates the state and society, and how different actors move within it. In order to achieve this, it is necessary first to ascertain how both the state and society themselves have changed in recent years. As will be shown, both have changed in important ways, altering significantly the rules of the political game.

From intervention to privatisation: the role of the state

Avoiding the populist cycle which affected many of the larger Latin American countries in the 1930s and 1940s, the Peruvian state structure remained relatively laissez-faire and non-interventionist until the early 1960s.[2] During the late 1960s and early 1970s, this picture changed radically. In particular, with the military coup which brought General Juan Velasco to power in 1968, Peru entered a period of economic development in which the state sought to play a protagonistic role.[3] The military government saw the state as an independent actor, capable of achieving a more balanced pattern of economic growth that would benefit those previously at the margins of capitalist development. The state therefore placed itself at the very centre of society, seeking to channel and reconcile conflicting social demands in a typically corporatist way.

The Velasco government took over major previously foreign-owned businesses and extended its role in the spheres of regulation, planning and in the assignation of resources. Although it was not the intention of the Velasco regime to supplant the private sector (it saw its role as promoting national capitalism and industrialisation behind protective tariffs), the public sector during this time grew at the expense of the private. State enterprises came to be a dominant force not only in the productive sphere, but also in such fields as marketing and banking. So from being a country with a relatively backward state sector, Peru rapidly became one of the most interventionist countries in Latin America. However, the growth of the state brought to light a number of critical weaknesses and shortcomings.

Firstly, the pattern of state development lacked solid financial foundations.[4] Turning its back on foreign investment to finance development but lacking an efficient tax system to pay for its expanded role, the Velasco regime resorted to sovereign borrowing to cover its fiscal and balance-of-payments shortfalls. Many of the public companies which came into being were overstaffed and inefficiently run and, by operating at a loss, exacerbated fiscal problems. The debt crisis of the 1980s exposed the weakness of this new state-oriented model of development. In fact, the Peruvian debt crisis broke well before the 1982 Mexican default led to the suspension of bank lending to the rest of Latin America. During the so-called 'second phase' of the military regime (1975–80), the government found itself obliged by the IMF to embark on a structural adjustment programme, which sought to reduce the extent of state intervention and promote a more 'market-friendly' approach.[5] During the Belaúnde administration (1980–85), and especially after 1982, recurrent fiscal difficulties were exacerbated by the burden of debt repayment. This made Peru more susceptible to pressures emanating from the Washington-based multilateral institutions, which sought to promote policies of trade liberalisation, economic deregulation and the privatisation of state-owned companies.

Secondly, the quality of state services was poor and uneven. Although the state at this time assumed many new responsibilities and functions, its ability to carry out such functions was limited. Its authority, especially in rural areas far from the capital, was weak. The administrative apparatus established by Velasco was highly centralised, and despite rhetoric to the contrary, the primacy of Lima over the rest of Peru at this time was further underlined, at the expense of provincial towns and cities. For many, especially in rural areas, the state appeared more of a burden than a facilitator, taking more in taxes than what it returned in services.

Thirdly, the growth in the economic activity of the state failed in its objective to reduce social tensions. Rather, the state became the focus of different pressure-groups in society, each seeking to influence public policy to protect its perceived interests. Politics therefore became more confrontational. Indeed, it had been the fear that the situation was rapidly getting out of control which prompted Velasco's ouster in 1975. The threat of losing social conquests led to widespread labour unrest in the late 1970s, involving a sequence of general strikes. The labour movement and the political parties of the Left doggedly resisted the timid attempts of the Belaúnde government to push ahead with economic liberalisation.

The García government (1985–90) brought about the denouement of the statist model.[6] Turning his back on the liberalising Washington consensus, García sought to implement a poorly planned heterodox model in which the state once again played a central role in the assignation of resources.[7] In part, the thinking resembled that of the Velasco period, with the state once again asserting itself in mediating conflicting interests from various sectors of society. Just as most other Latin American countries – many reluctantly – were being forced by the fiscal logic of the debt crisis to embrace neoliberal economics, the García government sought to swim against the tide. The consequence of these policies was an inflationary explosion and a bout of extreme recession, which both effectively bankrupted the public sector and exposed the inability of the state to resolve the country's deep social problems. The crisis of hyperinflation also coincided with the climax of political violence perpetrated by the Maoist-inspired Sendero Luminoso (SL, Shining Path), whose violent campaign to overthrow the state revealed the latter's inability even to guarantee law and order.[8] These twin crises combined with each other, shaking public confidence in the state and its capacities and thereby creating the necessary political conditions for an abrupt change.

Under Fujimori, the role of the state changed substantially. With the encouragement of the IMF and the World Bank, the government pursued an aggressive policy of economic liberalisation. This took various forms.[9] In 1990 and 1991, Fujimori did away with the system of protection which had sheltered Peruvian firms from foreign competition for the best part of thirty years. Markets were deregulated, including financial markets. Labour contracts were made more flexible, allowing employers to hire and fire at will. Finally, the government announced in 1991 its intention to sell off all state-owned industries by 1995. The first Fujimori government (1990–95) pursued this agenda with vigour and determination. The consequence was a rapid transformation of the economy into one where the private sector, both foreign and Peruvian, became the mainspring of economic activity, with the state withdrawing to a largely supervisory role. State-sector employment slumped dramatically as most industries were privatised, even though by 1998 some key sectors still remained in state hands. There was a major shake-out in the labour market, with the private sector failing to absorb labour displaced from the public sector. The process of privatisation generated substantial foreign investment, helping to provide much-needed capital for firms long starved of adequate funding, generating both increased production and (for instance in the case of telecommunications) some improvement in the quality of services.[10]

The fiscal revenue generated by privatisation increased the resources available to the state to undertake other activities, whilst price stabilisation also helped restore fiscal order. Also, a much-needed tax reform extended the efficacy of the tax system, reducing tax evasion and helping to bring within the tax net both the wealthy and the large number of not-so-wealthy members of the informal sector. The reforms thus sharply increased the number of registered taxpayers.[11] With its income thus enhanced, the state apparatus was therefore better placed to improve the quality of its performance. However, in this respect, the results were mixed. Some state institutions were undoubtedly streamlined, becoming much more efficient. Other than the tax authority itself (SUNAT) and the customs office, an illustrative example was the traditionally inefficient intelligence system (SIN), which greatly expanded the range of its activities. The Fujimori government was able to expand social expenditure through the ministry of the presidency, although many observers criticised such spending programmes, arguing that they were more significant in building political support for the government than dealing with the causes of poverty. In other areas, the quality of state activity was not noticeably improved. For instance, both the Education and Health Ministries remained bereft of funds and were not subjected to 'root-and-branch' reforms to cut back bureaucracy and improve efficacy.

Notwithstanding such limitations, the state underwent a process of significant change under Fujimori, becoming smaller and in some respects more efficient. In part, the bankruptcy of the public sector, exposed by the debt crisis, admitted no real alternative course of action. The radical nature of the Fujimori reforms was a reflection of the profound crisis which had effectively paralysed most state activity by the late 1980s. Indeed, without such a profound crisis, the conditions for change would probably not have existed. Nevertheless, it remained an open question whether the shift from state capitalism towards a more liberal economy would resolve the deep social cleavages which had prompted an interventionist model in the first place.

From collective action to individualism: processes of social change

As we have seen, the expansion of state activity was partly attributable to an attempt to respond to deep structural problems arising from Peru's traditional pattern of development. The country had long been one in which income disparities had been among the most pronounced in Latin America and poverty most abject.[12] The extent and degree of rural poverty were the mainspring for the migration from rural to urban areas, which began in the 1940s, but which accelerated through the 1950s and 1960s. By the late 1970s, Peru was roughly two-thirds 'urban' in its population make-up and one-third rural, whereas 30 years before the proportions had been the reverse.[13] At the same time, rapid population growth was encouraged by the substantial increase in life expectancy (especially as a result of a sharp fall in infant mortality). This demographic trend was only mitigated by a fall in the birth rate in the 1980s and 1990s.

Information on poverty in Peru is more abundant and probably more reliable than data on income distribution.[14] Per capita GDP provides an overall impression of the incidence of poverty. Between 1950 and 1975, per capita GDP grew by an annual average of 2.5 per cent, suggesting that poverty was somewhat reduced during that period. Since 1975, per capita GDP has pursued a volatile but downward path, falling particularly quickly in the period of hyperinflation at the end of the 1980s. It has recovered somewhat in the 1990s, with the recovery in growth rates. The fall in real wages since 1975 has been steeper than the fall in GDP per capita, although most of the very poor do not take part in the wage economy. Headcount surveys suggest that whereas 42 per cent of the population was 'poor' or 'very poor' (using a World Bank definition) in 1985, by the mid-1990s more than half the population could be so described.[15] Data on income distribution are more impressionistic, the most recent detailed study dating from the mid-1970s.[16] However, most analysts agree that the pattern of income distribution has not improved markedly since then, with income still highly concentrated in a relatively small affluent elite, and with extreme poverty widespread in the rural highlands but also pervading the urban population. Although the restoration of price stability was undoubtedly beneficial for the poorest in society (those least able to defend themselves from inflation), there is little evidence to suggest that the restoration of economic growth since 1992 brought much by way of tangible benefits to most Peruvians. However, it appears to be the case that privatisation and export-led growth have benefited the elite a great deal, thereby probably widening the income divisions in Peruvian society.

Popular organisation is well embedded in Peru, strengthened by a culture of collective action which has perpetuated itself at the community level. Nevertheless, for much of the twentieth century this organisation failed to articulate itself in national politics; unlike other countries in Latin America, popular movements failed to break the control of the elite or to force it to negotiate their inclusion in the political system. Oddly, it was the military government of the late 1960s which sought to mobilise popular pressure in order to channel it into regime support. In response to the reforms of the Velasco era, popular organisation took on more assertive characteristics. In the sphere of organised labour, trade unions grew greatly in membership and political strength, largely in response to the sudden growth of the public sector.[17] Organised labour acquired important new rights, of which the labour communities were perhaps the most significant. In the rural sphere, peasant federations became a more influential voice, stimulated by both the process of land reform and the feelings of dissatisfaction and frustration that it engendered.[18] In urban shanty towns, new forms of organisation emerged at the community level, nurtured by demands for land, housing and basic services like water and electricity. These forms of popular organisation were all strengthened by the conviction that only through collective action would social demands be attended to.

The political and economic changes of the 1980s, and particularly the twin effects of hyperinflation and political violence, had profound effects on the nature of social organisation.[19] Trade unions proved themselves unable to prevent the sharp deterioration in real living standards experienced by the working class during the late 1980s, as real wages fell and the contraction in formal-sector employment gave rise to the further expansion of the informal economy. Helped by the García government's measures to facilitate short-term employment, workers lost many of the legal rights that they had gained during the Velasco period. Many were prepared to accept lower wages if it defended their jobs, a shift in outlook which rendered union activity largely superfluous.[20] The collapse in the power and influence of labour unions facilitated the process of privatisation, weakening the resistance of those most diametrically opposed to it.[21] Privatisation, in turn, further weakened the unions and their ability to negotiate collective contracts. In the rural sphere, peasant federations and the rural cooperatives created by the agrarian reform similarly encountered an adverse situation. In particular, the spread of SL throughout much of highland Peru during the 1980s and the concomitant militarisation of the areas affected helped break the power of peasant organisation. Peasants were typically caught in the crossfire between Sendero Luminoso and the armed forces, threatened by both sides. In such circumstances, autonomous organisation became impossible. Many thousands were forced to seek refuge in urban areas as *desplazados* (displaced peoples). Others sought more gainful, albeit precarious employment in the coca plantations of the upper Huallaga valley, whose rapid expansion in the 1980s helped cushion rural unemployment.[22] Finally, in the urban shanty towns, also afflicted by both hyperinflation and the rise in violence, popular organisation came to focus on the day-to-day concerns of community survival rather than pursuing more overtly political demands. Organisations like *comedores populares* (district soup kitchens) multiplied in number, often supported by church-backed groups, but these were concerned primarily with finding more efficient methods to distribute sufficient food to stave off malnutrition.

Popular organisation therefore became less political in its orientation, since the potential for collective action was more circumscribed than before, thereby further debilitating political parties, especially those on the left, for which such organisation had provided the nucleus of their organised support in society. The reduced profile of collective identities became particularly evident in the labour market, where the expansion of the informal sector in the late 1980s created intense competition for employment of any kind.[23] The informal sector was characterised not so much by unemployment but employment at very low rates of remuneration. Low wages forced informal workers to undertake several forms of employment at the same time. Also, many workers were at once members of both sectors, therefore blurring the frontiers between the two. For example, it was not uncommon to find teachers or other state employees working as taxi drivers, street salesmen or newspaper vendors. Between those working the streets, economic relations were more ones of fierce competition for a very limited market, where the scope for collective action was limited. Similarly, in the shanty towns, many of the initial activities which encouraged collective action, such as defence of land, acquisition of land titles and the struggle for basic services, became less important as these communities became more consolidated, and the critical problem facing households was lack of employment.[24] Particularly in the urban sphere, an ever more important part of the whole, collective responses to social problems appeared less attractive or viable as strategies than previously. The overriding problem of lack of adequate employment induced competitive rather than collaborative responses. In such circumstances, urban society (also rural society to a lesser extent) became increasingly atomised and fragmented – albeit more complex – in the ways in which it was structured. The demands placed on the authorities became more individualistic and less collective. Political responses therefore changed as a consequence.

Fujimori's Peru: authoritarianism and democracy

Having addressed the ways in which the state underwent a transformation in the late 1980s and early 1990s and the ways in which Peruvian society itself changed, it becomes easier to comprehend the emergence of a government which sought to establish what it called 'direct democracy', by which it meant a direct rapport between a president and his people that excluded other political forces. In fact such political styles have a long track record in Peru and are, therefore, nothing new in themselves. Political leaders of widely differing persuasions have sought to establish 'top-down' styles of governance, at once personalist and clientelist. However, the Fujimori government has taken this to new lengths, taking full advantage of the twin crises that preceded it to provide a political underpinning for the neoliberal economic model.

The need for an authoritative, if not authoritarian government had been demanded by the country's armed forces, alarmed by the speed at which the country appeared to be entering a period of chaos at the end of the 1980s. In 1988, in a document referred to as 'the green book', the military argued that in order to implement and consolidate a new free-market economic system in Peru, it would take possibly fifteen years of decisive government that would not be blown off course by the pressures of democratic politics.[25] The model of Chilean dictator Augusto Pinochet, who in 1988 had initiated his country's slow and conditional return to civilian government following 15 years of dictatorship, may have influenced this thinking. The problem would be how to achieve such a model without overtly violating democratic institutions.

The weakness of political parties made Fujimori's task easier. The changes we have observed in the nature of society, coupled with the effective bankruptcy of the state, affected those institutions such as parties whose function it was to provide a 'bridge' between the state and society. The weakening of the state made parties less relevant as a mechanism by which specific groups in society could gain access to state institutions. Social change, with the increased salience of individual competition at the expense of collective action, also helped undermine the role played by political parties. However, it is important to stress that the party system in Peru had never been very strong, and that the country lacked a strong legacy of democratic institutionality. Indeed, it is possible to argue that although political parties played an important albeit fluctuating role in the country's political development during the twentieth century, a party system as such only really took root in the 1980s, the very point when new challenges were surfacing which would impede democratic consolidation.[26]

In the years following the return to civilian rule, four main political parties sought to put down roots in society, representing a wide range of ideological points of view. At one end of the spectrum, the right-wing Partido Popular Cristiano (PPC, Popular Christian Party) became the political expression of business interests; at the other, the Izquierda Unida (IU, United Left) emerged as an alliance of different facets of the Marxist Left. In between, Acción Popular (AP, Popular Action), an elitist party with a popular following, was an expression of the centre-right, whilst the Alianza Popular Revolucionaria Americana (APRA, Popular American Revolutionary Alliance), Peru's oldest mass-based party, occupied a space on the centre-left. The political and economic pressures facing government made for volatility in voting behaviour. AP, which won power in 1990 with 47 per cent of the vote, received only 7 per cent of the vote in 1985; APRA, which won the 1985 elections with 54 per cent of the vote, won only 20 per cent in the 1990 elections. The IU, which won the mayoralty of Lima in 1983 and came second only to APRA in the 1985 elections, entered the 1990 elections split in two, attracting only 11 per cent of the vote. Electoral data both for presidential and municipal elections suggest that party loyalties were fluctuating, with many voters switching their preferences between parties on very pragmatic lines.

The demise of Peru's political parties was evident well before Fujimori's victory in the 1990 presidential elections. Indeed, Fujimori, a quintessential 'outsider', owed his political debut to a deep public revulsion towards conventional party leaders, who were widely viewed as exacerbating rather than resolving the country's problems. Weeks before the first round of elections, few had ever heard of the one-time rector of the Universidad Agraria (Agrarian University), whose main claim to fame had been a weekly radio programme that he had hosted. Fujimori's electoral feat in winning second place in the first round of elections in 1990, then to defeat the front-running Mario Vargas Llosa in the second eliminating ballot, was indicative of the unrequited search for new political leadership untainted by any connection with the discredited political parties.[27] However, Fujimori contributed to the parties' decline, noting that his own popularity in opinion polls (his key political asset) was directly related to his ability to orchestrate discontent with parties and their leaders. The *autogolpe* of April 1992, when Fujimori shut down Congress and dismissed the members of the Supreme Court, was vindicated by him on the grounds that he was aiming to free Peru of what he called the *partidocracia*, as if the party system had become the very antithesis of democratic government. As a consequence of the *autogolpe*, Fujimori's public support surged in the opinion polls. The election of a new Congress in November 1992 with a large pro-Fujimori majority was a further blow to the major parties, whilst the subsequent lifting of the constitutional bar on immediate re-election (which allowed Fujimori to stand again in 1995) made it more difficult for the parties to resuscitate themselves. The exiling of Alan García in the wake of the *autogolpe* removed from the political scene a potential party-based rival to Fujimori.

Fujimori was thus able to develop a rapport with the electorate that benefited from the lack of alternative forms of political mediation. Whilst his popularity, especially during his first government (1990–95), owed much to his success in stabilising the economy and then disarticulating SL, he proved himself an adept politician in using the resources of his office to enhance his public standing.[28] Not only did he constantly travel the country responding to public needs of one type or another, but through the ministry of the presidency used substantial fiscal resources in ways which promoted his grassroot political support. His reelection in 1995 with 62 per cent of the vote was in part a vindication of such tactics. The political parties between them managed to win a paltry 5 per cent of the vote. In the following three years, at least, there were few obvious signs of the parties emerging phoenix-like from the ashes of their 1990 debacle.The task of government was also rendered easier by the presidentialist system in Peru and the relatively subordinate roles played by the legislature and the judiciary. The 1979 Constitution had reinforced some of the presidentialist characteristics of previous constitutions, and during the governments of both Belaúnde and García such executive biases were reinforced by the fact that the ruling party could rely on an absolute majority in Congress.[29] When he came to office in July 1990, Fujimori was the first president since the Constitution came into force not to have a majority in Congress, although on many matters (especially in the area of economic policy) he could count on the support of congressmen elected under Vargas Llosa's *Fredemo* ticket (basically an amalgam of PPC and AP supporters, with members of Vargas Llosa's own *Libertad* grouping). Signs of tension between Congress and the Executive over questions of counter-insurgency and human rights were among the factors which led to the 1992 *autogolpe*. The Congress elected subsequently gave Fujimori an absolute majority. It also approved the new 1993 Constitution which further extended executive powers vis-à-vis the judiciary. In his second government, which began in 1995, Fujimori supporters also won the majority of seats in Congress, further reducing representation in the hands of traditional parties. This pro-government majority greatly facilitated the passage of contentious legislation, although repeatedly the *Fujimoristas* in Congress employed devices to minimise parliamentary debate on more politically sensitive issues.

The *autogolpe* also gave Fujimori the chance to dismiss the Supreme Court, most of whose members had been appointed during the preceding García administration. Indeed, one of the pretexts for the coup was Fujimori's promise to restructure the judicial authority, which, he argued, was permeated by corruption. That there was a need for reorganisation in the judiciary was clear, and some of the reforms introduced promised to yield improvements, especially in the administration of justice. One of the pretexts for the 1992 *autogolpe* had been the need to deal with judicial inefficiency and corruption. However, although the 1993 constitution proclaimed the need for greater judicial autonomy, subsequent legislation tended to reinforce executive domination over judicial appointments. Meanwhile the role of the Supreme Court, and in particular its President, was diluted in favour of an Executive-dominated legal commission. Through its majority in Congress, the Executive also passed laws which reduced the autonomy of the Constitutional Tribunal.[30]

Furthermore, the military lent decided support to Fujimori, not only providing his government with overt backing at critical junctures like the *autogolpe*, but also acting almost as a surrogate political party; indeed, the armed forces represented (alongside the Church) one of the few institutions that retained a strong, organised presence in society.[31] That military strategists were looking for tough-minded political leadership was made evident by the 'green book' mentioned above. They had been dismayed by the apparent chaos of García's last two years in office and in particular the failure of both the García and Belaúnde governments to stem the advance of SL. In backing Fujimori, the armed forces sought the powers they considered necessary to defeat SL militarily; it was precisely congressional opposition to the extension of those powers that helped precipitate the *autogolpe*. The armed forces enthusiastically supported the *autogolpe*, providing the military muscle to carry it out. The relationship between Fujimori and the armed forces had been close from the time the former had been waiting in the wings to replace García in July 1990. It became more so after the designation of General Nicolás Hermoza del Bari as Commander-in-Chief of the army in 1991.[32] The *autogolpe* also led to a change in the way in which promotions were conducted. Up until 1992 the commanders of the three services had held office for only a year, being replaced on the basis of seniority; thereafter, Fujimori retained Hermoza indefinitely, strengthening both his position and those of his supporters in the high command. The opponents of Hermoza were effectively weeded out following the failure of an attempted coup in November 1992. Whilst Fujimori was protected by the support of the armed forces, he was at pains to ensure that the armed forces were in turn protected from litigation over human rights. This became particularly evident in response to evidence of military involvement in the 1993 Cantuta killings. It was also made manifest by the controversial amnesty law of 1994, which protected all members of the armed forces from previous responsibility for killings and other abuses committed in the course of duty.

It was Fujimori's ability to orchestrate and sustain genuine public sympathy which provided him with his most precious political asset, and there can be no doubt that popularity in the opinion polls became one of the key measures of regime legitimacy. Throughout his first administration and on into his second, Fujimori managed to maintain much higher approval ratings than either of his two immediate predecessors. This was made more remarkable by the social cost involved in the original stabilisation package and the failure of the benefits of subsequent growth to 'trickle down' to the mass of the population. Although Fujimori managed to reap substantial political profit from his government's success in bringing both inflation and political violence under control, his popularity owed much to his success in projecting an image of hard work, consistency and efficacy, all values which his predecessors had failed to impress on public opinion. Furthermore, in view of Fujimori's ability to prevent other political actors or intermediaries from stealing the limelight, his personal popularity underscored the popularity of the government as a whole.

The Fujimori government has been described as 'populist' and 'neopopulist' in its orientation, a tendency that is also discernible in other Latin American countries, but which receives its clearest expression in Peru.[33] The term refers to the breakdown of political mediation between state and society and its replacement with a personalist regime in which the direct relationship between the President and 'his' people is underscored. Under such a system, representative institutions are routinely bypassed or ignored, and political power emanates from a concept of legitimacy based on presidential popularity. Although there is a long history of populist responses in Peru and democratic institutions have traditionally been weak, the new conjuncture (neopopulism) is derived from important changes which have taken place both within the nature of the state and that of society itself. It is these that are likely to prevent any return to the status quo ante.

Some pointers to the future

Crystal ball-gazing is a risky endeavour, particularly for a country like Peru where the political scene routinely seems to throw up unforeseeable events. Nevertheless, one of the purposes of contemporary political analysis is to provide a historically rooted framework which enables us to make sense of the present and to provide some pointers towards the future. Here, I would simply like to project forward some of the variables we have been examining in this chapter.

First, it seems unlikely that there will be a quick return to the old matrix of state intervention. The state apparatus created in the 1960s and 1970s proved unwieldy, inefficient, susceptible to arbitrariness and corruption and, in the long run, unfinanceable. It is not impossible to imagine the reappearance of demands for the nationalisation of key economic sectors, especially those in the hands of foreign multinationals. It is even more likely that political pressure will emerge to ensure that foreign firms are adequately regulated, especially when they are monopoly producers of goods and services. However, it is most improbable that there will be any resort to the kind of state capitalism envisioned by the military under General Velasco. One of the major challenges facing governments will be how to respond to problems of poverty and deprivation, a sphere in which the private sector can provide few answers. This will require an overhaul of the state machinery in sectors like health and education. Even if the state withdraws entirely from the productive sphere, social pressures will militate against a minimalist state.

Second, and following on from the first point, the free-market, export-oriented economy may not be the best vehicle for reducing social exclusion. The development of dynamic export industries in such areas as mining and hydrocarbons may resolve deeply rooted balance-of-payments problems, but are unlikely to generate mass employment. The employment needs of the population will make themselves more felt as urbanisation continues and as the offspring of the last generation of very high demographic growth enter the labour market. The bifurcation between a small, relatively skilled labour force, fairly well organised and in receipt of comparatively high rates of remuneration, will therefore contrast with a growing informal sector where skills are few, organisation weak and incomes very low. The historically rooted pattern of extreme income inequality is therefore in danger of becoming more pronounced, although continued migration from rural areas may reduce somewhat the absolute numbers of the 'very poor'.

Third, and in response to the changes noted in both the state and society, patterns of political intermediation will be affected. In view of the profundity of the crisis affecting political parties since the late 1980s, it seems unlikely that the parties which were influential up until then will stage a come back. Some of the parties (like AP) tended to be personalistic in nature and have encountered grave difficulties in renewing their old leadership. Others, especially those of the Marxist Left, held ideological positions out of kilter with the new international or domestic situations. Whilst more populist parties like APRA could regain their old standing by exploiting discontent in society, it seems likely that business interests (probably with the support of the army) would rally round to prevent this happening. Renewed electoral activity – with presidential elections scheduled for 2000 and 2005, might provide new incentives for party organisation, but the poor performance of the political parties in the 1995 elections pointed more towards the emergence of amorphous coalitions rather than renewed partisan zeal.

The question therefore that arises from this is how social inequalities will express themselves politically if (or perhaps when) discontent with governments like that of Alberto Fujimori became more widespread. Although guerrilla organisations like SL or the Movimento Revolucianario Túpac Amaru (MRTA, Túpac Amaru Revolutionary Movement) may have been largely snuffed out in the 1990s, the social conditions which had engendered their development in the 1980s remain largely unattended. The potential therefore exists for renewed social violence, although an ever more urbanised society might make this easier to control than in the rural hinterland.

Fourth, and more specifically, the debate that seems likely to have potentially destabilising consequences relates to the issue of *continuismo* (continuity). Looking forward from 1998 at least, the politics of the last two years of Fujimori's second administration seem likely to be dominated by presidential re-election and whether or not this is constitutional. One of the problems inherent in personalist styles of government is that of succession; in the absence of personally designated successors the transfer of authority to others can easily become disruptive. Fujimori at least seemed keen to press the argument that he had been elected in 1995 under a new constitution (that of 1993) and that therefore re-election would be legitimate since it would be his first re-election under the new rules.[34] Much, of course, was likely to depend on Fujimori's ability to orchestrate popularity among the mass population on the one hand and to continue enjoying the confidence of the business class and the military on the other. Whether or not he would attain a third term of government was unclear, but it is hard to avoid the conclusion that, if successful, Fujimori would eventually have to deal with the emergence of new social forces and political actors, whilst the problem of succession would remain. Unless remarkably skilled in adapting himself to new circumstances, a third period in office might prove politically more turbulent than his first two. Such a possibility seemed likely to give Fujimori's erstwhile backers among businessmen and within the military high command some food for thought.

Notes

1 Recent books on Peru under Fujimori include: J. Crabtree and J. Thomas (eds), *Fujimori's Peru* (London, Institute of Latin American Studies (ILAS), 1998); M. Cameron and P. Mauceri (eds), *The Peruvian Labyrinth: Polity, Society, Economy* (University Park, Penn State University Press, 1997); P. Mauceri, *State under Siege: Development and Policy Making in Peru* (Boulder, West-view, 1996); and J. Tulchin and G. Bland (eds), *Peru in Crisis: Dictatorship or Democracy* (Boul-der, Lynne Rienner, 1994).
2 R. Thorp and G. Bertram, *Peru 1890–1977: Growth and Policy in an Open Economy* (London, Macmillan, 1978).
3 A. Lowenthal, *The Peruvian Experiment: Continuity and Change under Military Rule* (Prince-ton, Princeton University Press, 1975). See also G. Philip, *The Rise and Fall of the Peruvian Mil-itary Radicals 1968–78* (London, Athlone, 1978).
4 E. Fitzgerald, 'State Capitalism in Peru: a Model of Economic Development and its Limita-tions', in C. McClintock and A. Lowenthal (eds), *The Peruvian Experiment Reconsidered* (Princeton, Princeton University Press, 1983).
5 T. Scheetz, *Peru and the International Monetary Fund* (Pittsburgh, Pittsburgh University Press, 1986).
6 J. Crabtree, *Peru under García: An Opportunity Lost* (Basingstoke, Macmillan, 1992).
7 D. Carbonetto, *El Perú heterodoxo* (Lima, INP, 1986).
8 There is a considerable literature on SL. This includes: C. Degregori, *Sendero Luminoso I. Los hondos y mortales desencuentros II. Lucha armada y utopia autoritaria* (Lima, IEP, 1986); G. Gorriti, *Sendero: Historia de la guerra milenaria en el Perú* (Lima, Apoyo, 1990); and S. Strong, *Shining Path: The World's Deadliest Revolutionary Force* (London, Harper Collins, 1992).
9 O. Dancourt, *Reformas estructurales y política macroeconómica en el Perú, 1990–96* (Lima, PUCP, 1997); and B. Seminario, *Reformas estructurales y política de estabilización* (Lima, CIUP, 1995).
10 'Privatización en el Perú', *Perú Económico*, 27:6 (June 1994).
11 F. Durand and R. Thorp, 'Tax Reform: The SUNAT Experience', in Crabtree and Thomas (eds), *Fujimori's Peru*.
12 R. Webb and A. Figueroa, *Distribución del ingreso en el Perú* (Lima, IEP, 1975).
13 J. Matos Mar, *Desborde popular y crisis del estado* (Lima, IEP, 1984). Also see D. Cotlear, H. Martínez, J. León and J. Portugal, *Perú: La población migrante* (Lima, Amidep, 1987).
14 *Instituto Cuanto*, 'Perú 1997: Anuario Estadístico' (Lima, Cuanto, 1997).
15 *Cuanto*, 6:68 (December 1994).
16 R. Webb, *Government Policy and the Distribution of Income in Peru* (Cambridge, MA, Harvard University Press, 1977).
17 D. Sulmont, *Movimiento obrero peruano (1890–1980)* (Lima, Tarea, 1981).
18 J. Matos Mar and J. Manuel Mejía, *La reforma agraria en el Perú* (Lima, IEP, 1980).
19 S. Stein and C. Monge, *La crisis del estado patrimonial en el Perú* (Lima, IEP, 1988).
20 C. Balbi, 'Politics and Trade Unions in Peru', in M. Cameron and P. Mauceri (eds), *Peruvian Labyrinth*.
21 Crabtree, *Peru under García*, pp. 152–7.
22 E. Morales, *Cocaine: White Gold Rush in Peru* (Tucson, University of Arizona Press, 1985).
23 R. Infante, *Perú: Ajuste del mercado laboral urbano y sus efectos sociales* (Lima, OIT, 1995).

24 M. Tanaka, 'From Movimientismo to Media Politics: The Changing Boundaries between Society and Politics in Fujimori's Peru', in Crabtree and Thomas (eds), Fujimori's Peru.

25 Oiga, no. 647, 12 July 1993 contains textual excerpts from this document.

26 J. Crabtree, 'The 1995 Elections: End of the Line for the Party System?' Institute of Latin American Studies (ILAS, London) Occasional Papers (1995).

27 C. Degregori and R. Grompone, Elecciones 1990, demonios y redentores: Una tragedia en dos vueltas (Lima, IEP, 1991). Also see M. Vargas Llosa, El pez en el agua (Barcelona, Seix Barral, 1993).

28 On the relationship between fiscal outlays and electoral outcomes, see C. Graham and C. Kane, 'Opportunistic Government or Sustaining Reform? Electoral Trends and Public Expenditure Patterns in Peru, 1990–95', Latin American Research Review, 33:1 (1998).

29 During the second Belaúnde government (1980–85), AP reached an agreement with the Partido Popular Cristiano (PPC, Popular Christian Party), which gave it an absolute majority. In 1985 García won an absolute majority without need for alliances.

30 In January 1997, the Constitutional Tribunal, set up under the aegis of the 1993 Constitution, was called upon to rule on the constitutionality of a law which would have allowed Fujimori to stand for re-election in 2000. Its majority verdict effectively challenged Fujimori. Congress subsequently voted in favour of a constitutional accusation which dismissed those members of the Tribunal who had voted the original law unconstitutional.

31 Mauceri, State under Siege.

32 E. Obando has developed the theory of 'rings' in which individual military leaders command the loyalties of those of lesser rank whose careers depend on the promotion of those leaders. He argues that under Hermoza, the changes to the system of military promotions rendered obsolete the old system of rings. Thereafter, there was but one ring, with Hermoza at its centre. See E. Obando, 'Fujimori and the Military', in Crabtree and Thomas (eds), Fujimori's Peru.

33 See, for example, B. Kay, 'Fujipopulism and the Liberal State in Peru', Journal of Inter-American Studies and World Affairs, 38:4 (1996); J. Crabtree, 'Populismo y neopopulismo: La experiencia peruana', Apuntes, 40, 1st semester (1997); and A. Panfichi and C. Sanborn, 'Democracia y neopopulismo en el Perú contemporáneo', Márgenes, 13/14 (November 1995).

34 In common with most other Latin American constitutions, the 1979 Peruvian Constitution barred immediate re-election. The 1993 Constitution removed this restriction but stipulated that a president could be re-elected only for one single term.

6

Mexico

Howard Handelman

This chapter is a revised version of material that previously appeared in Howard Handelman: Mexican Politics: The Dynamics of Change (St. Martin's Press, 1997)

Most historians date Mexico's industrial growth back to the times of Porfirio Díaz (1876–1911). However, economic modernisation and actual industrialisation did not take off until the late 1930s, when the last remains of the revolutionary turmoil began to fade away. In the decades that followed, the country managed to transform itself from a rural, mainly illiterate, agricultural-based society to a largely literate, considerably industrialised and primarily urban nation. At that moment in time, many scholars hailed such development, commonly known as the 'Mexican economic miracle', as a model for the Third World to follow. Nonetheless, the country's development process showed serious flaws.

The net benefits of the apparent growth were notoriously unequally distributed. Much of the private sector was noted for its low productivity rates, while the enormous public sector was characterised by inefficiency and corruption. Industrial growth was paradoxically linked to large fiscal and trade deficits that subsequently brought about serious financial difficulties. Despite such setbacks, Mexico's growth rates remained constant and robust from 1940 through to the mid-1970s, when President Luis Echeverría's administration mismanaged the economy and stirred up conflicts with the private sector, events that resulted in the precipitation of a severe financial crisis. By the end of that decade, with the discovery of vast oil reserves and extensive foreign borrowing by the López Portillo administration, Mexico resumed economic growth at a spectacular rate. Yet the oil boom proved to be very brief, and by 1982 Mexico's excessive external indebtedness brought any signs of growth to a halt. The well-known 'debt crisis' that came about sent not only Mexico but all of Latin America plunging into the worst economic decline since the Great Depression of the late 1920s.

The subsequent administrations of Presidents Miguel De La Madrid (1982–88) and Carlos Salinas de Gortari (1988–94) faced the crisis by redesigning Mexico's economic development model. They implemented 'liberalisation' policies that reduced the state's economic involvement substantially and opened up the country's formerly protected economy to foreign trade and investment flows. By joining the General Agreement on Tariffs and Trade (GATT) in 1986 and embarking into the North American Free-Trade Agreement (NAFTA), Mexico embraced free trade and developed closer ties to the world market, especially to its northern neighbours – the United States and Canada. However, as Salinas's term drew to an end and 'neoliberal' reforms seemed to have curbed inflation and brought about economic stability, the realities of Mexico's political economy of the 1990s degenerated into political tensions that triggered the Zapatista uprising, and into a sizeable balance-of-payments deficit that resulted in the unexpected 1994 devaluation of the Mexican peso by the newly elected administration of President Ernesto Zedillo.

The economic decline inherited by Zedillo seemed to be easing by 1996. But the second major recession in less than two decades, coming relatively soon after the country had apparently emerged successfully from the first, badly shook popular confidence in the political and economic systems. This has led to a process of rethinking among the Mexican people about the country's democratic structures, as the government it (doubtfully) elected has apparently not lived up to expectations.

Neoliberal economic restructuring

The 'debt crisis' of the early 1980s and its resulting effects on Mexico's economy caused the nation's leaders to reassess the country's development model. Latin American industrialisation had been inward looking, built on import substitution and protectionism, in contrast with the East Asian export-based manufacturing model. For several decades, the import-substitution model stimulated constant economic growth and rising living standards. However, it also began generating massive trade and budget deficits. As a consequence of such trends, subsequent administrations liberalised the economy dramatically, reducing state intervention and opening the domestic market to international trade. This 'economic restructuring' was started by the De La Madrid administration and accelerated greatly during Salinas's presidential term. Economic policy under Zedillo has been mostly preoccupied with the country's financial crisis. Nonetheless, since Zedillo was part of the group that designed and implemented Salinas's economic policies, he has continued to follow his predecessors' neoliberal path. In any case, Mexico's course of liberalisation is far too advanced to be reversed.

A few months before De La Madrid took office in 1982, Mexico signed an accord with the IMF calling for a reduced budget deficit, diminished state subsidies and lower real wages in order to reduce inflation. The agreement certainly set the tone for subsequent Mexican economic policy. De La Madrid put an end to his predecessors' strategies for stimulating economic growth through extensive deficit spending and external borrowing. He implemented severe budget cuts that slashed consumer subsidies and welfare programmes, while wage hikes lagged well behind price increases. The payoffs for these painful austerity measures were not apparent under De La Madrid, especially since he tried to restimulate growth prematurely midway through his presidential term, triggering renewed inflation and a further decline in production. As a consequence, he left office as the first post-war Mexican president to preside over an overall decline in the country's GDP during his term. Cumulative inflation from 1982 to 1988 was ten times higher than the rate under his predecessor López Portillo, reaching 4,600 per cent.[1]

Nevertheless, De La Madrid began to turn the corner towards economic recovery in his last year in office by adding a new instrument to the government's anti-inflationary repertoire. So far, his administration had relied unsuccessfully on the standard anti-inflationary measures prescribed by the IMF. However, in December 1987, representatives of government, business and labour agreed to an Economic Solidarity Pact binding each of the three sectors to anti-inflationary restraints. The government committed itself to additional cuts in the fiscal deficit, tightening of the monetary supply and further trade liberalisation, while the labour, business and commercial farming sectors agreed to wage controls as well as price controls on many consumer goods. The Pact had a specific time span but was renewed periodically in subsequent years.[2]

The main component of these anti-inflationary strategies was business and labour's voluntary agreement to wage and price controls. Similar approaches to confronting inflation have been tried elsewhere in Latin America, but generally without long-term success. However, in Mexico the Pact (and its renewals) were introduced after the prescribed IMF measures had already begun to bring the fiscal and trade deficits under control.[3] Soon after Salinas took office in 1988, the combination of anti-inflationary measures and the Pact started to reduce the inflation rate substantially. Additionally, Mexico showed an extended period of economic growth for the first time since the oil boom, though at a slower pace. The economy grew during each of Salinas's first three years in power (1989–91), the most sustained period of growth since the 1982 foreign-debt crash. During those years, GDP growth ranged from 3.3 per cent to 4.5 per cent, levels that were reached only once in the previous seven years.[4]

At the start of his presidential term, Salinas devised a revised accord entitled the Pacto por la Estabilidad y el Crecimiento Económico (PECE, Pact for Stability and Economic Growth). The Pact's new name signalled that inflation was practically under control and that it was time to start restimulating the economy.[5] Salinas restored some of the funding directed to education, health and welfare that had been slashed by the De La Madrid administration. However, he remained strongly committed to neoliberal policies, including the deregulation of prices and reduced budget deficits. Most of the government-imposed price controls were lifted between 1990 and 1991 and the budget deficit, which had reached 14 per cent of GDP in 1982, was in actual surplus by 1992.[6]

It also needs to be said that these apparently stringent monetary policies were accompanied by fundamental structural changes that would prove to have a long-term impact. In contrast with the enormous rate at which it grew during the presidential terms of Echeverría and López Portillo, state intervention in the economy was reduced dramatically during the De La Madrid and Salinas administrations. Although it was De La Madrid who initiated the changes, Salinas implemented the structural reforms, such as the privatisation of state-owned enterprises, which proved to be one of the hallmarks of his administration. The number of state-owned enterprises was reduced from 1,155 to 280 between 1982 and 1990.[7] The firms that were privatised included Teléfonos de México (the Latin American telecommunications giant), Mexicana de Aviación and Aeroméxico (Mexico's leading airlines), sugar refineries, copper mines, steel mills, food-processing plants and hundreds of smaller companies from a wide range of industries. From the sale of its ten largest firms, the government earned in excess of $3 billion, resources that were directed to support social spending and other 'needed' programmes.[8] Nonetheless, certain enterprises such as PEMEX (the petroleum monopoly), the railways (Ferrocarriles Nacionales), and CONASUPO (the state food distribution agency) were to remain under state control for strategic and security reasons.

One of the fundamental policy changes implemented both by the De La Madrid and the Salinas administrations was the dismantling of the import-substitution model in favour of export-oriented development. Two specific events symbolised the 'opening-up' of the Mexican economy to the world: the joining of the GATT in 1986 and the signing of the NAFTA seven years later, irreversibly linking its economy to those of the United States and Canada. The GATT was mainly a negotiation forum created after the Second World War to facilitate trade between the world's capitalist nations by removing trade barriers. Many countries joined the GATT over the years as it continued to reduce tariffs through its many negotiation rounds. Mexico stayed out of the group because of the logic of its import-substitution model of industrialisation and a notable domestic protectionist sentiment. When De La Madrid finally committed the country to joining the Agreement in 1986, the decision provoked considerable opposition. Many Mexicans thought the move threatened less efficient companies that had long been protected from import competition. As a matter of fact, earlier attempts to join the GATT had been abandoned due to strong opposition from segments of the private sector that saw it as a major threat to their operations. Additionally, the CTM (Confederación de Trabajadores de Mexico, Mexico's trade union confederation) opposed free trade, as it threatened jobs in a range of non-competitive industries and contradicted its 'nationalist' ideology. It was not until the economic advantages of export-oriented development were demonstrated by the East Asian Newly Industrialised Economies (NIEs) that Mexico fully embraced the world market. Deprived of their traditional protectionist trade barriers, Mexican firms were forced to become more competitive both domestically and internationally. Manufacturers were encouraged to produce for the export as well as the domestic markets, a move that many large enterprises underwent quite successfully. Mexico's trade balance improved due to an increase in manufactured exports, reducing dependence on petroleum-related exports. Nonetheless, by the end of Salinas' presidential term the nation once again suffered from a negative trade balance, but this time due to ever-increasing imports.

The Salinas administration proposed the establishment of the NAFTA in order to integrate the Mexican and American economies more fully, thereby strengthening Mexico's ability to compete in the world market. Under the Agreement, Mexican consumers have gained greater access to North American products, and competitive Mexican companies can now sell more easily both in the US and Canadian markets. Most importantly, the NAFTA reassured Mexican businessmen and foreign investors that the transition to an open economy was irreversible, thus avoiding the shifts in government economic policy that had affected them in the past.[9]

Farmland reform

An additional aspect that deserves special attention regarding the neoliberal policies implemented in Mexico is the farmland ownership reform or 'new *ejido* law', as it came to be known. Since the Mexican Revolution, over half the country's farmland has been distributed among more than three million peasant families in communes called *ejidos*. The land in each of these *ejidos* is communally controlled, with the state regulating its administration and sale. However, in practice only grazing and forest land (a little under 75 per cent of the total *ejido* land) is maintained communally, while agricultural land itself has been divided into family parcels that can be passed from generation to generation. Because one of the central issues of the Mexican Revolution was the peasants' struggle for land, maintaining the *ejido* concept has been considered inviolable by all Mexicans who still believe in the ideals of the Revolution. In order to prevent the members of the *ejido* commune, the *ejidatarios*, from losing their holdings to richer, more powerful commercial farmers, the law prohibited the sale of *ejido* land to those outside the commune.[10] Since the *ejido* structure has been considered to be one of the Revolution's greatest achievements, altering it has been unthinkable in Mexican political rhetoric, as would be the abolition of the National Health Service in the United Kingdom or the Social Security system in the United States.

Without a doubt, the establishment of the *ejido* system contributed to rural political stability. The Mexican peasantry – once amongst the most rebellious in Latin America – has generally been co-opted one way or another into the political system. However, in most instances, *ejidos* have not been economically viable. Members of *ejido* communes – with their small land parcels and limited access to scarce water supplies – have become dependent on the state for credit, technical assistance, irrigation, fertilisers, and other agricultural inputs. Consequently, they are at the mercy of corrupt and arbitrary bureaucrats from government and the ruling Partido Revolucionario Institucional (PRI, Institutional Revolutionary Party). Additionally, many of them are also exploited by political bosses from their own ranks (better known as *caciques*), who maintain control over access to government agencies and to state funds. For the most part, communal farming in Mexico has not been sufficiently productive. Peasants have not received enough government assistance since the early 1940s.[11] Even though Presidents Echeverría and López Portillo increased rural aid, few incentives were offered to members of the *ejido* communes to actually farm more efficiently. In the contemporary period, most grow corn with very low yields per acre for subsistence or for *tortilla* production.

The 1980s were a very difficult decade for Mexican farmers, with crop prices falling nearly 50 per cent in relation to the cost of agricultural inputs.[12] The effect of this decline was initially mitigated by improved export opportunities and surprisingly appropriate growing weather. Nonetheless, since the late 1980s, weak crop prices and declining government aid have worsened farmers' living standards. Anti-poverty programmes such as the Programa Nacional de Solidaridad (PRONASOL, National Solidarity Programme) and temporary subsidies have been somewhat helpful; nonetheless, the long-term prospects for agricultural smallholders are not optimistic. Additionally, the Salinas administration did not believe that members of *ejido* communes could ever become competitive, and opposed substantial spending to support them, regardless of countless critics that contended that Mexico's *ejido* problems could be solved by extending state aid and by giving them more independence from 'exploitative' government agencies such as BANRURAL, the Mexican agricultural credit bank.[13]

Furthermore, Mexico's entry into the NAFTA poses additional problems for Mexican farmers since their US counterparts produce on average four times as much per acre as they do. The removal of trade protection that the NAFTA signifies means that it is generally cheaper to import most of the current crops than to grow them. It has been the clear perception for some time now, that government (neoliberal) planners expect Mexican farmers to either switch to the production of higher-value crops that can be exported to the North American markets (such as tropical fruits and vegetables, or ornamental flowers), or to abandon their farming activities and sell their farms and land to more productive farmers. Article 27 of the Mexican Constitution (related to land property) was amended in 1992 by the Mexican Congress and thus the 'new *ejido* law' was passed. The main objectives of such changes were to 'permit and even encourage – but not compel – the privatisation of previously inalienable community-held "*ejido*" land'.[14] The Mexican government's constitutional obligation to redistribute land to the farmers was thereby terminated, an event that marked the official ending of one of the Revolution's most idealised programmes. As a result, *ejido* landowners are now free to rent, sell or use their parcels as collateral for agricultural loans. They can even enter, if luck is on their side and their productivity justifies it, into alliances with outside investors, including foreign companies, which can now own up to 49 per cent of the farm (including the land).

The 'new *ejido* law' was passed in the hope that outside investment and a more open land market would increase production for both the domestic and export markets. However, those who opposed it fear that the law will enable richer, more powerful outsiders to buy out poorer farmers, contributing to a reconcentration of farmland, which can result in an increased migration to the cities by displaced farmers. Nonetheless, it is still too early to judge the results.

Government credibility

Restoring the credibility of the Mexican government and business confidence in the Mexican economy have been other important government objectives since the early 1980s. A deep wedge had been driven between the private sector and the government both by Echeverría's populism and by the nationalisation of the banking sector under López Portillo. Thus, by the mid-1980s, businessmen had transferred their funds into property, government securities and deposits in the United States as they distrusted their government and showed serious concerns about the declining value of the Mexican currency.[15]

Presidents De La Madrid and Salinas both tried, in the wake of the debt crisis, to restore the credibility of the Mexican government and regain the confidence and trust of three crucial groups. The first was the Mexican private sector and the middle class, as sustained economic recovery required renewed business investment and the repatriation of capital from abroad. The second group were foreign investors, who could provide urgently needed additional capital and technological skills. Finally, reassuring foreign governments (especially the United States), international financial institutions and foreign commercial banks regarding Mexico's economic reliability was an objective of uppermost importance. All of these groups needed to be convinced that the Mexican government would follow consistent, predictable and transparent policies, and that the peso would remain relatively stable over time. Therefore, the De La Madrid, Salinas, and, most recently, Zedillo administrations secured Washington's support to restructure the debt and reassure the international financial community.

This has certainly not been an easy task. The anti-government hostility triggered by Echeverría and López Portillo within the business community proved to be too difficult for the De La Madrid administration to overcome. By the mid-1980s, a considerable proportion of Mexican business leaders had not only turned their backs on the PRI, but had become active in the opposition, pro-business Partido Acción Nacional (PAN, National Action Party). Furthermore, the De La Madrid government undermined its confidence-building campaign when policy mistakes generated a renewed wave of inflation between 1985 and 1986. Additionally, De La Madrid strained Mexican relations with the United States for most of his presidential term through his administration's support for the revolutionary Sandinista regime in Nicaragua and its sympathy for El Salvador's Marxist guerrillas, the Frente Farabundo Martí de Liberación Nacional (FMLN, Farabundo Martí Front for National Liberation), which infuriated the Reagan administration.

In contrast, after a controversial electoral victory, Salinas rapidly gained the confidence of the Mexican private sector and the international financial community. No other Mexican president had ever achieved comparable recognition at home and abroad. Salinas followed in De La Madrid's neoliberal footsteps, though with more positive results, and accelerated the privatisation of state-owned enterprises and other free-market economic policies. Under Salinas's leadership, the government finally managed to bring inflation under control and the economy began to undergo sustained growth. Foreign investors and international financial agencies were impressed by Salinas' bold initiatives such as the NAFTA and by his consistent and apparently clear policies. His economic team's seeming ability to always make the right moves inspired trust within the business community and in Washington. Only after he left office did the seriousness of his administration's policy mistakes emerge. It is now quite clear that the financial and social crises that Mexico faced soon after Zedillo took office were inherited from the previous administration's policy errors.

A proper balance of economic objectives

Surprisingly, by the start of the 1990s, Mexico seemed to have achieved a broad consensus over the general outlines of economic reform. Indeed, even the leader of the left-wing opposition Partido de la Revolución Democrática (PRD, Democratic Revolution Party), Cuauhtémoc Cárdenas,[16] appeared to have softened his opposition to the NAFTA and accepted some aspects of the new 'neoliberal' order. However, there still remained the problem of how to properly implement the neoliberal policies and how the Mexican population should share the burden of the required austerity measures. The economic policies that make up any attempt at economic restructuring are simultaneously closely intertwined and often in conflict with each other. As a consequence, the task facing the Mexican government since the early 1980s has been that of achieving the proper balance of economic objectives. It is true that government policies needed to address one problem (such as hyperinflation) often aggravate another (such as unemployment). Therefore, remedial solutions should not be introduced too early or too late. They cannot be applied too narrowly or too broadly, nor sustained for too short a period of time or for too long.

The huge budget deficits faced by Mexico between the late 1970s and early 1980s contributed to mounting inflation rates that, coupled with large bal-

ance-of-trade deficits, had weakened the peso and required substantial external borrowing. As inflation rates surpassed 100 per cent in 1983 and as the balance-of-payments deficit increased, the Mexican government was forced to
introduce several austerity measures, such as reduced spending, higher taxes,
more comprehensive tax collection, higher interest rates and a devaluation of
the peso. These policies, designed to restrain the economy, by their very nature
inhibit economic growth and result in unemployment. Therefore, governments must be careful not to deflate the economy too much or for too long.
On the other hand, on these same lines, they should not restimulate the economy too quickly, as was the case with the De La Madrid administration when
in 1984, convinced that inflation was under control after two years of declining GDP, it decided to restimulate the economy through boosting government
spending. As a result of such a premature action, the economy overheated at a
time when international interest rates were rising and oil prices declined, and
to top it all, Mexico City suffered a devastating earthquake whose cost was calculated at between $4 and $5 billion. The economy resumed its plunge with a
3.8 per cent decrease in GDP and an inflation rate that reached 132 per cent
in 1986 and 1987 respectively.[17] Consequently, severe austerity measures were
reimposed.

Countries facing severe balance-of-payments deficits, such as Mexico, must
normally devalue their currency to stimulate exports (by reducing their apparent cost in foreign currencies), while decreasing imports (by increasing their
domestic cost). Over time, improvements of the balance of trade reduce debt
dependency. However, in the short term, devaluation is inflationary because,
among other things, it pushes the price of imported consumer goods up and
increases the cost of imported raw materials and capital equipment needed by
local industries. Unfortunately, there are other immediate consequences that
result from the type of long-term economic objectives mentioned above. For
example, reducing inflation rates requires a reduction in government spending
as large budget deficits tend to generate inflationary pressures. In Latin America, this means cutting consumer subsidies. However, in the short run these cuts
influence increases in the price of basic necessities, contributing to inflation.
Similarly, almost immediately after trade barriers are removed or reduced,
floods of imports result in an increased trade deficit. This is an effect that certainly seems contrary to the aim of trade liberalisation, which is to improve the
balance of trade over time by forcing national industries to become competitive
exporters through exposing them to more competitive imports.

As we have seen, achieving a proper balance of economic objectives did not
prove an easy task in the case of Mexico. Certainly, the job was made more difficult by the decline in oil prices and the Mexico City earthquake. Nonetheless,
by the time Salinas took office in 1988, the Mexican economy had begun to
show signs of recovery. As noted, during the first half of his presidential term
growth rates were modest but averaging in excess of 3 per cent per annum, and
the inflation rate had declined from 114 per cent during De La Madrid's last

year to 18.8 per cent in 1991.[18] Indeed, the Salinas administration stimulated growth, intensified the privatisation of state-owned enterprises and reduced protectionism. These free-market reforms were so impressive that Salinas was often compared to Margaret Thatcher as a radical 'neoliberalist'. Convinced by the reforms, many Mexican businessmen began repatriating capital from abroad and foreign investment began flowing into the country, encouraged by a stable peso and the prospects of preferential access to the North American market through the NAFTA. From 1988 to 1994 foreign investment flows increased by over $40 billion, most of it through the Mexican stock market.[19] Lower trade barriers forced Mexican firms to become more competitive as the NAFTA expanded prospective opportunities for export. By 1995, manufac- tured exports accounted for over 82 per cent of total exports, reducing the country's traditional dependency on oil earnings.[20]

Economic crisis revisited!
When Salinas left office, he did so with considerable public support and posi- tive evaluations of his performance. International organisations such as the Organization for Economic Cooperation and Development (OECD) (which Mexico joined during Salinas's last year in office) issued favourable evaluations of the Mexican economy and its prospects. However, the economy was in fact more fragile than most realised or wished to admit. Additionally, the Salinas administration enhanced the PRI's position by boosting the economy through increased government spending and by hiding the magnitude of the budget deficit in the run-up to the 1994 presidential elections. Unaware of the dangers of the seriously growing balance-of-trade deficit, Mexican consumers and busi- nesses overextended their credit lines and increased their acquisition of imported goods, naively raising the prospects of an acute crisis.

Although most economists agreed that the Mexican peso was overvalued, and members of Salinas's administration considered the prospects of a devalu- ation a reasonable measure at the time, Salinas preferred to ignore the matter, as his term was coming to an end and he had no intention of assuming respon- sibility for implementing such an unpopular measure. Therefore, less than three weeks after Zedillo took office in 1994, the currency was finally devalued. Ini- tially, it was designed to lower the value of the Mexican peso by around 16 per cent (from 3.46 to 4 pesos to the dollar), but the value of the peso declined by 70 per cent within just a few weeks (to about 6.80 pesos to the dollar by the end of March 1995), as panicked private-sector investors rushed to dispose of their pesos.[21] Furthermore, as the peso continued to weaken, the Mexican stock market plunged as foreign investors, who had acquired stock in Mexico while counting on a stable currency, withdrew their funds. The resulting recession was characterised by high unemployment levels and a steep decline in living standards.

The social costs of neoliberal restructuring

The reforms and structural adjustments that Mexico introduced in the 1980s were directed to lowering inflation rates and reducing fiscal and balance-of-payments deficits. However, they imposed an enormous economic strain on the population, particularly on the poorer sectors.[22] As the reforms were among the most far-reaching in the region, they were consequently among the most painful for the general population.

One of the most important elements of the Mexican government's anti-inflationary policies was to maintain wage increases lagging behind rises in the cost of living. Such deflationary wage policies had several effects; production costs were held down for private firms, lower real salaries for public-sector employees helped reduce the budget deficit, and as consumer demand declined with falling real wages, inflationary pressures were reduced.[23] In order to lower real wages, the government held down the salaries of the public-sector employees, raised the minimum wage level at a rate lower than inflation and put pressure on trade unions (particularly those affiliated to the PRI) to mitigate their wage increase demands.[24] By doing this, the government produced negative growth rates for some years as well as higher unemployment, two factors that exerted further downward pressure on wages. As a result, the 1980s were characterised by a 9 per cent decline in per capita income, a cumulative decline of over 41 per cent in the levels of real wages, and the doubling of unemployment levels from 6 per cent to over 12 per cent.[25] Overall, it can be stated with certainty that the living standards of the poor, working class and much of the middle class fell sharply in that decade.

Government spending cuts were also quite painful, particularly when they involved consumer subsidies. The price of basic foods such as tortillas, rice, beans, cooking oil, bread and eggs had been subsidised for all Mexican consumers, regardless of socio-economic level. Since these measures for rich and poor alike could not be sustained in times of austerity, they were replaced by specific targeted subsidies (similar to food stamps in the United States) aimed at the most needy. However, these new subsidies were not as generous as the ones they replaced and failed to reach many of the poor, especially in secluded rural areas. Government expenditure for education and for health also declined, resulting in an increase in school drop-out rates, as many children were obliged to work to support their family income.[26]

Reviving social spending

By the time of the 1988 presidential elections, Mexico's economy had started a slow recovery that was perceivable through a declining inflation rate and gradually diminishing unemployment. When Salinas took office that year, he did so with the lowest percentage of the vote of any PRI presidential candidate, and there are still many doubts among political historians that he actually won the election. He therefore knew how much the economic crisis had diminished support for and the credibility of the government. As a consequence, one of the Salinas administration's major initiatives was the PRONASOL, aimed precisely at restoring support for the government.

Restoring some of the social spending that was cut in the 1980s and address-ing the needs of the poor that had been neglected in the past were the Pro-gramme's clearest objectives. Such programmes helped build infrastructure, provided social services and attempted a reduction of both urban and rural poverty. Typical projects included building and refurbishing public schools, community electrification, street paving and road construction, potable water, health care, housing and legal aid, among others.[27] In the first half of Salinas's presidential term, the PRONASOL's budget grew from $950 million to $2.5 billion, and by the end of his presidency, the Programme's annual expenditure equalled nearly 2 per cent of Mexican GDP.[28] The Programme clearly repre-sented an innovative approach to formulating social development programmes, particularly in lower-income areas. Instead of having the government design projects in a top-down manner, the PRONASOL required input directly from the aid recipients, or at least from organisations representing them. In conse-quence, the particular projects were more likely to address the actual problems of the beneficiaries rather than what government planners thought good for the poor, regardless of how well intentioned they were. In order to accomplish such a task, the programme incorporated a broad range of grass-roots organi-sations that represented peasants and the urban poor into its decision-making process.

The PRONASOL embodied a fundamental departure from 'politics as usual' in another respect. It was a massive programme that linked the poorer sectors of Mexican society to the government outside the ruling party's corporatist structure. Thus, community groups had access to the Programme's officials, who were generally members of their communities, rather than having to work with government or party bureaucrats.[29] Beyond its manifest goal of combating and alleviating poverty, the PRONASOL also had important political objec-tives. Two events demonstrated how severely the economic crisis of the 1980s had undermined the government's legitimacy and reduced support for the PRI. First, Cuauhtémoc Cárdenas's surprisingly good performance in the 1988 pres-idential elections, where he received an astonishing 32.5 per cent of the votes; and secondly, the Opposition's strong showing in that year's congressional elec-tion, where they received 47.6 per cent of the total votes against a slightly larger 50.4 per cent for the PRI.[30] Furthermore, Salinas's controversial presi-dential victory meant that he had taken office without a clear popular mandate. PRONASOL seems to have been designed to restore some support for the then 'newly elected' government and the PRI. Its broadly advertised projects pro-vided an effective 'populist' counterbalance to the administration's neoliberal economic reforms.[31]

Initially, such a political strategy seemed to work. The PRI clearly won the

1991 state and congressional elections, the 1994 congressional elections, and the 1994 presidential race. The programme also helped to enormously improve Salinas's popular approval, which collapsed only after he left office in 1994. The trend reverted more recently. Support for the PRI fell sharply in the 1994 state elections, in spite of substantial PRONASOL funds and government investment being directed to Chiapas following the Ejército Zapatista de Liberación Nacional (EZLN, Zapatista National Liberation Army) uprising.[32] Furthermore, the government had to accept three state governorship victories for the opposition PAN in 1995.

The PRONASOL's most important accomplishment was the revival of government social spending, which rose during Salinas's presidential term from 14.9 per cent to over 26 per cent of the national budget. Even if the Programme's funds were 'misused' for political purposes, they still reached the poorer sectors of the Mexican population more effectively than any previous schemes to fight poverty. Furthermore, although Zedillo replaced the PRONASOL with his 'Alliance for the Well-being' (a programme with almost identical social goals), according to the *New York Times* $1.6 billion were budgeted in 1995 for such programmes.[33]

Mexican democracy

Although the Mexican electoral and party system seems to be quite competitive and clearly characterised by a multi-party contention, appearances are quite deceiving. It is true that, unlike most authoritarian regimes, Mexico has elections that are vigorously contested. Nonetheless, Mexican electoral competition only goes so far. The PRI and its predecessor, the Partido Nacional Revolucionario (PNR, National Revolutionary Party), have won every presidential race since the formation of an official party in the mid-1920s and, prior to 1988, had won virtually every election that bore some importance. Only in the past two presidential elections of 1988 and 1994 have the PRI candidates faced serious opposition. Therefore, until quite recently, national elections in Mexico served a completely different function than they do in most pluralist democratic states. Their objective was not necessarily to determine any winners, normally a foregone conclusion, but rather to provide the Mexican public with a sense of participation in the political processes and therefore to legitimise PRI control. It is not surprising to recognise that for many years the government's primary electoral concern was to ensure sufficient electoral opposition in order to maintain the façade of truly contested elections. As Knight stated: 'without formal opposition, elections would be meaningless. And without elections, the system would lose its mask of democratic legitimacy'.[34]

It is clear that overall, Mexico has had quite a good record of industrialisation and economic growth. Such growth meant increased urbanisation, expansion of the middle and working classes and rising literacy rates that surpassed

90 per cent by the start of the 1990s. According to the United Nations Development Programme (UNDP), Mexico's Human Development Index (HDI) ranks 52nd among the world's nations. Moreover, a real per capita GDP of $6,000 places it 15th in the world. However, while having surpassed the 50 per cent literacy rate considered to be a threshold for achieving democracy over half a century ago, Mexico still does not meet convincing criteria for democratic government – particularly fair elections and a truly competitive political party system that would guarantee the real possibility of alternating political power. Although modernisation has certainly increased the country's chances of meeting such criteria, it has not succeeded in effectively democratising Mexico or eradicating the pervasive corruption that characterises its political order.

The strong performance of Cuauhtémoc Cárdenas in the 1988 presidential elections raised hopes that Mexico might finally be moving towards a competitive party system. But once Salinas took office, his strong leadership, breakthrough neoliberal reforms and popular programmes (such as the PRONASOL) restored support for the government and indirectly for the PRI. Simultaneously, Cárdenas's followers proved to be divided and poorly organised. Thus, it was no surprise that the PRI won the 1991 congressional elections convincingly only three years after Salinas's controversial victory. However, as we have seen, by the last year of Salinas' term the Zapatista uprising in Chiapas (which coincidentally started the same day that the NAFTA entered into force) refocused attention on Mexico's political and economic deficiencies [35] and, coupled with the unsolved assassinations of Luís Donaldo Colosio and José Francisco Ruíz-Massieu,[36] renewed popular doubts about the government and contributed to strong PAN results in the 1994 presidential elections. Since then, Zedillo's administration has been undermined by the economic crisis it inherited and by endless revelations of corruption in the Salinas family. These factors undoubtedly contributed to the three impressive PAN victories in the 1995 state elections.

Beyond these changes, some trends can be discerned that are likely to continue in the future. Primarily, the PRI's electoral dominance is less pronounced than it has ever been. While it had been impossible for an opposition-party candidate to win a single governorship race until the late 1980s, the PAN won three in 1995 alone, and the PRD won the first-ever governorship election for Mexico City's Federal District in 1997.[37] Zedillo has been more willing than any of his predecessors to accept opposition victories of that magnitude. Some analysts have identified that socio-economic development in Mexico has contributed to a more democratic society by increasing the competitiveness of its electoral system. In other words, opposition parties have performed better in areas that are more urban, more industrialised and more highly educated. In contrast, the PRI draws its strongest vote in poor, uneducated and rural areas. Therefore, as Mexico's population becomes more educated and urban and as the middle class expands, support for opposition parties is likely to grow further. Additionally, it is precisely the poor, uneducated and rural areas where the

PRI found its strongest supporters in the past that are now 'blossoming' with anti-government and anti-PRI movements. Such is the case of the Mexican states of Chiapas and Guerrero.

While socio-economic modernisation has been important in Mexico's democratisation, the nation's severe economic crises of the 1980s and 1990s have also been important catalysts for change. The traditional electoral success and the base of political support for the PRI (and for the government itself) had been closely linked to the state's ability to distribute assistance and economic subsidies. The regime had subsidised basic foods, medical care, petrol, energy and housing, both for consumers and for businesses alike, while also distributing jobs through the state bureaucracy and state-owned firms. However, the country's economic crises and the neoliberal reforms undertaken to restore its economic health have deprived the PRI of the capacity to maintain its traditional corporatist system. Additionally, if the 1996 Electoral Reform Law has succeeded in reducing media bias and the PRI's financial advantage in campaigns, then it could be said that Mexico has finally achieved a reasonably fair and competitive electoral system. But as we know, merely accomplishing such a task will certainly not prove sufficient to transform Mexico into a fully democratic society.

The 'current' crisis

Most analysts were relatively optimistic about Mexico's economic future as Salinas's term drew to an end. The neoliberal reforms appeared to have controlled inflation and improved the country's general economic health, the NAFTA seemed to provide Mexican industry with new market opportunities and the Mexican stock market prospered considerably in the closing years of the Salinas administration, boosted by the seemingly favourable economic prospects and heavy foreign investment. Yet there were certain factors that seriously threatened the recovery.

First, the government overextended its debt obligations by issuing nearly $30 billion-worth of short-term treasury bonds (*tesobonos*) due in 1995. Secondly, as the economy expanded and free-trade policies encouraged the inflow of foreign goods, imports grew at a much faster rate than exports, reviving the balance-of-payments deficit and increasing pressure to devalue the peso. Fearing that a devaluation would taint his achievements and negatively influence the PRI's performance in the 1994 presidential elections, Salinas refused to act promptly and hoped that the negative tendency would revert itself before it became too serious. Finally, the unresolved Zapatista uprising, the spate of political assassinations and increasing instability within the PRI sent jitters down the spines of foreign investors, who were ready to disinvest at the first signs of trouble or a weakened peso. In addition, rising interest rates in the United States increased the threat of capital flight. To worsen the situation, the new Zedillo administration complicated Salinas's mistakes by assuring investors that a devaluation would not take place. However, the newly elected President's credibility was completely undermined when the continuing trade deficit finally forced a devaluation only a few days after his administration's initial announcement. Thus, the peso plummeted from 3.46 to the dollar in December 1994 to 6.31 per dollar by June 1995 and to 7.54 by the start of 1996.[38] The devaluation's intended purpose of stimulating exports was accomplished. In 1995, the value of Mexican exports rose 30.6 per cent over the previous year, while imports fell only 8.7 per cent, moving the country's economy from a considerable $18.5 billion trade deficit in 1994 to a $7.1 billion surplus.[39] Mexico suffered a severe economic setback when a $50 billion international rescue package organised early in 1995 required the implementation of a painful economic stabilisation programme in order to bring its finances under control. Inflation, which had dropped to 7.1 per cent in December 1994, jumped to over 50 per cent a year later.[40] The declining purchasing power created a slump that resulted in many firms shutting down operations. By December 1995, most factories were operating at around 40 per cent of installed capacity and over a million people were left without work. GDP declined by 6.2 per cent, 2 per cent more than in 1983 – the steepest fall of the 'debt crisis' years.[41]

It is generally understood that President Zedillo inherited a serious balance-of-payments problem and most would agree that his administration had to devalue the peso. Few expected the massive disinvestment by foreign investors after the devaluation was announced at the end of 1994. The economic decline seemed to be easing by 1996 when GDP grew 5.1 per cent and 1997 showed clear signs of recovery. Nonetheless, the second major recession in less than two decades has badly affected the Mexican people's confidence in their government, their institutions and their political and economic systems.

Prospects for the future

As one of the world's major developing nations, Mexico seemed confident to take off economically. The country has a relatively well-educated and well-trained workforce, extensive natural resources and an enormous potential market in its North American neighbours. However, over the past decades it has been tormented by serious government policy errors. It followed an ISI model for too long and neglected opportunities to develop and benefit from manufactured and other non-traditional exports – like most of Latin America. Industries became inefficient and uncompetitive due to excessive protectionism and previous presidents spent and borrowed excessively, exacerbating the problem. It came as no surprise that Salinas was widely recognised for opening up the economy to foreign trade and investment flows, privatising state-owned enterprises and reducing the size of the state, while bringing the fiscal deficit and inflation under control. Unfortunately, Mexico's neoliberal revolution has failed to live up to its alleged virtues. Under the new order established by the

Salinas administration, market forces (rather than political or social pressures) were supposed to guide economic decisions. But the Mexican government allowed the trade deficit to become uncontrollable because it was politically hindered to devalue the peso.

While the neoliberal model has some obvious virtues, particularly in its greater efficiencies, it may worsen Mexico's huge disparity in wealth and income, one of the country's most troublesome economic failings. Mexico differs from similarly developed nations in that its income and wealth are far more concentrated and education is less ubiquitous. Additionally, if Mexico fails to achieve a modern democratic society and greater social justice in the near future, it will face serious political difficulties that will undoubtedly affect its recovery and further development. Unless it can rapidly come to grips with these inequities, it will face future political and economic setbacks even if it resumes sustained growth. In order to transform Mexico into a fully democratic society, more extensive reform of government and social institutions are needed. On one side, the Mexican government has been overly centralised. That is, the federal government has complete control over state and local governments, and within itself, power is highly concentrated in the executive branch, in other words, the President. The administrations of De La Madrid, Salinas and currently Zedillo, have made legislative and administrative efforts to decentralise public administration and policy making. Very little progress has been made.

Zedillo has opened dialogue with congressional leaders and tried to raise the profile of the government's legislative branch as part of his commitment to reducing 'presidentialism'. He has even gone as far as consulting on policy with the opposition parties' leaders, both the PAN and PRD. In an unprecedented act, Zedillo appointed Antonio Lozano, a member of the PAN, to the post of Attorney-General and even trusted him with the task of investigating government corruption and the murders of Colosio and Ruiz-Massieu. Zedillo has also begun to separate the PRI from the government by reducing his own control over the official party. In this sense, he has allowed the PRI's state organisations total liberty in selecting their own governorship candidates, whereas previously they were selected, or at least approved, by the President. In this same line, he has vowed to end Mexico's long-established practice of presidents naming the next PRI presidential candidate.

Zedillo's efforts to reduce presidential power and strengthen the other branches of government at the federal, state and local levels, are long overdue. Such a decentralisation of power is an essential component of democratisation. Unfortunately, in the case of Mexico, such a transition may have undesirable short-term consequences. An immediate consequence from decentralisation would be a shift of power from the President to state and even local political bosses, who may be less responsive to the electorate and who may manipulate the electoral processes. Hence real democratisation would ultimately require reforms to state and local politics parallel to the ones at federal level. Furthermore, a real process of democratisation must extend to Mexican culture and social institutions which have authoritarian aspects that need to be addressed. Traditionally, Mexicans have been fearful of change, even democracy, with the PRI exacerbating this tendency by suggesting that an opposition-party presidential victory would lead to anarchy or extremist dictatorship.[42] It would be fair to say that a substantial number of the people who voted for the PRI in the past two presidential elections did so because they were fearful of change and did not want to risk giving the opposition a chance to govern. However, based on the latest congressional, governorship and even presidential electoral results, this kind of behaviour has certainly decreased.

Additionally, if real democratisation is to take place, a number of other politically important institutions also need to change. Trade unions are amongst the country's most authoritarian organisations. Even if Mexico developed a truly democratic political system, its labour organisations would not necessarily be affected. There is considerable evidence both from industrial democracies and from developing nations that trade unions help shape their member's political attitudes and behaviour. Hence, working-class political participation and support for democratic political institutions would very likely increase if Mexican unions were 'democratised'. Moreover, in the rural communities the problem of authoritarian village *caciques* is even more severe and deferential values amongst the quiet masses of peasants are more deeply rooted. Thus, democratising labour unions and rural village governments will require considerable grass-roots mobilisation and withdrawal of government and PRI support for corrupt and authoritarian bosses.

In the near future, Mexico's leaders must find a way to restore sustained economic growth with controlled inflation and minimal foreign indebtedness. Simultaneously, the country's ability to achieve greater democracy and social justice will result in the long awaited political stability required for real economic development. Such tasks are tremendous, but very much within reach.

Notes

1 Data taken from the Mexican Central Bank's annual publication of statistical information. See Banco de México, *The Mexican Economy 1995* (Mexico City, Banco de México, 1995).

2 For a convincing analysis of the Pact, see N. Lustig, 'México, el Pacto de Solidaridad Económica: La heterodoxia puesta en marcha', in G. Rozenwurcel (ed.), *Elecciones y política económica en América Latina* (Buenos Aires, Grupo Editorial Norma, 1991).

3 *The Mexican Economy 1995*, p. 208.

4 *The Mexican Economy 1995*.

5 Like its predecessor, the new Pact was ratified and extended several times and then renamed the Pact for Stability, Competitiveness and Employment, to account for the immediate realities of the Mexican economy.

6 *The Mexican Economy 1995*, pp. 60–75.

7 Banco de México, *The Mexican Economy 1991* (Mexico City, Banco de México, 1991), p. 119. On the privatisation process, see E. Quintana, 'Empresas privatizadas: Divorcios y conflictos', *Este País*, 9 (December 1991), pp. 12–13.

8 *The Mexican Economy 1991*, pp. 106–7.

9 See N. Phillips, 'Global and Regional Linkages', in J. Buxton and N. Phillips (eds), *Developments in Latin American Political Economy: States, Markets and Actors* (Manchester, Manchester University Press, 1999).

10 In reality, such restrictions have constantly been evaded.

11 Although the small size of most *ejidos* poses problems, small agricultural parcels are not inherently unproductive, as many farmers elsewhere in the world have proved. For example, farmers in East Asia have very high yields on much smaller plots of land.

12 See M. Gates, *In Default: Peasants, the Debt Crisis, and the Agricultural Challenge in Mexico* (Boulder, Westview, 1993), p. 12.

13 See H. Handelman, *Mexican Politics: The Dynamics of Change* (New York, St Martin's Press, 1997), pp. 129–130.

14 See C. Salinas, 'Tercer informe de gobierno', *Excelsior* (Mexico, 2 September 1992).

15 It is believed that over 80 per cent of Mexico's $97 billion foreign debt by 1985 was accounted for by capital flight over the previous ten years.

16 Cuauhtémoc Cárdenas has had an interesting political career in Mexico. He was once governor of the state of Michoacán for the PRI. He is the son of former President Lázaro Cárdenas, who nationalised the oil industry in the 1930s. He was elected as the first governor of the Federal District within Mexico City, where the federal government is located.

17 Data taken from N. Lustig, *Mexico: The Remaking of an Economy* (Washington DC, Brookings Institution, 1992), pp. 40–1.

18 *The Mexican Economy 1995*, pp. 8–9, 30–5, and Banco de México, *The Mexican Economy 1997* (Mexico City, Banco de México, 1997), pp. 23–5.

19 *The Mexican Economy 1995*, p. 103.

20 *The Mexican Economy 1995*, p. 79.

21 *The Mexican Economy 1995*, p. 268.

22 See D. Green, 'The Impact of Neoliberalism', in Buxton and Phillips (eds), *Developments*.

23 'Real' wages are a measure of purchasing power. Thus, when wage increases are lower than the rate of inflation, 'real' wages decrease.

24 According to Lustig, as of 1980, 40 per cent of the Mexican population were earning less than the legal minimum wage. See Lustig, *Mexico*, p. 65.

25 Lustig, *Mexico*, pp. 73–5.

26 Lustig, *Mexico*, p. 88.

27 See W. Cornelius, A. Craig and J. Fox, 'Mexico's National Solidarity Program: An Overview', in W. Cornelius *et al.* (eds), *Transforming State–Society Relations in Mexico: the National Solidarity Strategy* (San Diego, University of California Center for US–Mexican Studies, 1994), p. 3.

28 Cornelius, Craig and Fox, 'Mexico's Natonal Solidarity Program'.

29 PRONASOL officials were generally young, enthusiastic, and of diverse backgrounds. Some had links to new 'social movements' (independent grassroots movements) of the 1980s and some were even associated with radical political groups. In this regard, see A. Knight, 'Solidarity: Historical Continuities and Contemporary Implications', in Cornelius *et al.* (eds), *Transforming State–Society Relations*, p. 39.

30 Comisión Federal Electoral and Instituto Federal Electoral (IFE), *Reporte de resultados electorales: 1976 – 1991* (Mexico City, IFE, 1992).

31 President Salinas frequently appeared on television in seemingly well-orchestrated PRONASOL events. Media coverage showed him walking casually through crowds of cheering masses without bodyguards.

32 In March 1994, two months after the Zapatista (EZLN) uprising, the government announced over 2,500 new PRONASOL projects for Chiapas with a total budget in excess of $235 million. See *Excelsior*, 14 March 1994.

33 *The New York Times*, 3 July 1995.

34 See A. Riding, *Distant Neighbours* (New York, Vintage, 1984), p. 135.

35 Until the Zapatista rebellion, Chiapas had suffered from some of the country's most authori-

tarian political practices (strong PRI domination, extensive corruption, far-reaching electoral fraud and serious human-rights violations). The region's severe poverty highlights major contradictions in the Mexican economy. While Mexico's per capita income is among the highest in the developing world, the majority of its rural population remains impoverished, especially in the poorer states of Chiapas, Oaxaca, Guerrero and Hidalgo. For an overview of the Zapatistas see P. Calvert, 'Guerrilla Movements', in Buxton and Phillips (eds), *Developments*.

36 Luís Donaldo Colosio was the PRI's initial presidential candidate. He was assassinated in March 1994, only to be replaced by Ernesto Zedillo in the presidential race. José Francisco Ruíz-Massieu was the PRI's secretary-general when he was assassinated a few months later. Their assassinations still remain unsolved, leading experts to believe that Salinas might have been involved.

37 Previously, Mexico City's Federal District was governed by a City Major appointed by the President. In 1997, the fist-ever democratically elected 'governor' of Mexico City took office. Ironically, it was Cuauhtémoc Cárdenas who, after coming a close second in the 1988 presidential elections, subsequently governed the world's largest city.

38 *The Mexican Economy 1997*, p. 268.

39 *The Mexican Economy 1997*, p. 286.

40 *The Mexican Economy 1997*, p. 24.

41 *The Mexican Economy 1997*, p. 243.

42 See D. Levy and K. Bruhn, 'Mexico: Sustained Civilian Rule without Democracy', in L. Diamond *et al.* (eds), *Politics in Developing Countries: Comparing Experiences with Democracy* (Boulder, Lynne Rienner, 1995), pp. 196–210.

7

Colombia

BRIAN McBETH

In the mid-1980s, Colombia had become one of the most violent countries in Latin America, yet at the same time a strong democratic tradition continued, with competent bureaucrats administering the state. In the early 1990s the policy of *apertura* (economic opening-up) pursued by the administration of President César Gaviria Trujillo had a fundamental impact on the structure of the economy, while the new political Constitution adopted by a National Assembly in 1991 brought about fundamental structural changes in the institutional framework for political and economic activity. As a result, the Colombian economy changed from a closed, provincial system, to one capable of competing in overseas markets. This chapter looks at economic and political events in Colombia in the 1990s in order to draw lessons for the future.

Historical perspective

In the early 1960s and throughout the 1970s Colombia adopted an economic strategy similar to many of its regional neighbours. This was characterised by import substitution and a protectionist scheme designed to allow infant industries to dominate the internal market, with the state playing a significant role in managing the economy. Foreign companies and investment were largely excluded from the domestic market and foreign exchange was earned through the export of primary products such as coffee which, until relatively recently, accounted for almost 50 per cent of the country's foreign earnings. Although the importance of coffee in the economy has diminished in recent years, it still remains an immensely important sector because any fluctuation in coffee prices has an immediate impact on the well-being of the country owing to the large number of growers and people indirectly associated with the industry.[1] During the 1955–65 period coffee prices declined, leading to a fall in industrial output with the effect of increasing protectionist and import substitution policies. This situation remained an important source of growth for heavy industry as well as consumer durables and intermediate capital goods in the period 1958–67.

For over 20 years the government's major single instrument of economic policy has been the exchange-rate mechanism, which was based on the 'crawling-peg system' of daily mini-devaluations. This acted as a stabilising influence by minimising distortions in the allocation of resources and maintaining the competitiveness of the country's exports, as well as helping to prevent balance-of-payments difficulties owing to the importance of the external sector in the economy. At the same time, the public sector continued its commitment to liberalise trade and investment relations with foreign countries, working towards the development of a national economic programme designed to eradicate extreme poverty. This was accomplished in part by a joint effort involving both private and public capital, relying on the entrepreneurial flair of private capital for economic growth, while the government limited its domestic role to coordinating fiscal and monetary policy, providing funds for public-sector and infrastructure development, and establishing a political environment conducive to investment and industrial development.

Limits of the traditional economic model

In the 1980s Colombia's cumulative economic growth of 33.4 per cent was the highest in Latin America, where the average was 14.2 per cent. Throughout the 1980s the economy grew at rates above 3.5 per cent per annum, reaching 6.9 per cent in 1986 and growing by a staggering 46.8 per cent in the period 1981–91 compared with Chilean, Brazilian and Venezuelan growth of 39.3 per cent, 18.1 per cent and 12 per cent respectively. Despite sustained growth levels, Colombia had a highly skewed income distribution and a relatively low per capita income of $1,222 in 1989. The economy was also more concentrated in the hands of a smaller minority than its neighbours, while the unemployment rate throughout the 1980s remained relatively high. Despite growth in manufacturing and mining as well as continued support from more traditional sectors such as agriculture, the economy seemed unable to absorb enough workers to reduce the unemployment rate below 10 per cent. The drug trade, which was partially responsible for Colombia's economic growth in the 1970s and 1980s caused numerous socio-economic problems, not least of which was that the political and economic power of narcotics traffickers (hereafter referred to as 'narcos'), specifically of the Calí and Medellín cartels, appeared to rival that of the national government. The unequal income distribution patterns in certain areas associated with cocaine and marijuana trafficking increased inflationary pressures because of a steady influx of US dollars. This had the effect of disproportionately expanding the growth of the property and construction industries because of their capacity to absorb laundered drugs money. Further to this, the drug trade spread corruption and violence through society, particularly the public sector, exacerbating the country's economic and social problems.[2]

Despite the successful aspects of the import-substitution growth model, its limitations became apparent towards the end of the Barco administration (1986–90).[3] The increasing importance of exports had become especially evident, along with the need to internationalise Colombia's economy, making it essential to rationalise and gradually reduce the levels of protection afforded to domestic industries. In 1989 five industries were studied in depth for restructuring: the agro-industry, automobiles, leather, textiles and steel. It was found that all suffered from low-grade technology, inadequate levels of machinery, high interest rates, low-quality inputs, and expensive foreign capital goods, as well as being handicapped with high transport costs, because the industries were located at the centre of the country far away from export outlets. As a consequence of the findings, a macroeconomic programme was instigated in 1989 which was the precursor of Gaviria's *apertura* policy. Its main aims were to promote growth, reduce inflation and improve the performance of the export sector, with the government forecasting GDP growth of 4.5 per cent in 1989 and 1990. Additionally, pressure from the World Bank (which was owed $3.7 billion) forced the Barco administration in February 1990 to initiate a strategy of opening up the economy, with the liberalisation of imports and the restructuring of the industrial sector a precondition for new loans. Barco's Programme of Modernisation of the Colombian Economy was therefore a structural change to stimulate medium to long-term growth. The main thrust of the economic Programme was that trade policy would be modified in order to increase the competitiveness of the Colombian economy, complemented by changes in the industrial and financial sectors and the reform of the public sector in order to increase productivity.[4]

Apertura – *economic opening-up*

When President César Gaviria Trujillo came to power in August 1990 he accelerated the restructuring of the economy initiated by Barco. The new economic thinking of *apertura* closely followed World Bank adjustment programmes on three basic arguments. First it was felt that the slowdown in Colombia's economic growth, from an average of 5 per cent per annum in the 1960s and 1970s to just over 4 per cent in the 1980s, was the result of declining productivity related to the lack of internal market competition. It was accepted that there was a strong correlation between productivity increases and industrial development, hence the inability of the country's industrial sector to lead an economic recovery was worrying. It was also felt that the system of import licences used to protect national industries was counterproductive because they generated enormous economic rents as well as administrative corruption. Finally, the system of protectionist tariffs and controls limited the growth potential of the export sector. It was concluded that long-term economic growth in Colombia required structural change and an improvement in foreign-exchange reserves. The Colombian government therefore faced two major challenges in 1990 which posed a contradiction between long-term and short-term objectives, namely to reduce trade barriers with the least disruption to the domestic economy while lowering the rate of inflation, which in 1990 stood at 32.4 per cent. The policy of *apertura* aimed to inject new dynamism into the economy by eliminating the inherent anti-export bias among local business leaders, as well as improving Colombia's infrastructure to facilitate export growth. In addition, the elimination of tariffs and barriers would reduce the costs of imported raw materials and capital equipment. At the same time labour and market distortions would be eliminated and the financial sector boosted, leading to a more competitive exchange rate. The privatisation of state assets, trade reform, and significant changes to the foreign investment and financial regime, together with legal and labour reforms, were also critical elements of the comprehensive economic package. The trade reform initiatives were designed to remove the legal restrictions which barred foreign investment and private enterprise in Colombia in order to stimulate development and higher growth by subjecting the private sector to market forces. Finally, the Central Bank was transformed to fit the new framework with a new independent monetary board.[5]

Violence in the economy

When analysing the economic performance of Colombia, the impact of the drugs trade and the operations of the various guerrilla factions cannot be ignored. In the late 1980s continuous violence had surprisingly little economic impact at the national level. The social and political climate was regarded as a secondary factor in industrialists' investment decisions. It was perceived as no more important than the level of domestic demand or the level of import duties, and at least two-thirds of all industrial firms expanded their production capacity during the late 1980s. The adverse effects of the drug trade have to be offset against the investment possibilities it stimulated, especially in construction and property. In the short run it would appear that violence and economic growth are not mutually exclusive, but the effects of social instability and violence are cumulative and their impact will not be known for some time. In the long term, illegal drug money is a potential source of instability because it tends to encourage a process of 'dollarisation' in the economy that could seriously curtail the efficacy of stabilisation policies in the future.

Income generated by Colombian drug barons has been estimated at between $1.5 billion to $4 billion, of which between $900 to $1.4 billion enter the country, equivalent to 2 per cent of GDP. The guerrillas are also a source of illicit money. According to the army, in 1992 the Fuerzas Armadas Revolucionarias de Colombia (FARC, Revolutionary Armed Forces of Colombia) and the Ejército de Liberación Nacional (ELN, National Liberation Army) earned $120 million and $96 million respectively, mainly from kidnappings and extortion. It was recently calculated by *Portafolio* that the direct cost of the war against the guerrillas between 1990 and 1994 was 1.5 per cent of GDP, equivalent to $1.1 billion per annum. The figure does not include the indirect costs of loss of investment and the additional costs of doing business in Colombia.[6]

Samper's new government

The two main presidential candidates in 1994 were defined ideologically with Ernesto Samper Pisano at the centre-left, representing the Liberal Party, and Andrés Pastrana Arango at the centre-right, representing the Conservatives. Samper was perceived as a liberal heavyweight who favoured state intervention on behalf of the underprivileged and centred his campaign on the issue of employment, promising to create 1.5 million new jobs during his four-year term by revitalising the economy, which he projected would grow by at least 6 per cent per annum.[7] The Samper campaign had history on its side. Since 1930, a united Liberal Party had never lost a presidential election, losing only when divided as in 1946 and 1982. The odds favoured Samper, who not only had the backing of the powerful Liberal Party election machinery, but also most of the Liberal Deputies and Senators in Congress. The mainly Liberal press also supported his candidacy, and when Humberto de la Calle was chosen as Vice-President, presidential candidate Samper secured the support of Gaviria's government, unifying the party. Pastrana believed in giving the private sector an unfettered hand. As such he was closer to the incumbent government's economic policies, with Pastrana's policy platform almost identical to that of Gaviria's *Revolución Pacífica* (Peaceful Revolution) of 1990. Pastrana was viewed as an intellectual lightweight whose main claim to fame was being the son of former President Misael Pastrana. He had a successful turn as Mayor of Bogotá, the second most important and powerful political post in the country, and was a popular presenter of a television news programme.

The presidential elections of 1994 were not marred by the violence of four years previously when three presidential candidates were assassinated. For the first time there would be a second round if no candidate gained 50 per cent of votes cast. As there was no clear majority winner following the first round on 29 May, a second ballot between the two front-runners took place three weeks later. The result was extremely close, with Samper winning 50.4 per cent against 48.6 per cent to Pastrana. Pundits had predicted a high level of abstention because of voter 'fatigue' and the World Cup, but in the second round both candidates obtained more than one million additional votes in an election which had the highest number of votes cast in Colombia's history. Although the abstention level was considerably lower than in previous elections, only 3.6 million voters out of a total of 17 million decided who the next president would be.

The victory of Samper was immediately surrounded by controversy when Pastrana, initially viewed as a sore loser, accused the President's election team of receiving $6 million 'narco-funding' from the Calí drug cartel to finance his campaign. Although Samper moved quickly to cushion the allegations – ordering a full investigation – Colombia was placed in the spotlight, which, together with murky allegations about the World Cup performance of the Colombian football team in the USA, badly damaged the new administration's image. The Samper government would be haunted by these allegations throughout its four-year term, producing a 'lame-duck' presidency and generating a lack of confidence in the administration which extra-legal groups such as the guerrillas and the paramilitaries took advantage of by increasing their armed activities.

Breaking with tradition, Samper named his key ministers before he was sworn in as President in August. Horacio Serpa was named Interior Minister, a post he occupied briefly in the Barco government. Guillermo Perry Rubio, an electrical engineer with a doctorate in economics from the Massachusetts Institute of Technology, was appointed Finance Minister. Rodrigo Pardo, the former Colombian Ambassador to Venezuela, became Foreign Relations Minister. Samper continued Gaviria's initiative of appointing a civilian as Defence Minister, naming Fernando Botero, his presidential campaign organiser and a former Deputy Interior Minister. Néstor Humberto Martínez Neira, who had held a number of posts in the financial world and who at the time worked for the Inter-American Development Bank (IDB), was the new Justice Minister. Finally, Juan Manuel Turbay, one of Samper's closest advisers was later appointed Communications Minister.

Economic continuity – with a human face

In his inaugural speech Samper reiterated his government's commitment to fight subversion, terrorism, paramilitarism and street crime. The struggle against drug trafficking, corruption and organised crime received top priority. Although the new government would continue the previous administration's economic policy of *apertura*, there was a clear change in focus aimed at preventing the peso from strengthening further while consolidating and diversifying the productive sector, with special emphasis on infrastructure and agriculture.[8] The government's efforts – with foreign investors encouraged to take part – were also aimed at the improvement and revitalisation of the road system, telecommunications, ports and power plants to bring them up to international standards. The overall economic goal of Samper's government was to achieve an annual GDP growth rate of 6.5 per cent which, with higher coffee prices and rising commodity prices such as coal, nickel and oil, would not be impossible to achieve.

As part of the government's effort to fight inflation, it negotiated a Social Pact in 1994 (similar to the one which had operated in Mexico – see Chapter 6), in which a commission formed by representatives of government, business and labour reached an agreement on wage and price increases in order to reduce inflation in 1995 to 18 per cent from 22.6 per cent in 1994. The three sectors agreed to raise prices of food, public services and other basic necessities by no more than 18 per cent, with the result that public-sector salaries, which affected about 4 million people, were increased in 1995 by an average of 18.2 per cent compared with the previous year's rise of 20.5 per cent. The agreement on a minimum wage increase was a big achievement for the new administration because during the previous eight years the government had set increases by decree after failing to reach a consensus with business and labour leaders. The agreement on the minimum wage was part of a government initiative to control wage and price increases during the next four years in order to reduce inflation to 10 per cent by 1998.

The government's 1994 inflation target of 18 per cent proved difficult to achieve. Despite the curb in credit expansion, higher coffee revenues percolated through the economy which, together with a substantial rise in oil exports, drove prices upwards. These inflationary pressures persisted in 1995, aggravated by the government's 20.5 per cent budget increase. In 1994 the high cost and restrictions on consumer credit began to hurt the business sector, with interest rates on car loans, for example, exceeding 45 per cent. At the beginning of 1995 interest rates were lowered by the Central Bank by between 1.5 to 5 per cent, generating the expectation that they would continue to fall, easing the pressure on the appreciating peso whilst giving local businesses breathing space. The peso was devalued in nominal terms at an annual rate of 13.6 per cent, which meant that with an expected inflation rate of 24 per cent, the currency in real terms would be revalued by over 10 per cent during the course of the year. Control of the peso's appreciation would be problematic given the large foreign investments made during the year in the country's oilfield developments. The Samper administration pursued incompatible economic policies, maintaining high interest rates without reducing inflation which stayed persistently above government forecasts.

Further inflationary pressure was added when Samper launched an ambitious $800 million plan to create 1.5 million new jobs. This increased public spending from 30 per cent of GDP to 34 per cent by 1998, financed by short-term borrowing and additional tax revenues raised from tax reforms, something which most observers believed would be extremely difficult to achieve. The fiscal deficit projected, assuming a successful tax reform, would have been in the region of 4–5 per cent of GDP, financed by borrowing internally with the total debt increasing from C$3.3 trillion in 1994 to C$11.7 trillion in 1998, placing further pressure on interest rates, something which the government was trying to avoid in order to maintain growth in the economy. At the same time the Central Bank (as an independent institution from the government) applied the brakes in March 1995 in order to prevent the economy from overheating, creating a liquidity crisis by increasing the minimum reserve requirements banks held on deposits at the Banco de la República. Consequently, the monetary base fell from an annual rate of 40 per cent in 1994 to 20 per cent the following year. The tight money policy and strong demand for credit meant that interest rates remained high, at around 40 per cent.

In addition, Samper wanted his administration to achieve a 'great social leap', calling on all sectors to support his plans for fundamental social change in Colombia. At the core of the development programme was the generation of new jobs in an expanding export sector, support for small businesses, increased social investment in health, education and housing, infrastructural expansion and the reactivation of the moribund agricultural sector. In addition, in order to incorporate 12 million 'unreachable' Colombians not included in the government's social programme, the Samper administration launched a social solidarity programme, Red de Solidaridad Social (Social Solidarity Network), to provide direct economic support a week after coming to power. More than 1 per cent of GDP was assigned to the programme by the end of 1998, with the government aiming to create 110,000 new jobs in both the rural and urban sectors in addition to the 1.5 million additional jobs Samper had promised to create.[9]

Drugs and government

In spite of its good intentions, the Samper administration was preoccupied for the duration of its term by the initial accusations made by Pastrana. The allegations damaged the government on an international level, strengthening the US critique of narcotics funding and political corruption in the country. Although the Colombian government had poured vast sums of money into the fight against drugs, with limited effect, up until 1994 it had successfully argued that the drug problem was not one of supply but demand, and that more was needed to curb drug use in the United States and Europe. This position was undermined by the Pastrana claims and the subsequent controversy sparked by Gustavo de Greiff, the Prosecutor-General, who stated the war on drug trafficking was a failure,[10] and called for a study of the effects drug legalisation would have in Colombia.

These developments strengthened the Clinton administration's contention that the Colombian government was a 'narcodemocracy', corrupted by drug money and with a weak appetite to fight the narcos. The US State Department's annual report on drugs in 1994 criticised lenient sentences given to surrendering traffickers, concluding that widespread corruption and intimidation by traffickers was undermining Colombian institutions. In addition, Senator John Kerry, the Chairman of the Foreign Relations Sub-Committee on terrorism and narcotics, warned that Colombia had capitulated to the Calí cartel, which, according to the American senator, had now penetrated the country's main business interests, including banking, finance, shipping, mining, coffee and cut flowers. The US Senate voted early in 1994 to stop aid to Colombia unless President Clinton certified that the Colombian government was fully co-operating in counter-narcotics operations. Under continuous US pressure the Samper administration was unable to recover the political initiative, since the 'narco cassettes' were released soon after the presidental elections ended in June 1994.

At the beginning of 1995, the political crisis remained unresolved, with opinion polls showing that 60 per cent of the population wanted Samper to resign. In August, Defence Minister Fernando Botero resigned over his alleged involvement in accepting drug money in the 1994 presidential campaign as Liberal Party campaign manager. The resignation of two other Samper advisers and Ministers (Rodrigo Pardo at Foreign Affairs and Juan Manuel Turbay, the Communications Minister, both also involved in the Samper campaign) soon followed. Together with Interior Minister Horacio Serpa, they were accused of breaching the total campaign funds allowed under the electoral rules. Soon afterwards, campaign treasurer Santiago Medina implicated the President directly with receiving funds from the Calí cartel to use in the campaign. In addition, Samper's lawyer was almost murdered in an assassination attempt that was interpreted as a direct warning to the President that he should resign.

The survival of the Samper administration was increasingly dependent on manipulation of certain sectors of the judiciary, a worrying sign reflecting the extent to which the Executive was determined to stay in power. Following the November 1995 ruling by the Electoral Council that both the Samper and Pastrana campaigns had breached spending curbs set at $4 million (by $7 million and $1 million respectively), the Council of State court ruled the curbs illegal. As a result neither Samper nor Pastrana were subject to penalties or criminal charges. The ruling weakened the case against the three detained Ministers, who avoided imprisonment when the Fiscal-General was forced to drop charges against them. The Fiscal-General did, however, continue to investigate Serpa, Pardo and Turbay's involvement in electoral fraud, illegal enrichment and a cover-up of funds received. A congressional commission in December 1995 subsequently exonerated Samper and his campaign advisers owing to a lack of evidence. The Clinton administration interpreted this as a cover-up. Most of the commission members were from Samper's Liberal Party and some were themselves under investigation for drug corruption.

Towards the end of 1995 the political situation was rapidly deteriorating in an ever-decreasing spiral of corruption charges and political assassinations. Under such a shaky political situation, economic policy was at a standstill. Economic pressure grew as groups such as the Asociación Nacional de Industriales (ANDI, National Industrialists Association), which initially supported the President, withdrew their backing, and as a result foreign investment (apart from oil) showed a marked slowdown. In conjunction with declining output in the construction and manufacturing sectors, economic growth only managed to reach 5 per cent, inflation was not under control and the exchange rate moved above the C$1,000 to US$1 level, which only served to accelerate the rise of the retail price index.

Proceso 8000

In January 1996 Fernando Botero Zea, the detained former Defence Minister, declared that Samper was aware drug money had been used during the election campaign. The allegations by Samper's confidant made the President's position appear untenable. As a result of Botero's allegation, the Fiscal-General indicted Samper and several Ministers for electoral fraud, illicit enrichment and for covering up the affair. The congressional commission which had closed its enquiry in December 1995 was reopened with the new evidence provided by the Fiscal-General and became known as *Proceso 8000*. If the Commission decided there was sufficient evidence for formal charges the case would be heard by the full House of Representatives, which could send the President to be tried by the Senate, leading ultimately to impeachment, with the Supreme Court ruling separately on any criminal charges.

It was felt the process could take months, if not years, leading to the paralysis of a government which was facing serious problems on both social and economic fronts. This moved the main private-sector lobby organisations and over one thousand business leaders in Medellín to urge Samper to step down while he conducted his defence, with the Church joining the chorus and students demonstrating against the President. The only institutional support which Samper received came from the labour unions, although he continued to command popular support, much of which stemmed from populist speeches given as he toured Colombia promising to spend additional funds in the regions. The Central Bank sought to counter these measures, and when pressure was placed by the government to curtail the independence of the Central Bank, the Finance Minister Guillermo Perry resigned at the end of April 1996.

Samper was boosted when Heyne Mogollón, a member of the three-man congressional team investigating corruption charges against the President, cleared him of any wrongdoing in May 1996 on the grounds that there was not enough evidence to recommend impeachment. Mogollón's report was forwarded to the Committee of Accusations of the House of Representatives, which voted against a resolution recommending that Samper be accused of criminal wrongdoing before the full House. It further recommended that Congress should shelve its probe as there was insufficient evidence to justify impeachment proceedings. The panel's findings were submitted to the Liberal-dominated Chamber of Representatives which voted in June 1996 to absolve Samper of any wrongdoing during his presidential campaign. A strong plea was sent to the United States to accept Samper's innocence and not to impose further sanctions, a move which the State Department diplomatically rejected, with the Clinton administration giving a clear impression it wanted Samper to resign.

Samper still faced possible impeachment proceedings stemming from charges that he approved the use of the Calí contributions to bankroll his campaign. However, the President appeared to be in a stronger political position, but with a weakening economy, a relatively large budget deficit, pressure from the United States and a disgruntled private sector, Samper found it increasingly difficult to govern. It was evident that the Samper administration would continue from one crisis to another, achieving very little of substance, especially in the area of social change, which was one of his main political promises. The record of the Samper government up to 1996 shows a deterioration of the social indices, whilst high interest rates and political uncertainty led to a decline in economic activity. GDP growth for 1996 was 2.1 per cent compared with 5.2 per cent during 1995. Unemployment increased 2 per cent, non-traditional exports fell 7 per cent and coffee exports declined by 26 per cent compared with the previous year. The Central Bank spent almost $500 million support-ing the peso. The government was also running a large budget deficit estimated at 4 per cent of GDP, with government expenditure increasing during the first four months of the year by 66 per cent compared to 1995, and with revenues increasing by only 36 per cent. There was no sign that the large budget deficit could be curbed, with the government promising instead more expenditure to maintain its popularity, preferring to increase its borrowing requirements to balance its books.

US–Colombian relations continued to deteriorate. In 1996 the Clinton administration demanded the extradition of a number of Calí drug barons, including Gilberto and Miguel Rodríguez Orejuela, so they could be brought to trial in the United States. Although the 1991 Colombian constitution specifi-cally excluded extradition, US Attorney-General Janet Reno argued that the 1979 US–Colombia extradition treaty remained in force. The Colombian gov-ernment countered that the bilateral treaty could not take precedence over the 1991 Constitution. Further pressure was placed on Samper when a confidential memorandum written by Myles Frechette, the US Ambassador, came to light, calling on the United States to impose economic sanctions on Colombia because of the government's lack of commitment to fighting the narcos. It was evident that the United States was not satisfied with the Chamber of Represen-tatives vote to absolve Samper, demanding an enquiry into links between drug cartels and certain congressmen close to the President. The longer Samper remained in power the less negotiating space he had with the United States on matters not related to drugs, which would in turn severely undermine his sup-port among powerful industrialists such as Julio Mario Santo Domingo, reported to have been the largest contributor to his campaign. Consequently, in order to placate the United States, the Samper administration introduced a series of judicial reforms, including stiff new penalties for organised crime and money laundering. The process would take decades to become law and it was doubtful whether the United States was convinced of the government's inten-tions to fight the drug cartels. It appeared that both countries were inexorably moving towards a major clash. The approval of an extradition treaty with the United States remained a point of contention. Previous Colombian govern-ments had shied away from the extradition issue as it was an immensely unpop-ular subject. The Samper administration was no exception, with opinion polls showing that 70 per cent of the people polled were against extradition.

The political situation in Colombia in 1997 continued to deteriorate, at times resembling a surreal farce, with coca-growers striking to demand the right to grow illegal crops while outlawed guerrilla factions proposed amendments to the 1991 Constitution. The former Attorney-General, who had spent 43 days in jail, was countersuing the Fiscal-General for wrongful arrest whilst the United States continued to threaten economic sanctions in the forlorn hope of removing Samper. In order to appease the Clinton administration, Samper proposed a number of anti-narcotics (including extradition) and constitutional changes, including the abolition of the post of vice-president and the second round of elections, and that Senators be elected by a departmental electorate rather than national ballot. Clearly the most important constitutional amendment from the American point of view was the introduction of an extradition treaty with the United States. In the past there had been strong opposition to such a measure, with the former Medellín cartel unleashing a terror campaign to deter the Gaviria government from approving such a treaty, but this time around there was less opposition to it in order to appease the wrath of the Clinton administration. Ultimately, a toothless extradition treaty was approved by Congress without a retroactive clause, which meant that the powerful Calí cartel barons, amongst others, would not be extradited to the United States.

What about the future?

The *apertura* programme set in place economic reforms designed to reduce the role of the state in the economy by opening the domestic market to external trade and investment, privatising state assets, investing in new infrastructure and integrating Colombia more closely with neighbouring economies. It was not welcomed by many because of its alleged adverse social impact.[11] The main argument against *apertura* is that it was implemented too quickly, with the benefits accruing to the richest 3 per cent of the population. The improvised and accelerated way in which the *apertura* policies were applied resulted in little capital accumulation, with the savings ratio falling from 20 per cent of GDP in 1990 to 8.8 per cent in 1996, fuelling a consumption boom stimulated by cheap imports and narco-dollars. Critics have also argued that the reduction in import tariffs increased unemployment and lowered salary levels because in many instances local industry could not compete with imports. This was especially true for the agricultural sector.[12] But the rural sector had been in decline since the 1950s when it accounted for nearly half of GDP. In the 1990s, the decline continued and the agricultural sector is now on par with the manufacturing sector, accounting for a fifth of total GDP. Foreign trade also changed, with coffee exports representing 64 per cent of total exports in 1965 declining to less than 25 per cent in 1996, with oil, coal and bananas increasing in importance.

It is clear that any form of protectionism, be it for agricultural production or any other sector, distorts the market with consumers paying higher prices because of production and distribution inefficiencies. Many of these critics fail to see that the *apertura* allowed for a more transparent, fairer economy which was intended to have an impact on the four strong economic groups which monopolise the Colombian economy. Instead the Samper administration has strengthened the position of these groups. At the same time, a closed financial system meant that credit was difficult to achieve for small entrepreneurial firms. Colombia, like other Latin American countries, has a remarkable number of budding entrepreneurs who, with a more open financial system, could achieve remarkable results. The stranglehold that the four powerful economic groups have on the country would be unacceptable in many countries simply because of a lack of any form of competition. The intention of *apertura* was for local economic groups to compete with international products which were assumed to be produced at the most cost-effective basis. In this way Colombian consumers would not have to pay for the inefficiencies of local producers operating in a protected market. A throwback to a quasi-protectionist policy would only ensure the well-being of the powerful economic groups and not the economy as a whole.

The Samper administration slowed down the effects of *apertura* and sought, as one of its main objectives, to address the social problems which the Gaviria government had allegedly failed to tackle or had exacerbated, particularly in the agricultural sector. Such an argument has served as a good excuse for the insecurity and difficult living conditions brought on by the action of the narcos and guerrillas as a result of a lack of state protection. In 1997 over a million people fled their rural districts in search of security.

The long-term prospects for Colombia are closely tied to the behaviour of mineral exports, which are now the main source of foreign reserves, and almost double those of coffee. The energy and mining sectors have continued to increase their share of GDP, reaching a peak in the late 1990s. As oil has gained in importance as a source of external revenue, the economy is more prone to 'Dutch-disease' problems. Whereas in the past Colombia managed its coffee booms relatively well, oil shocks are essentially different in character, and some of the policies implemented to manage coffee bonanzas may not be appropriate or even applicable. The main difference is that with coffee, Colombia had some degree of commodity-supply control and thus could influence price, but the price of oil is determined by the international oil market and will not be influenced in any way by a change in production in Colombia.

Without the acceptance of the benefits of an open economy Colombia will not fulfil its potential. It is clear that a large number of opinion makers find the intellectual premises on which the economic programme of *apertura* is based too painful to contemplate. Although it is difficult to assess the overall number, it is clear that many feel an open economy is unjust and unfair without realising that the alternative leaves the very people whom they want to help worse off. The reliance on the state to provide a solution is still prevalent. Agueldo Villa, for instance, believes that market forces alone do not stimulate capital accumulation. Using the country's oil industry as an example, he argues that the problem is one of 'how to turn oil revenues into investment in industry and agriculture and how to raise and direct savings to finance the local currency base which a programme of priority economic investment would demand',[13] which only state intervention could deliver. The merits of an open economy should win in the end, but it will take time before it is generally accepted by the vast majority of opinion makers.

Political developments in the future

While the country sank into economic malaise due to the mismanagement of the Samper administration, the political situation was even worse. The general view that the Colombian state 'has been poor, its coverage insufficient and a good part of its bureaucracy, of clientelist origin, is inept and corrupt',[14] was borne out in 1997 when the narco-political crisis deepened, weakening the political system, which had to cope with a rise in public and private dishonesty, with five ministers resigning as a result of sordid business deals and a number of Congressmen and Senators indicted for corruption, together with an increase in political violence and petty delinquency.[15] Added to these problems was the discrediting of the institution of the presidency, the slowdown of the economy and worsening international relations.

The political system as a whole has been weakened by the erosion of the bi-party system, a lack of strong political opposition and the inadequate management of public-order problems. These three factors have deprived the Colombian electorate of adequate channels for political expression. Moreover, the *Proceso 8000* has had the insidious result of making the presidency and Congress bow to pressure groups in order to remain politically alive. In addition, the *Proceso 8000* has shown the direct links between politics and the narcos, further weakening the authority of the government and the state in general, allowing the guerrillas and narcos greater freedom of action to act with the result that they have increased their control on parts of the country. The narcos in particular, through a number of flexible and changing alliances, have contributed to foster a climate of permanent confrontation with the state, placing the government on a semi-permanent warfooting. This is because the narcos and other extra-legal forces have benefited most from the lack of state control in a great part of the country, highlighting the fact that 'the judiciary and the armed forces need to deploy their resources on different fronts as long as the drugs sector carries on its illegal trade'.[16] The extra-legal entities have time on their side because of their long-term objectives, whereas the politicians and government have a short-term horizon of two to four years and hence go for quick-fix solutions which will increase their electoral standing. Consequently, although the 1991 Constitution opened up the political system to new political parties, young activists, ethnic groups and other minorities, some have argued that it played a similar role to the 1886 Constitution it replaced. Both tried to end conflict and ensure the hegemony of certain power groups: the coffee growers in 1886 and the narcos in 1991. The experience of *apertura* and the 1991 Constitution 'aimed to make the transition from authoritarian political and economic governance to democratic and political governance, but acknowledged that the implementation of this strategy ran the risk of implosion'.[17]

Under such a scenario the 1991 Constitution has been interpreted as an armistice with the narcos because it did not allow extradition (Article 35), while the guerrillas and paramilitaries found in it 'an instrument to redefine the rules of the game with the state'.[18] At the regional level there has also been a fundamental change. with the emphasis on decentralisation which has led to the popular election of mayors, and the presence and/or *de facto* control by the guerrillas in a large number of municipalities. The inability of the Samper administration to govern because of its preoccupation with drug money allowed guerrilla forces to make significant territorial gains and humiliate the army in a number of bloody confrontations such as Patascoy in December 1997. This has led in turn to a greater division of the country among the guerrillas, narcos and paramilitaries.

The intention of the 1991 Constitution was to end the old model of political behaviour which stemmed from regional coalitions 'in which the expansion of the regional and political market had the effect, through power games and local alliances, of the territorial diversification of the national economy (coffee, cotton, sugar, banana, precious metals and coca producing areas)'.[19] Soon after the National Assembly drafted the new Constitution, parliamentary elections took place which had the unfortunate result of strengthening 'precisely that traditional political class, the only one capable of effectively mobilising, through the practice of clientelism, a captive electoral base, while emerging or independent tendencies did not have truly democratic resources with which to obtain at least the same presence in Congress as they had in 1990'.[20]

According to Valdivieso, the former Fiscal-General, Colombia is the victim of 'a sinister trick, which converted the electoral reforms, designed to perfect democracy into mechanisms for definitively liquidating the party organisations as intermediaries of popular expression'.[21] The result is that only mavericks remain on the political scene as 'the institutions and political parties disappear and hence, by whatever means, individual dealings, secret pacts, shady deals and business negotiations are facilitated'.[22] In addition, the decay and weakening of the political system and parties opened the door to the 'growing involvement of plutocratic interests in politics, destroying neoliberal freedoms'.[23] This can be seen by the influence the powerful financial groups exercise currently on the political system by taking a more active interest in running Colombia's powerful economic guilds and by building powerful media groups.

The March 1998 congressional elections reinforced the tendency to move away from the party machinery, with the electorate favouring strong personalities who had fought corruption. Although the 1991 Constitution established democratic pluralism there is a need for parties to offer clear ideological differences with many arguing that 'the big failing of Colombian democracy is the decay of the political parties, which are responsible for organising citizens' participation for public action'.[24] A major criticism is that 'we lack good parties which are open and present in society, transparent in their workings and exemplary in the conduct of their representatives'.[25] The lack of strong political parties is attributed by Agueldo Villa to the 'nationalist front' mentality because 'the truth is that they were slapdash with the division of bureaucracy and government and they allowed clientelism, bureaucratism and dishonesty in the management of public money and became established in the state'.[26] The large abstention rate in elections is a symptom of popular perception that the system is unlikely to change. Although the 1998 congressional elections did not change the composition of the two Houses, a surprisingly large number of candidates running on independent tickets won significant segments of public opinion. Ingrid Betancourt, running on an anti-corruption platform, was elected to the Senate with the highest number of votes. The left-wing parties failed to obtain a single representative in the Senate and only two in the Chamber of Representatives. The abstention level was 56 per cent compared with 67 per cent in 1994, with the larger than expected turnout interpreted as a desire to clean up the deep-rooted corruption in Congress, but only 15 per cent of the new intake were new faces.

The difficulties which the Colombian government has faced in recent times are a direct result of failing to confront the problems with sufficient timeliness. Hence the governing leaders have stimulated the belief that the problem lies with 'the institutions created [the 1991 Constitution] and not in the behaviour of the people'.[27] Moreover:

> The excessive presidentialism which lasted until the 1991 Constitution and the system of rents and privileges which prevailed before globalisation, accustomed Colombians to not differentiate the actions of the various powers of the state. All decision making was perceived to be monolithic, which in effect it was, as the Executive exercised mechanisms of control-veto with respect to the initiatives of the other powers. Today the institutions of the state have greater identity and autonomy in spite of the activities of some corrupt leaders. The role of the Fiscal-General has represented significant progress for judicial culture, as it demonstrates that there is not a single monolithic power and that the crisis did not stem from the design of bad institutions but rather from the actions of bad rulers.[28]

Many of the problems which the Samper administration faced have been present for some time in the Colombian political system. During the 1980s the magnitude of the drugs problem was smaller than during the mid-1990s, but in the past it suited the government for economic reasons to have the dollar receipts which entered the country illegally or through the 'back door' at the Central Bank. The same can be said about the guerrilla problem, which a number of governments have tried to solve. At the beginning it was felt that there was a need to incorporate left-wing groups in order to achieve a peaceful transition but there has been no real will on either side to achieve a lasting peace agreement. At times it was politically convenient for the government to tolerate the activities of left-wing groups, while the guerrillas continue with their left-wing rhetoric only to concentrate on the business of kidnappings and extortion.[29]

Many political scientists believe Colombia's political system needs to change in order to make politics more acceptable to the electorate. Agueldo Villa argues that the most important item for Colombian democracy is the need to reconstruct the political system in order to curtail the degenerative effects that so far have affected politics. Sarmiento postulates the establishment of a completely new state as a way out of the current malaise, which would not intervene in all economic areas but which would have to 'carry out a series of concrete tasks to reach general objectives with high levels of acceptance such as economic growth and income distribution'.[30] The new state would implement an economic model 'of high growth with equity, to act directly to reduce poverty and improve income distribution, harmonise stability with productive activity and create the conditions for the long-term achievement of a growth strategy based on knowledge'.[31] The instrument at the disposal of the new state would be a series of rules for official intervention and a number of regulators which would operate independently of the government. According to Sarmiento, what is needed is a government which 'would operate selectively, stimulating competitiveness in those sectors which are prepared to support it, but also ... would implement industrialisation, exchange-rate and commercial policies to guarantee the protection and promotion of certain activities that are able to incorporate spending in science and technology and diffuse it in the rest of the country'.[32]

This does not mean a return to a generalised form of protectionism but rather to a selective and dynamic one, with tariffs erected in order to protect targeted industries. The two writers reflect what many feel about the future of the political system in Colombia, but fail in what they are trying to achieve. It is clear that all Colombian governments have sustained economic growth rates and low unemployment as their goal. The problem is that they fail to deliver on their promises in many instances, not because the system *per se* was at fault but because the human resources to implement polices were not available. The political system, with a free press and fair elections, is strong and healthy, dealing with the problems of the Samper administration more than adequately.[33] The issue of corrupt politicians is clearly not present in Colombia alone and can be dealt with by the courts. What is needed in the future is for the electorate to have greater faith in its politicians, and this can only be achieved by political parties fielding honest politicians and a more rigorous selection of candidates.

There is a hint that this is currently happening. The congressional elections in March 1998 returned Ingrid Betancourt, the most vociferous and strongest opponent of Samper in Congress, to the Senate with the largest number of votes cast in the elections. The presidential race in 1998 was between Andrés

Pastrana Arango, with Gustavo Bell Lemus (former Governor of the Atlantic Department) as his running mate as the Vice-President for the Conservatives, and Horacio Serpa, who was accompanied by María Emma Mejía (the former Foreign Affairs Minister) as his Vice-President, for the Liberal Party. As the country prepared to elect a new president in May 1998 it appeared that it was tired of the current Liberal malaise and was desperately seeking a solution to the guerrilla problem. Pastrana sought to encapsulate the country's mood by calling for an *Alianza por el Cambio* (Alliance for Change) in which all sectors could unite with him to end the current crisis. Moreover, there appeared to be a groundswell of interest from all social groups to prevent Serpa winning because it would mean continuity with the economic policies of Samper. Pastrana's campaign was given a boost in March 1998 when Alfonso Valdivieso and other *galanistas,* such as Gloria Pachón de Galán, Luis Carlos Galán's widow, all members of the Liberal Party, gave their support to him. Many other prominent Colombians not associated with the Conservatives, such as the novelist Gabriel García Márquez, Enrique Santos Calderón, editor of the *El Tiempo* newspaper, Julio Sánchez Cristo of the *Radio Cadena Nacional* radio chain, Humberto de la Calle, Samper's former Vice-President, Rudolf Hommes, former Finance Minister in the Gaviria government and others came out supporting Pastrana. The conservative ticket of Pastrana/Bell won the presidential elections in June at the run-off with Serpa after the first round, with a relatively large margin and increasing the total number of votes cast by 6 million, the highest for any presidential election.

It would be pleasing to believe that, after the fracas of the Samper administration, the Colombian electorate is tired of the old-style, tainted politics. But such a view is probably misguided as the end result is such a coveted prize, with so much riding on it, that it would be hard for the political establishment to give it up. It can be expected that the current party-political structure will continue, albeit sufficiently cleaned up to allow a semblance of normal governance to take place. The Pastrana administration will need to tackle a number of fundamental problems. There is an urgent need to have a proper foreign policy, for example. The Samper administration showed that Colombia was ill-prepared to deal with hostility from the United States. It will also be essential to stimulate economic activity on the microeconomic level. In the same way that Colombian economists have been very good at managing the economy on a macro level, there is now a need to focus on the requirements of middle and small enterprises which have the potential of significantly increasing employment. Finally, and most importantly, there is a need to re-establish governability in areas of the country which are controlled by extra-legal entities. This will not be easy, but until this is achieved Colombia will continue to drift from one political crisis to another.

Notes

1 See M. Palacios, *Coffee in Colombia, 1850–1970: An Economic, Social and Political History* (Cambridge, Cambridge University Press, 1979); M. Cárdenas, *Coffee Exports, Endogenous State Policy and the Business Cycle* (Berkeley, University of California Press, 1991).

2 See L. Buitrago and L. Zamosa (eds), *Al filo del caos: Crisis política en la Colombia de los años '80* (Bogotá, Tercer Mundo Editores, 1991).

3 Luis Jorge Garay, *Colombia y la crisis de la deuda* (Santa fé de Bogotá, CINEP, 1991).

4 INCOMEX, 'Material seleccionado, proceso de modernización de la economía colombiana', mimeo, Santa fé de Bogotá, 17 April 1990.

5 B. McBeth (ed.), *Colombia* (London, Euromoney Publications, 1993).

6 'El costo de la guerra', *El Tiempo*, 11 March 1998.

7 For a detailed discussion, see J. Ocampo, 'The Economic Policy of the Samper Administration', mimeo (London, Institute of Latin American Studies, 1996); M. Cárdenas and R. Córdoba, 'Recent economic policy in Colombia. The view from the Outside', mimeo (London, Institute of Latin American Studies, 1996); and *Estralegia* 5.9.94.

8 *La República Empresarial*, 8 August 1994.

9 The programme turned out to be a failure. The Comptroller-General's office concluded in March 1998 that after three and a half years the programme had distributed C$438 billion compared with a promised C$1900 billion. In addition, only 1.8 million people out of the 12 million targeted had been helped directly. *Semana*, 23 March 1998.

10 As consumption of marijuana, cocaine and heroin had increased, with less than 10 per cent of the illegal drugs entering the United States seized by narcotics agents. In early May 1995, the Constitutional Court overturned the existing legislation and decriminalised the use of some drugs, including marijuana and cocaine.

11 J. Child, 'Apertura y privatización', pp. 63–95, L. Botero, 'Apertura económica y reforma laboral', pp. 14–62, C. Navanjo, 'La apertura económica', pp. 96–126, in J. Child (ed.), *Neoliberalismo y subdesarrollo: Un análisis crítico de la apertura económica* (Santa fé de Bogotá, El Ancora Editores, 1995).

12 E. Sarmiento Palacio, *Apertura y crecimiento económico: De la desilusión al nuevo estado* (Bogotá, Tercer Mundo Editores, 1996).

13 H. Agudelo Villa, *La revolución liberal: Un proyecto político inconcluso* (Santa fé de Bogotá, Tercer Mundo Editores, 1996), p. 51.

14 L. Restrepo, 'Colombia: Una nación en peligro', in IEPRI, Universidad Nacional, *Síntesis '97: Anuario social, político y económico de Colombia* (Santa fé de Bogotá, Universidad Nacional, 1997), p. 10.

15 According to the Comptroller-General, some C$400,000 million were stolen from government coffers in 1997, equivalent to 10 per cent of the fiscal deficit. *Semana*, 22 December 1997.

16 E. Revéiz, *El estado como mercado: La gobernabilidad económica y política en Colombia antes y después de 1991* (Santa fé de Bogotá, Fonade, Carlos Valencia Editores, 1996), p. 171.

17 Reveiz, *El estado*, p. 24.

18 Reveiz, *El estado*, p. 173.

19 Reveiz, *El estado*, p. 81.

20 E. Rojas Morales, *Colombia a la deriva: Una mirada ética a la política y un juicio moral a la campaña 'Samper Presidente'* (Bogotá, Fundación para la Investigación y Desarrollo de la Ciencia Política, 1997), p. 7.

21 Rojas Morales, *Colombia*, p. 21.

22 Rojas Morales, *Colombia*, p. 21.

23 Agudelo Villa, *La revolución liberal*, p. 183.

24 Agudelo Villa, *La revolución liberal*, p. 182.

25 Agudelo Villa, *La revolución liberal*, p. 182.

26 Agudelo Villa, *La revolución liberal*, p. 182.

27 Revéiz, *El estado*, p. 310.

28 Revéiz, *El estado*, p. 313.
29 Note that Serpa, one of the leading presidential candidates in 1998, feels that 'nobody is going to win this war between the guerrillas and the state'. *Semana*, 23 March 1998.
30 Sarmiento Palacio, *Apertura y crecimiento económico*, p. 20.
31 Sarmiento Palacio, *Apertura y crecimiento económico*, p. 20.
32 Sarmiento Palacio, *Apertura y crecimiento económico*, p. 179.
33 Without the strong intervention of the United States, it is doubtful whether the Proceso 8000 would have had such far-reaching effects. Although it is unacceptable for one country to dictate policy to another, it is clear that without the United States pursuing an active role against the drugs barons, many of the recent changes in Colombia would not have taken place.

8

Venezuela

JULIA BUXTON

Venezuela has always been something of a paradox within Latin America, constantly countering regional trends. As Latin America moved incrementally towards democratic forms in the first half of the twentieth century, Venezuela was subject to authoritarian government until 1958,[1] when a pacted transition allowed for the installation of a democratic regime. Democratic government was sustained throughout the following three decades, whilst regional neighbours experienced democratic collapse and military authoritarianism. In the 1990s Venezuela faced pronounced popular disaffection with the political status quo, culminating in two coup attempts, the impeachment of a president, mass rioting and surging abstention, whilst regional neighbours consolidated democratic transitions. Venezuela's exceptionalism has been most clearly pronounced in the field of economic policy. The generalised acceptance and application of neoliberal stabilisation and structural adjustment measures across many Latin American states at the end of the 1990s find limited parallels in Venezuela. Whilst the majority of Latin American countries have shifted from protected inward-looking development to a globally competitive, diversi- fied export strategy led by the private sector, Venezuela remains dependent on a single export – oil, with revenues flowing directly to the state.

The particularly negative consequences of oil on Venezuela's economic development since the 1920s has been vastly documented.[2] Vulnerability to swings in the international oil markets, the overvaluation of the currency[3] and limited diversification of the economic base have been the most salient features. In political terms, oil revenue (and the illusion of it) has sustained a restricted form of democracy, with the oil income channelled through the dominant two-party system in a highly inequitable and clientelistic manner. Economic reform would therefore undermine the political model – and those with vested interests in its maintenance, ranging from the protected private sector to the party-affiliated unions – and more critically from the dominant parties themselves. This underlines the inability of successive Venezuelan governments to adopt and sustain stabilisation and structural adjustment measures, specifically when favoured by a temporary upward swing in the price of oil.

Background to recent stabilisation efforts

Successive Venezuelan governments resisted stabilisation policies throughout the 1970s and 1980s despite sustained fiscal and monetary problems. In 1989 the incoming government of Carlos Andrés Pérez implemented a drastic reversal of Venezuela's highly flawed import-substitution development strategy. The new policy orientation, dubbed *El Gran Viraje* (the Great Turnaround), was a two-stage model seeking to restore macroeconomic balance in the first phase, complemented by major structural reform in the second phase. Despite enviable economic results, including the highest level of Venezuelan GDP growth in 35 years,[4] *el paquete* (the package) met with fierce and sustained opposition from virtually all segments of Venezuelan society including the President's own party, Acción Democrática (AD, Democratic Action). The consolidation of the new economic direction was arrested by the impeachment of the President on charges of corruption and his replacement by an interim President until elections in December 1993. The subsequent presidential victory of Rafael Caldera (1993–98) was predicated upon his vociferous opposition to the policies of Carlos Andrés Pérez and his reputation as an honest politician. Whilst Caldera's immediate policy actions – including the suspension of economic guarantees, a halt to the privatisation process and the imposition of price and foreign-exchange controls – were largely determined by the collapse of the banking sector in 1994, they demonstrated his elemental commitment to a return to Venezuela's statist past.

Although interventionist measures stabilised a precarious political situation, they brought the economy closer to collapse. Having provided the equivalent of 12.7 per cent and 3 per cent of GDP in 1994 and 1995 respectively in financial assistance to the banking sector, the government faced acute economic crisis. With no realistic alternative, the anti-IMF government began negotiations with the Fund in 1995, announcing a two-phase adjustment programme, the *Agenda Venezuela*, in April 1996. In its initial stages, the application of the *Agenda* reaped economic dividends. Then the government opted not to pursue structural reforms as foreign investment capital poured into the country following the opening of the oil sector to private participation, and as oil prices improved.[5] When oil prices nosedived in 1998, the vulnerability of this strategy was exposed and the economy fell once again into deep crisis. This drastic economic downturn occurred in an election year, with popular hostility to the government's economic strategy channelled through Colonel Hugo Chávez, leader of the failed coup attempt of February 1992, who campaigned (like Caldera in 1993) on an anti-IMF platform.

This chapter examines the social, political and cultural obstacles to the application of adjustment policies in Venezuela and the constraints on economic policy-making. The first section provides a brief overview of the Venezuelan democratic model, moving on to an examination of recent economic policy. The final section explores the political limitations to economic reform. It will be argued that continuity in the traditional statist model is a prerequisite for the survival of the political status quo. That is to say that the future legitimacy of Venezuelan democracy is predicated upon continuity with the economic direction of the past.

Oil and politics

Venezuela's model of economic development has been classified as 'capitalist rentist'.[6] Since exploitation of the country's oil resources began in the 1920s, oil has been the mainstay of the economy.[7] The transition to an oil economy had the immediate effect of displacing the *latifundia* structures (large agricultural estates) which had characterised the agricultural economy. As the profitability of agro-exports declined, the rural oligarchy shifted into the service sector, generating a rentier bourgeoisie dependent on state dispersion of the oil revenues. Rent-seeking activities restricted diversification from the oil economy whilst entrenching the model of state-directed development. The decline of the agricultural sector prompted massive and rapid internal migration to urban areas. According to Karl, these social changes had the effect of undermining the structural preconditions of authoritarian rule, generating intense pressure for democratisation from the burgeoning middle class.[8]

Due to sustained and repressive authoritarianism, Venezuelan civil society was profoundly weak, with limited organisational and associative experience. As a result, in the covert conditions of political organisation during the Gómez periods (1908–29 and 1931–35), the emerging parties acquired highly verticalist organisational structures. Vanguardism was deployed to build the parties, using tactics of penetration and absorption to incorporate society into the political struggle. The two main parties, AD and the Comité de Organización Política Electoral Independiente (COPEI Committee for Independent Political Electoral Organisation), adopted a *policlasista* (multi-class) orientation, seeking to unite all classes in the struggle for democracy.[9] This led to the formation of disciplined, cross-national groups, rigidly controlled from the centre, an organisational profile particularly prominent in AD. According to Santana, 'This model was excellent for the worst type of dictatorship, but it is not going to be the best model for later.'[10] A brief democratic opening from 1945–48 was marked by heightened and increasingly violent competition for sectoral control, with the AD government deploying oil resources through the state administration to incorporate labour and build peasant organisations. This initial attempt at establishing a functioning democratic system was terminated by military intervention in 1948. The ensuing ten years of authoritarian control forced the leading parties, AD, COPEI and the Unión Radical Democrática (URD, Radical Democratic Union) to bury sectarian and ideological differences in order to overthrow the Pérez Jiménez government in 1958.

The partidocratic state

The structural framework for the post-1958 party system was determined by the series of inter-party elite agreements which characterised the transition to democracy. Whilst the 1958 Pact of Punto Fijo and the series of economic guarantees which followed were initially credited with facilitating the transition to and consolidation of Venezuelan democracy,[11] it is evident that in the long term the Pact impeded democratic deepening and reform. In political terms, the Pact strengthened the verticalist, centralising tendencies within the parties, committing the leadership to control and containment of their parties and political constituencies. This led to a concentration of political authority in the party elite (the *cogollo*), which was seen as a prerequisite for sustaining the Pact and safeguarding vested interests in the democratic regime. In economic terms, the Pact locked the country into a highly dysfunctional model of state paternalism and rent-seeking behaviour. Extensive protectionism and subsidisation was extended across social groups, with the state constitutionally committed to a highly interventionist role. In linking the process of democratisation with economic redistribution, Punto Fijo structured a material rather than a normative commitment to the new democratic state. As a result, the legitimacy of the political system was highly contingent on its capacity for sustained economic redistribution to the lower classes and protectionist, clientelistic relations with the oligopolistic private sector. This 'populist system of elite conciliation'[12] institutionalised in the 1961 Constitution was, according to Kornblith, dependent on the maintenance of three core variables: an abundance of oil revenue to satisfy group demands; the limiting of sectoral demands; and the aggregation of these demands.[13] A change in any of the three key variables would undermine the new democratic state.

The articulation of social interests was monopolised by the parties, leading to the characterisation of Venezuelan democracy as 'partidocratic', defined by Granier and Yepes as 'a situation in which the parties have been converted into virtual monopolisers of a political system which is formally competitive and open'.[14] Autonomously organised interests were viewed as implicitly destabilising. Practices of penetration, co-optation and control, funded by the dispersion of oil revenues, impeded the emergence of independent interest organisations, with all forms of sectoral, functional and social representation incorporated through a network of corporatist ties and clientelistic links. This was most clearly pronounced in the trade-union movement.[15] The judiciary, the military, the state administration and even the electoral council were subject to clientelistic placement and intensive politicisation, with appointment dependent on party contacts.

This limited form of representation gained institutional form through the electoral system. Despite Venezuela's federal status, political authority was cen-tralised in Caracas, with state governors appointed by the President rather than being popularly elected. The election of congressional candidates was based on the closed-block list system. Candidates for the list were determined by the cen-tral party elite, undermining accountability between representatives and repre-sented, as a premium was placed on party loyalty.[16] With popular choice limited to a single preference in the 'large ballot' for the presidency and the 'small bal-lot' – which simultaneously elected Congress, Senate, local assemblies, mayors and councillors – the expression of popular choice was highly controlled. The electoral system strongly favoured nationally organised parties, numerically capable of fielding candidates at all levels of elective government. With the elec-torate prevented from ticket splitting, the electoral system structurally induced dominant party hegemony, as minor parties were incapable of consolidating regional authority because of the single preference in elections. In addition, pragmatic agreement and convergence between AD and the COPEI and their clientelistic dispersion of oil revenues further constrained the emergence of minor parties.[17] State funding of elections also worked against the emergence of opposition parties as it was distributed on the basis of previous electoral per-formance, giving AD and the COPEI an inbuilt financial advantage. This was reinforced by dominant party relations with the Venezuelan private sector, whose campaign contributions were exchanged for access to government and guaranteed economic protection and benefits.

In their early party programmes, AD made explicit their position that the state was an engine for Venezuelan development.[18] Committed to 'sowing the oil', the first AD government of Rómulo Betancourt (1958–63) established Cordiplan to draw up five-yearly economic plans. The first laid the framework for ISI, a tardy introduction in comparison to the rest of the region. The entre-preneurial state – controlled by the parties – became the principal distributor of oil revenue in a highly protected and subsidised economy. Relative stability in the international oil market provided a constant flow of fiscal income, allow-ing Venezuela to become one of the most successful economies in the world, with annual economic growth rates averaging 6 per cent throughout the 1950s and 1960s. This parlayed into democratic stability, despite a guerrilla uprising in the mid-1960s.[19] The popularity and legitimacy of the leading parties and the democratic system are evidenced from electoral results between 1958 and 1973. An initially fragmented party system gradually gave way to a two-party system in 1973, characterised by pragmatic convergence between AD and the COPEI, high levels of partisan alignment and low rates of abstention.[20]

The oil boom – and bust
Economic stability ended during the first government of Carlos Andrés Pérez (1973–78), when the Yom Kippur war and Arab oil embargo led to a surge in world oil prices – and Venezuelan revenue, which the administration proved incapable of handling judiciously.[21] The excess oil income led to a burst of

Table 8.1 *National election results, Venezuela, 1958–73*

Year	Presidential candidate	Party	% of presidential vote	% of congressional vote	Abstention %
1958	R. Betancourt	AD	49	50	6.6
	W. Larrazabal	URD	35	27	
	R. Caldera	COPEI	16	15	
	Others			8	
1963	R. Leoni	AD	33	33	7.8
	R. Caldera	COPEI	20	21	
	J. Villalba	URD	19	17	
	Others		28	29	
1968	R. Caldera	COPEI	29	24	3.3
	G. Barrios	AD	28	26	
	M. Burelli	URD	22	9	
	A. Prieto	MEP[a]	19	13	
	Others		2	28	
1973	C. Pérez	AD	49	44	3.4
	L. Fernández	COPEI	37	30	
	Others		14	26	

Note: a Movimiento Electoral del Pueblo (People's Electoral Movement).
Source: Consejo Supremo Electoral, *Tomo de Elecciones.*

investment and growth directed through the bloated and highly inefficient state apparatus, with government efforts focusing on diversification into steel, aluminium, hydroelectricity and other non-oil activities. The oil, iron-ore and natural-gas industries were nationalised, with the government taking over foreign investment in the utilities sector. The expansion of the state's role exacerbated the rentier profile of the Venezuelan private sector. Whilst the state remained locked in the highly expensive development of extractive industries, the private sector focused on quick-profit, low-risk investments in banking and finance.

For Naím, the oil wealth created popular expectations and illusions leading to major policy mistakes. These where initially masked by the inflow of income.[22] Attempts to neutralise the revenue inflows through investment outside Venezuela met with political opposition, with both parties and society pressuring for the distribution of benefits. Extensive social programmes, tax breaks, indiscriminate subsidies, presidentially decreed labour benefits, and a rapid expansion in state employment led to a precipitous rise in living standards, with annual per capita income increasing from $1,340 in 1972 to $2,900 in 1976, 'creating a psychology of wealth which permeated all sectors'.[23] The massive influx of oil revenue served to reveal major imbalances in the ISI model. With domestic demand exceeding domestic production capacity, imports rose rapidly, spurred by an overvalued currency. Between 1976 to 1977 imports increased by 40 per cent whilst exports rose by only 3.4 per cent.[24] In the medium to long term, this import pattern generated severe balance-of-payments difficulties. Adding to the disequilibrium, the government maintained artificially low interest rates, encouraging excessive spending and limiting savings. Taxation of the non-oil sector remained low to negligible as the government was able to meet three-quarters of its financial needs through oil.

Government expenditure failed to respond to changes in the international oil market. Massive investment outlays were not revised when the price of oil began to fall, with the government opting to acquire international debt rather than scale down public spending. Assisted by initially favourable lending terms, ISI was maintained despite being highly unproductive, inefficient and endemically corrupt. From the Pérez period onwards, a pattern emerges of successive Venezuelan governments pledging themselves to economic reform and budget expenditure restraint during periods of low oil prices, then promptly shelving reform when oil price increases reduced fiscal pressures. This is most clearly represented by the policies of the COPEI government of Luis Herrera Campins (1978–83) and the AD government of Jaime Lusinchi (1983–88). The incoming COPEI administration inherited a bleak economic outlook with the government initially committing itself to austerity measures. Wider international circumstances left the administration with little alternative. The 1979 oil-price shock prefigured sharply declining terms of trade for commodity exporters in a period of rising international interest rates, and in an attempt to stabilise oil prices, Venezuela was forced to reduce oil production. Compounding these economic difficulties, the closure of international capital markets following the Mexican debt default in 1982 led to a foreign-exchange crisis, whilst higher international interest rates made debt repayment increasingly problematic. Massive capital flight out of Venezuela was further stimulated by low domestic interest rates and the maintenance of an overvalued bolivar. The government reacted slowly to the deteriorating economic situation, exacerbating the problems with erratic economic policies. No attempts were made to revise the indiscriminate network of subsidies and state-owned industries continued to be poorly administered, often running at astronomical operating losses.[25] In February 1983, the Herrera Campins government devalued the bolivar and imposed foreign-exchange controls in attempt to curb capital flight.[26] The tiered exchange system, known by its acronym RECADI, distributed dollars at a preferential rate according to a set of government-determined priorities with a free market in non-essential areas. The controls became a major source of corruption. The existence of (and scramble for) the preferential rate heightened macroeconomic imbalances, leading to major distortions in trade, prices and output. Incapable of meeting payments on its public-sector debt, the government was forced to declare a partial moratorium in March 1983.

The incoming Lusinchi government attempted to sustain the populist system of distribution and no adjustments in the direction of economic policy were undertaken. The differential exchange-rate system was maintained, accelerating corruption within both the private sector and the top ranks of government. Wage and price controls were imposed, intensifying the recession which had begun to take hold under Herrera Campins, generating the highest level of unemployment in Venezuela for 25 years. Between 1985 and 1988 the government pursued an expansionary policy, despite a further collapse in oil prices in 1986 of around 8 per cent of GDP. The cost of economic stimulation was mounting inflationary pressures (fuelled by a further devaluation of the bolivar in December 1986), a widening fiscal deficit and a persistent fall in international reserves. Despite having reached agreement on modification to the payments of its public-sector debts in 1987,[27] the Lusinchi government was subsequently forced to suspend principal payments to commercial banks. The outwardly buoyant economic situation, with growth averaging 4.2 per cent per year, assisted AD in the 1988 presidential election, enabling Carlos Andrés Pérez to take the presidency for a second time. Nobody anticipated the economic policies that were to come.

El Gran Viraje

Pérez constantly evoked memories of the boom period of his first government throughout the 1988 election campaign. He promised jobs, economic growth and a return to the good times. On taking office, Pérez inherited a fiscal deficit equivalent to 9 per cent of GDP, operating reserves of $300 million and debt repayments totalling $5 billion per year.[28] Naím has identified three immediate problems with which Pérez had to contend.[29] First, the government had to tackle repressed inflation, induced by price controls and successive devaluations. Second; depressed oil prices, the weak performance of the non-oil sector, capital flight and debt-servicing obligations had generated a balance-of-payments crisis, exacerbated by the foreign-exchange regime. Third, government-administered interest rates were strongly negative, the 12.5 per cent rate in 1988 encouraging borrowing to purchase foreign currency.

Contrary to all expectations, Pérez sharply altered economic direction. The first indication of the changes to come was the appointment of a cabinet dominated by politically independent, foreign-trained technocrats. This was an unprecedented move, breaking with the long established tradition of appointing mediocre political loyalists. It was a personnel decision which infuriated the President's party, AD, setting Pérez on a collision course with AD power-brokers which was finally resolved in the Party's favour, with the President's impeachment in 1993.[30] This departure from traditional appointment practices was swiftly followed by negotiations with the IMF. Although not an unprecedented move in itself, the disbursement of a $7 billion extended fund facility marked the first loan Venezuela had ever received from the IMF. The loan was intended to support a package of stabilisation and structural reform measures, designed to move Venezuela from a planned, protected economy to a free market, creating the conditions for sustainable, non-oil-based economic growth.[31] It was a drastic and unanticipated change in approach which the government introduced with exceptional speed.

Under the first stage of the adjustment, price controls were lifted on private and a host of public goods, including utilities, and a range of subsidies abolished.[32] One of the most controversial measures adopted was a 100 per cent increase on the cost of heavily subsidised domestic petrol, which led to a steep rise in public transport costs. The move met with a response of unprecedented violence, the so-called *Caracazo*.[33] According to official estimates over 400 people died – unofficially the figure is over 1,000 – as major riots fanned outwards from Caracas to major cities.[34] Exchange-rate controls were lifted and the bolivar floated, leading to an immediate 170 per cent devaluation. Interest rates were freed and moved sharply upwards from 13 per cent to 40 per cent.[35] Public spending was cut, enabling the government to curb the fiscal deficit, and legislation was introduced to reform the taxation system, including the imposition of value-added tax (VAT) to boost ordinary revenues. The administration proceeded rapidly with renegotiating the country's $19.5 billion public debt with creditor banks, in line with the debt initiative launched by US treasury secretary Nicholas Brady. After offering creditors an array of debt-repayment options, the debt composition was altered, interest-rate payments lowered and a seven-year grace period on principal repayments of the restructured loans introduced.[36] Tight fiscal and monetary policy was complemented by a series of major structural reforms. Trade was liberalised and the tariff system was reformed, with the average tariff falling from 35 per cent in 1988 to just under 10 per cent in 1989. Non-tariff barriers covering an estimated 94 per cent of local manufactures were removed and special export permits eliminated. These changes were given an institutional form through free-trade negotiations with Colombia and Venezuelan entry into the GATT. A host of state companies were scheduled for privatisation and a new foreign investment regime was put into place, with restrictions on profit remittance lifted and the stock market opened to foreign investors for the first time.

The reforms exacted a high social cost and faced opposition from nearly every sector of Venezuelan society. Industry, farming and the financial sectors remained deeply opposed to economic liberalisation, fearing the loss of economic privileges and the prospect of competition. Unions and the state administration were opposed to the privatisation process which threatened jobs and powerful vested interests in state-owned companies. The main union confederation, the AD-controlled Confederación de Trabajadores Venezolanos (CTV, Confederation of Venezuelan Workers) took the unprecedented step of calling a general strike in 1991 to support wage demands. The popular sectors opposed the package for its obviously dire economic implications, whilst the middle class encountered a sharp contraction of privileges and subsidies. AD set itself firmly against the reforms, which not only limited their clientelistic capacities and their access to government but also damaged their already dwindling levels of political support. The accelerated decline in living standards had a severe impact on the military, which in conjunction with damaging allegations of top-level military corruption and intensive politicisation, triggered the abortive coup attempt by junior officers in February 1992.[37] This break with military non-intervention in conjunction with the *Caracazo* provided a clear indication that the traditional methods of party control and interest articulation had collapsed.

Despite the political opposition to the *paquete*, its economic results were impressive. Immediately following the introduction of the adjustment programme Venezuela fell into deep recession, with real GDP contracting by 8.3 per cent in 1989. Year-end inflation leapt to 80 per cent, unemployment rose to 10 per cent and informal-sector employment rose to 42.4 per cent of total employment. However, as imports collapsed and exports (particularly of non-traditional goods) soared, the balance-of-payments deficit was eliminated, moving back into surplus at the end of 1989. Inflation fell to 36.5 per cent in 1990 and down to 31 per cent in 1991 following the correction in relative prices. In that same year, Venezuela registered GDP growth of 9.2 per cent, a performance facilitated by increased oil revenues resulting from the Gulf war. Economic growth boosted employment opportunities, leading to a decline in unemployment which fell to 7.5 per cent in 1991. However, despite its commitment to fiscal restraint and a tight monetary policy, the Pérez government used the additional oil income to finance a substantial rise in state expenditure.

In 1992, serious economic problems began to develop. Public-sector finances were strained by a fall in oil prices below the budgeted $19 per barrel to $14.9 per barrel. Despite a shortfall of $2.3 billion in earnings, public spending continued to rise – by 19.4 per cent, generating a deficit equivalent to 3.6 per cent of GDP. With privatisation failing to compensate for the revenue shortfall, the administration resorted to domestic and foreign borrowing. But political events mitigated against renewed efforts to stabilise the economy. The two military coup attempts of 1992 critically undermined investor confidence and contributed to a sharp outflow of capital. The government attempted to counter this through increasing interest rates, which created major problems of capitalisation in the banking sector whilst exacerbating debt repayment problems. The government's fiscal difficulties were compounded by increasingly conflictive relations with Congress. Plans to levy VAT and a business assets tax were rejected, as was legislation to reform the financial sector to improve regulation and open the sector to foreign participation.[38] In May 1993, Pérez was impeached when the Supreme Court lifted his congressional immunity to bring charges of corruption related to the channelling of funds to the Chamorro government in Nicaragua. An interim government headed by independent senator Ramón Velásquez presided over the deteriorating political and economic situation, guiding the country to elections in December 1993.

The Agenda Venezuela

The Presidential victory of Rafael Caldera was based on his overt opposition to the Pérez adjustment programme, which he most controversially articulated in an emergency congressional session following the February 1992 coup attempt. The presidential campaign of the octogenarian founder of the COPEI [39] promised a 'letter of intent with the Venezuelan people', as opposed to the IMF, equity and an ill-defined programme of social solidarity. Support was also based on his association with the founding of Venezuelan democracy and his image as an honest politician, in sharp contrast to the legacy of corruption in the previous Pérez administration.

Immediately on taking office, Caldera reversed the Pérez reform programme. VAT was abolished on day one of the new administration and in March 1994 the government announced its own economic plans: the Sosa programme of tax and public-spending reforms. Although initially boosting non-oil revenue, any benefits of the Sosa programme were vitiated by the collapse of the banking system in 1994 – and arguably the government's handling of the crisis. The crisis first began to break at the end of 1993 when one of Venezuela's largest banks, the Banco Latino, failed to meet clearing house requirements. In 1994, the government decided to inject public funds into a number of financial institutions in an attempt to stabilise chronic problems of undercapitalisation. The decision to intervene in up to a third of the banking sector proved enormously costly. The government borrowed heavily from the Central Bank to fund its intervention strategy, leaving the Bank operating at a loss in 1996.[40] The banking crisis triggered massive capital flight out of the country, which the government attempted to arrest through strict exchange and price controls introduced by emergency decree in June 1994. The move received extensive popular support but failed to stabilise the economic situation. Despite successive devaluations, the bolivar remained overvalued, trading on the black market at a vastly depreciated implied rate. International reserves continued to decline and the government failed to curb public expenditure. With alternatives limited, negotiations with the IMF began in 1995. In April 1996, the government announced its own stabilisation package, the *Agenda Venezuela*, backed by a $1.4 billion standby loan.

As during the initial stages of macroeconomic stabilisation under Pérez, inflation surged to a year-end total of 103 per cent as interest-rate, price and exchange controls were lifted. After depreciating rapidly, the bolivar stabilised, and in July a crawling-peg exchange system was introduced with the intention of introducing a gradual and controlled depreciation of the bolivar. Domestic petrol prices were increased fivefold and the wholesale and luxury tax which replaced VAT was increased. The privatisation programme initiated under Pérez was restarted and the government negotiated a reform of the rigid and expensive severance-payment system with business and labour.[41] In contrast to the Pérez period, this dramatic policy U-turn met with minimal popular mobilisation. There were political costs, specifically the withdrawal of government allies Movimiento al Socialismo (MAS, Movement to Socialism) from the ruling coalition, which left President Caldera reliant on AD for the passage of legislation in Congress. However, the level of popular mobilisation and the industrial relations unrest which characterised the application of the *paquete* were not repeated, giving the government extensive room for manoeuvre in economic policy.

However, as if trying to duplicate exactly the course of economic policy failure navigated by Pérez, the Caldera government continued to increase public spending as oil prices rose above their budgeted level in 1997 and investment capital from the privatisation programme and oil-sector opening flooded into the country. Confident they could survive without further IMF assistance, the administration decided not to draw on further loan facilities, freeing themselves from agreed targets and structural reform commitments, including cuts to the public-sector workforce, judicial reform and the creation of a macroeconomic stabilisation fund.[42] The result of these policy decisions was a rerun of the events of 1993 and the 1970s and 1980s. A sharp fall in the price of oil in 1998[43] plunged the country into deep economic crisis, forcing the government into a rapid reversion to tight monetary and fiscal policy. This time, austerity met with pronounced public and political opposition, which was heightened by the proximity of national elections due at the end of that year. Government efforts to raise additional fiscal revenue were constrained by a resistant Congress,[44] and efforts to curb monetary expansion met with public-sector mobilisation for wage increases and employment security. Destabilising industrial relations conflicts persisted throughout 1998 and the government's privatisation efforts encountered the same problems as that experienced by Pérez, union and congressional opposition and vested interests on the part of state administrators. Despite his pre-election commitments to social solidarity, Caldera had done little to reverse mounting income inequality. In 1995, it was estimated that 41 per cent of Venezuelans were living in critical poverty.[45] Figures for 1996 showed that 80 per cent of the Venezuelan population were earning the minimum wage, while the top 10 per cent received half of the country's earnings. In 1996, 72 per cent of household income was spent on food and beverages in comparison to just 28 per cent in 1970,[46] and despite successive increases in the minimum wage, real purchasing power declined 35 per cent between 1989 and 1995.

Paralleling the elections of 1993, the deteriorating economic situation fed into support for the most ardent opponent of adjustment measures, with the anti-IMF mantle adopted by Hugo Chávez, whose lead in opinion polls rose to over 45 per cent in July 1998, six months before the elections. A presidential victory by Chávez represented a significant challenge to the political status quo in Venezuela, and was viewed as inherently dangerous by the elite.[47] Chávez's manifesto offered not only a rejection of neoliberalism but also an overhaul of existing political institutions. Controversially, Chávez promised to abolish

Congress if supported by a popular referendum and convoke an 'organic'[48] constituent assembly. At the end of the century, Venezuela stood on the threshold of intensive change, a change clearly not in the same direction as regional neighbours. The country lacked consensus over its future economic direction, with the potential for a pacific resolution to the impasse increasingly unlikely. Economically incapable of returning to the expansionary policies of the past, Venezuelan society remained reluctant to embrace critically needed economic reforms for the future, searching for charismatic saviours to take the country back to the boom period of the 1970s.

The inability to push economic-reform measures to their logical conclusion, to stick to agreed targets and break the cycle of boom–bust economics is a product of political convenience. Fundamentally, no previous government, specifically those of Pérez and Caldera, has been capable of consolidating reform because the measures lacked support and the government had no policy-making autonomy or political legitimacy. Incapable of isolating themselves from social pressures and facing organised sectoral and political resistance, governments shied away from the coherent application of stabilisation measures, perpetuating macroeconomic imbalances, oil dependency and fiscal crisis. The central reason for this is that economic reorientation would undermine the structural preconditions of the political system's legitimacy.

Accounting for the limitations to economic reform

In his analysis of the application of free-market policies in Latin America, Hojman points to a number of variables which influence the acceptability of the measures adopted.[49] A core explanatory factor for popular approval of neoliberal reforms is a specific country's experience of the debt crisis and its aftermath. According to this position, adjustment is likely to gain support if there has been pronounced economic crisis and hyperinflation, as for example in Peru, Argentina and Brazil during the 1980s. In addition, the emergence of an entrepreneurial middle class can be a favourable factor, specifically if there is widespread recognition that the ISI model has been exhausted. Hojman acknowledges that many of these factors were not present in Venezuela. Expansionary economic policies disguised the extent of economic decline, whilst oil revenues allowed the ISI model to be sustained despite its evident exhaustion. The country had no experience of hyperinflation and the Venezuelan middle class retained a rentier mentality, dependent on the state for continued privileges, subsidies and employment.

Whilst these factors clearly go far in accounting for popular resistance to neoliberal reforms in Venezuela, there are a number of other variables which have been posited to explain the intensity of political opposition. Looking specifically at the Pérez government, Navarro and Naím have pointed to a failed communication strategy on the part of the administration.[50] According to this line of analysis, adjustment measures faced social opposition because the government failed to give any indication of the reforms to be enacted, or provide a coherent, detailed explanation to the population as to why the measures were being taken. In addition, the administration was 'remote', creating the impression it was unconcerned about the social impact of the *paquete* and the costs entailed. In sharp contrast to the economic policy U-turns of President Menem in Argentina or Fujimori in Peru, the government failed to construct a 'coalition of potential beneficiaries', rendering the administration isolated with minimal support. Arguably these factors do not hold for the Caldera administration. Whilst the government can be criticised for major policy mistakes, specifically the over-reliance on oil revenue after 1997, major efforts were made to explain to the population the severity of the economic crisis when stabilisation efforts were undertaken in 1996 and 1998. Despite this, social opposition was pronounced, particularly in 1998.

Understanding the resistance to stabilisation should take into account not only the level of popular opposition, but also the marked reluctance of the Caldera government to pursue the structural reforms initiated in 1996 and the sustained hostility of the political parties. In this respect, a central paradox emerges. Whilst both society and the parties converged in their resistance to economic reorientation, the parties were not viewed as a legitimate channel for the expression of this opposition. The delegitimisation of state and political institutions had reached critical levels by the 1990s, with strong anti-party sentiments parlaying into support for 'independent' candidates in national and state elections. Figures like Hugo Chávez embodied social antipathy to stabilisation and a resistance to the imposition of IMF-inspired and sponsored neoliberal policies. In addition, he represented a rejection of existing political practices. There are perhaps parallels here with the political and economic situation in Peru in 1992, where the victory of Alberto Fujimori in the presidential elections was based on his expressed opposition to the traditional parties and his hostility to austerity measures. On taking office, his implementation of orthodox neoliberal policies received extensive social support, despite the evident break with pre-election promises and the social costs the policies entailed. In the Venezuelan case, the ability of Pérez and Caldera (after much delay), to follow the same economic strategy was far more constrained.

Equally, it could be projected that any incoming independent in the same vein as Fujimori would be unable to carry the majority of Venezuelan society with them in a process of economic reform. There are two key, interrelated factors which underline this hypothesis. First, vested interests in the maintenance of the traditional economic model in Venezuela are entrenched. Without a substantive overhaul of state institutions (a Venezuelan equivalent of a *fujimorazo*[51]) the capacity of government to implement economic reform will be impeded. Second, there is a 'cultural resistance'[52] to neoliberalism in Venezuela. This is a legacy of the democratic transition in the country and underscores the parallel process of economic decline and political delegitimisation.

The social conditionality of Punto Fijo

The transition to democracy in Venezuela was characterised by a trade-off, sub-stantive economic protection and guarantees in exchange for a restricted form of democracy – restricted in terms of popular input, social pluralism and sec-toral autonomy. During the early stages of Venezuela's democratic experience, this was relatively easy to sustain. A number of factors account for this. The most important is favourable economic conditions. Strong economic growth in the 1960s and early 1970s allowed the state to fulfil cross-sectoral demands, impeding the emergence of class-based conflicts whilst enabling the dominant parties to maintain their *policlasista* (multi-class) constituencies. Second, Venezuelan civil society was profoundly weak, with limited experience of autonomous organisation. This facilitated AD and COPEI control of social organisation and mobilisation. Third, memories of the authoritarian period were relatively fresh, enhancing popular support for the new democratic sys-tem. As a result of the confluence of these factors, the legitimacy of the politi-cal regime and the parties was unquestioned.

Table 8.2   *National election results, Venezuela, 1978–88*

Year	Presidential candidate	Party	% of presidential vote	% of congressional vote	Abstention %
1978	L. Campins	COPEI	47	40	12.4
	L. Pinerua	AD	43	40	
	Others		10	20	
1983	J. Lusinchi	AD	57	50	12.2
	R. Caldera	COPEI	35	29	
	Others		10	21	
1988	C. Perez	AD	53	43	18.1
	E. Fernández	COPEI	40	29	
	Others		7	28	

Source: Consejo Supremo Electoral, Tomo de Eleccionnes.

Research added to the impression that Venezuelan democracy had been rapidly consolidated. Surveys by Baloyra and Martz at the end of the 1970s demonstrated pronounced levels of popular support for democracy.[53] Of those interviewed, 73 per cent expressed opposition to military takeovers and a fur-ther 70 per cent viewed political parties as playing a central role in a democra-tic system.[54] However, underlying these apparently favourable indicators were the roots of the contemporary crisis. It is evident that Venezuelan society was disaffected with the suffocating presence of the parties, yet whilst economic performance and distributional capacity was maintained, these negative evalu-ations did not translate into rejection of AD or the COPEI. So, whilst 81 per cent of respondents were of the opinion that parties were instruments of powerful minorities, 87 per cent believed politicians were dishonest and 70 per cent claimed the only concern of politicians was to win elections, AD and the COPEI maintained their electoral hegemony.[55]

These findings correlate with a time series of polling by Walsh. The key column in Table 8.3 is popular confidence in the system's capacity to resolve national problems. As these perceptions deteriorated, support for AD and the COPEI began to recede.

Table 8.3 *Time series of polling, Venezuela, 1973–90 (%)*

Year	Believe political parties are democratic	Believe politicians are honest	No confidence in the system's capacity to resolve national problems
1973	13	13	27
1983	11	11	32
1990	4	3	49

Source: F. Walsh, attitudinal survey, *Nueva Sociedad*, 121 (1992).

The pronounced deterioration of the economy at the beginning of the 1980s removed one of the key structural preconditions sustaining the dominant party system and the legitimacy of Venezuela's political institutions. As the capacity for economic redistribution deteriorated, there was no corresponding relent in demands on the state or changes in social attitudes towards the intermediary role of the state. In 1979, the Baloyra and Martz survey revealed a strong consensus cutting across social classes in favour of state intervention.[56] These attitudes have persisted through to the 1990s. A survey by the Fundación Pensamiento y Acción (FPA, Thought and Action Foundation) in 1995 revealed that only a quarter of those polled agreed with Pérez's economic reforms, a finding supported by a Mercanalysis poll which showed only 21 per cent of respondents favoured an open economy.[57] In the absence of abundant oil resources, the finances which held the model of demand aggregation and articulation together began to collapse. This can be seen in a number of areas.

First, as the availability of resources dwindled, corruption became a central social and political preoccupation, with popular opinion turning forcibly against corruption in government and the state administration.[58] This accelerated the delegitimisation of state institutions, particularly of the judiciary, the state body responsible for the administration of elections – the Consejo Supremo Electoral (Supreme Electoral Council), the parties and Congress.

Corruption was cited as the central precipitating factor for the February 1992 coup attempt by its military participants and the issue also dominated the 1993 elections. Centrally, corruption has rendered the vast majority of Venezuelan society unwilling to bear the costs of economic adjustment, which

Table 8.4   *Public opinion polling, Venezuela, 1995*

What are the most negative aspects of democracy?		In which institutions do you have the most confidence?	
Aspect	Response (%)	Ranking	Institution
Corruption	38	1	Universities
System deformation	22	2	Catholic Church
Abuses of liberty	14	3	Media
Negative social effects	11	4	Armed forces
All negative	6	5	Neighbourhood groups
Don't know	8	6	Private sector
		7	Governors
		8	Judiciary
		9	Police
		10	Unions
		11	Congress
		12	Parties

Source: Fundación Pensamiento y Acción, 1995.

are viewed as being unequally distributed. In addition, opinion polls reveal that Venezuelans continue to view their country as rich, thereby negating the acceptance of adjustment measures. The current economic crisis is viewed as a product of corruption and not as a result of the state-dominated model of economic development.[59] This can be seen as a cultural constraint on economic reform.

Secondly, dominant party affiliated organisations were no longer capable of channelling resources and benefits to members. As a result, they began to face challenges from emerging independent organisations, and their monopolistic political position was questioned. A cogent example of this was the rise of *Nuevo Sindicalismo* (New Unionism), pioneered by La Causa Radical (LCR, Radical Cause) in Bolívar state, the home of Venezuela's main extractive industries. This presented a critical challenge to the AD-dominated CTV, which attempted to defuse the rise of LCR through collaboration with industrial managers, which resulted in a round of sackings of *Nuevo Sindicalismo* members and the suspension of the Union in 1979.[60] Increasingly, the state and parties were maintaining the partidocratic model through recourse to repression. Another increasingly overt method of restricting the emergence of opposition was electoral fraud.

The limits to political reform
Although AD and the COPEI continued to dominate the electoral system, elections were marked by increasing levels of abstention. In 1978, abstention rose by 9 per cent, taking abstention into double figures for the first time in the democratic period. Despite a small drop in 1983, abstention continued its

upward trend, reaching 18 per cent in 1988 before rising to an all-time high of 40 per cent in 1993. Accounting for rising abstention, the Consejo Supremo Electoral claimed that 'electoral abstention is not only a Venezuelan phenomenon; in the majority of countries where the vote is exercised, non-participation is the conduct of the indifferent'.[61] A second interpretation is that with the opportunities to 'exit' from the dominant parties constrained by the electoral system, voters began to express hostility to AD and the COPEI through abstention. Government actions indicate a covert acknowledgement of the roots of the problem. As President, Lusinchi established a commission to examine reform of the state, known by its acronym COPRE (Comisión Presidencial para la Reforma del Estado, Presidential Commission for the Reform of the State). In its subsequent reports, the COPRE pointed to popular disenchantment with AD and the COPEI and recommended internal democratisation of the parties, a reform of electoral funding and a major overhaul of the electoral system to counter institutional delegitimisation and political alienation. At the core of the proposals was decentralisation, seen as a means of reversing the highly centralist tendencies in the political system and as a way of increasing popular participation. In addition, the COPRE pointed to the benefits of changing from the closed-block list system of voting to open, named lists under which voters could split preferences for the different tiers of elective government whilst actually knowing who they were electing. This would force representatives to shift the focus of their loyalties from the party elite to constituents. Lusinchi shelved the recommendations, opting to maintain both the expansionary economic model of the past and its antidemocratic political counterpart.

On taking office in 1989, incoming President Pérez not only introduced a radical reorientation of economic policy, but he also acted on the COPRE reports. Under legislation introduced in 1989 the closed-block list system was abolished and decentralisation introduced. State governors and mayors were elected by direct, secret vote under the simple plurality system with national- and state-level elections separated. The move was bitterly opposed by the President's own party. In the first governorship elections in 1989 minority opposition parties were able, for the first time, to consolidate regional strongholds. LCR won the governorship of Bolívar state and the MAS took control in Aragua state. Both parties consolidated this hold in the second set of elections in 1992, with LCR retaining Bolívar and the MAS expanding their number of governorships to three. Both parties also made slow but significant advances in the mayoral elections, with the MAS gaining 15.5 per cent of the vote in 1989 and LCR gaining just 1.7 per cent, improving to 12.4 per cent and 7.3 per cent respectively in 1992. Of acute importance, LCR won the mayoralty of Caracas, taking control of local government in the capital.[62]

With political and economic reform running conjuncturally, Pérez allowed political opposition to his economic policy to be directed through the electoral system, to the detriment of the dominant parties' interests. This served to accelerate AD opposition to their own President. The electoral reforms had a further consequence which is of acute importance in understanding the limits to the autonomy of President Caldera and future Venezuelan governments. As a result of the introduction of open, named voting in national elections, there was a marked change in the distribution of political authority in the country. In 1993, congressional results demonstrated the breakdown of the traditional two-party system.

Table 8.5   *Presidential and Congressional elections, Venezuela, 1993*

Presidential election results, 1993		
Candidate	*Party*	*%*
R. Caldera	Convergencia	30.4
C. Fermín	AD	23.6
O. Alvarez Paz	COPEI	22.7
A. Velásquez	Causa R.	21.9

Congressional results, 1993		
Party	*Deputies*	*Senators*
AD	53	18
COPEI	48	14
Causa R	37	9
Convergencia	22	5
MAS	22	4
Independents	11	3
Minorities	10	0
Total	203	53[a]

Note: a   Excluding life senators.
Source: Consejo Supremo Electoral, Tomo de Elecciones.

In the absence of a congressional majority, President Caldera sought to 'salvage'[63] the traditional institutional pact with AD. In exchange the government did not impinge on AD's vested interests in state institutions. As a result, there was no overhaul of the corrupt judicial system, no consolidation of the electoral reforms introduced under Pérez and limited progress on privatisation. AD therefore managed to safeguard its clientelistic capacities and placements.

Applying economic reform in Venezuela therefore requires not only overcoming the ingrained statist legacy amongst the wider population, but also the entrenched vested interests of the dominant parties. This will not be easy. Recent research on electoral fraud points to the limitations on displacing AD and the COPEI despite their acute unpopularity, through democratic mechanisms.[64] Through their control of the electoral administration, AD and the COPEI have constantly conspired against the expression of the popular vote through gerrymandering, vote stealing and intimidation. Their determination to remain part of the political mainstream through recourse to undemocratic methods has severely destabilised the political system. For the first time in Venezuelan democratic history, the results of elections were openly challenged in 1993 by LCR, who claimed their candidate Andrés Velásquez had won.[65] Electoral fraud has also accelerated abstention: people no longer participate in Venezuelan elections, as they do not believe their vote will be recognised. Despite the efforts at political reform, the crisis of legitimacy and participation has not been assuaged. Abstention not only rose precipitously in the 1993 elections, but it has also become a marked feature of state elections, with nearly half of the electorate abstaining in the state elections of 1995. The machinations of the traditional parties also underlie support for Hugo Chávez in the run up to the 1998 election, with his proposal for a constituent assembly widely seen as the only method of overcoming dominant party control.[66]

By way of a brief conclusion

Despite an enviable array of natural resources and massive development potential, nearly half of the Venezuelan population live in critical poverty, there has been a dramatic reversal in social indices and basic public services have collapsed. At the same time nearly a third of the country's budget is dedicated to debt-service payments, a product of chronic economic mismanagement. Political institutions have no credibility and the legitimacy of government continues to be called into question. There is no consensus on the future direction of the country, in either economic or political terms. Without a major overhaul, a radical – perhaps even revolutionary – change to the existing political structures this dire economic situation will be maintained. In the absence of real political pluralism and the evolution of legitimate channels of interest articulation to negotiate the division and share the costs of economic reorientation, there will be no economic pluralism or reform in Venezuela. As a result, oil dependency and the appalling social effects of boom–bust growth cycles will be maintained.

Notes

1 With the exception of a brief three-year democratic period, the so-called *Trienio*, between 1945 and 1948.
2 See J. McCoy and W. Smith, *Venezuelan Democracy under Pressure* (New Brunswick, North–South Centre, 1995); M. Naím and R. Pinango, *El caso venezolano: Una ilusión de armonía* (Caracas, Ediciones IESA, 1984); D. Urbaneja, *Pueblo y petróleo en la política venezolana del siglo XX* (Caracas, CEPET, 1992); M. Granier and G. Yepes, *Más y mejor democracia* (Caracas, Roraima, 1987); R. Leon, *Los efectos perversos del petróleo* (Caracas, Capriles, 1990); and L. Goodman *et al.* (eds), *Lessons of the Venezuelan Experience* (Washington, Woodrow Wilson Centre Press, 1995).
3 The so-called 'Dutch disease', under which an overabundance of foreign exchange leads to a real appreciation of the domestic currency.
4 Registered in 1992. See the Economist Intelligence Unit, *Country Report, Venezuela 1991–1992* (London, EIU, 1992).

5 In 1991, the state oil company Petróleos de Venezuela (PdVSA) announced a new $65 billion investment plan, of which a third of capital was to come from the private sector.

6 B. Mommer and A. Baptista, *El petróleo en el pensamiento económico de Venezuela: Un ensayo* (Caracas, Ediciones IESA, 1992).

7 In 1996, oil revenue accounted for 59 per cent of government revenue and 70 per cent of export earnings.

8 T. L. Karl, 'Petroleum and Political Pacts: The Transition to Democracy in Venezuela', *Latin American Research Review*, 23:3 (1986).

9 Both AD (the Social Democrats) and the COPEI (Christian Democrats) emerged from the student opposition movement in 1928. For a discussion of political events in this period, see R. Alexander, *Rómulo Betancourt and the Transformation of Venezuela* (New Brunswick, Transaction Books, 1982); *The Venezuelan Democratic Revolution* (New Brunswick, Rutgers University Press, 1964); and Urbaneja, *Pueblo y petróleo*.

10 Interview with E. Santana of the School of Neighbours, in J. Buxton, 'The Venezuelan Party System 1988–1995, With Reference to the Rise and Decline of Radical Cause', Ph.D. Thesis, London School of Economics, 1998.

11 For a favourable evaluation of Venezuelan democracy see D. Levine, *Conflict and Political Change in Venezuela* (Princeton, Princeton University Press, 1973).

12 J. Rey cited in M. Kornblith, 'La crisis del sistema político venezolano', *Nueva Sociedad*, 140.

13 Kornblith, 'La crisis'.

14 Granier and Yepes, *Más y mejor democracia*.

15 See J. McCoy, 'Labour and the State in a Party Mediated Democracy', *Latin American Research Review*, 24 (1988); C. Bergquist, *Labour in Latin America* (Stanford, Stanford University Press, 1986); and D. Hellinger, 'Causa R and Nuevo Sindicalismo in Venezuela', *Latin American Perspectives*, 90:23, no. 3 (1996).

16 M. Coppedge, *Strong Parties and Lame Ducks: Presidential Partyarchy and Factionalism in Venezuela* (Stanford, Stanford University Press, 1994). See also D. Hellinger, *Venezuela: Tarnished Democracy* (Boulder, Westview, 1991).

17 AD and the COPEI moved towards the so-called *coincidencia* – working together in areas of common interest in the early 1960s in order to stifle Communist Party influence in the union movement. *Coincidencia* became a functional necessity following internal splits in AD in the 1960s.

18 R. Betancourt, *Venezuela's Oil* (London, Allen and Unwin, 1978).

19 The guerrilla conflict – motivated by events in Cuba – began in the early 1960s, led by disaffected sections of the AD youth wing (who were expelled after voicing opposition to the economic agreements with the private sector) and the Venezuelan Communist Party. The uprising generated little popular support and failed to present any major challenge to the new regime.

20 For an analysis of partisan alignment in Venezuela see A. Torres, *La experiencia política en una democracia partidista joven: El caso de Venezuela* Universidad Simón Bolívar (Caracas) paper 29 (1980).

21 From $2 per barrel to $14 per barrel over a one-year period.

22 M. Naím, 'The Launching of Radical Policy Changes, 1989–1991', in J. Tulchin and G. Bland (eds), *Venezuela in the Wake of Radical Reform* (Boulder, Lynne Rienner, 1993).

23 F. Jongkind, 'Venezuelan Industry Under the New Conditions of the 1989 Economic Policy', *European Review of Latin American and Caribbean Studies*, 54 (1993).

24 Jongkind, 'Venezuelan industry'.

25 For an analysis of the operations of the state-owned enterprises see the chapter by J. Kelly in Naím and Pinango, *El caso venezolano*.

26 Devaluation has traditionally been used as a means of restoring fiscal balance by increasing the local currency equivalent of each dollar derived from oil exports. Benefits of devaluation were, however, vitiated by the maintenance of subsidies which continued to cover all sectors of Venezuelan society.

27 This was negotiated without recourse to the IMF or World Bank.

28 The World Bank estimated that Venezuela's total stock of debt in 1989 stood at $34.1 billion.
29 M. Naím in Tulchin and Bland (eds), *Venezuela in the Wake of Radical Reform.*
30 Whilst Pérez was arrested on charges of corruption, according to many observers and local journalists the decision to prosecute the President was politically motivated (by his own party
   according to Pérez), in order to derail his reforms. See W. Smith and J. McCoy, 'Deconsoli-
   dación o reequilibrio democrático en Venezuela', *Nueva Sociedad*, 140 (1995). For an interesting, although obviously biased account see the collection of interviews and press reports
   supportive of Pérez in the collection edited by J. Catala, *El juicio político al ex-presidente de
   Venezuela Carlos Andrés Pérez: Verdades y mentiras en el juicio oral* (Caracas, Centauro, 1995).
31 For a detailed analysis of the structural adjustment package see M. Naím, *Paper Tigers and
   Minotaurs: The Politics of Venezuela's Economic Reforms* (Washington, DC, Carnegie Endowment for International Peace, 1993).
32 Indirect subsidies were replaced by targeting, a novel concept in Venezuela. Unfortunately this
   lack of experience and bureaucratic inefficiency meant that distribution was poor.
33 The price increase was chronically mistimed by being imposed at the end of the month – when
   finances are limited for the majority of Venezuelans, pending pay cheques at the beginning of
   the following month.
34 L. Salamanca, 'Venezuela: La crisis del rentismo', *Nueva Sociedad*, 131 (1994).
35 The Supreme Court subsequently annulled the liberalisation decree, forcing the government to
   reimpose interest-rate controls.
36 There had been a series of negotiations on the payment of the public-sector debt under the Lusinchi government in 1986. Further restructuring was required when Venezuela found it impossible to fulfil the revised conditions.
37 A nationalist group within the military had been planning a military coup since 1983. The coup
   attempt was launched in 1992 when the political situation was sen as clearly favourable, given
   the delegitimisation of state institutions and mass hostility to the economic reform package. See
   the chapter by F. Aguero in McCoy and Smith, *Venezuelan Democracy under Pressure.*
38 The financial sector was characterised by inadequate regulation and dangerously high levels of
   undercapitalisation, resulting from the build-up of bad debts, corruption and risky lending
   strategies.
39 Caldera split from the COPEI, the party he founded in 1928, when he was not selected as the
   party's presidential candidate for the 1993 elections and as the COPEI adopted a policy of
   offering constructive support to Pérez. Caldera went on to establish his own 17-party coalition
   organisation, Convergencia.
40 In December, Congress approved legislation allowing the government to refinance its debts
   with the bank through the placement of a $3.9 billion mega-bond.
41 Under the terms of the agreement the government was to pay $8 billion of labour liabilities over
   the following five years.
42 The aim of the macroeconomic stabilisation fund is to smooth the flow of fiscal revenue in periods of higher-than-budgeted oil prices.
43 The slump in oil prices in 1998 was related to overproduction by members and non-members
   of the Orgnization of Petroleum-Exporting Countries (OPEC), a mild winter in the northern
   hemisphere and the South-East Asian economic crisis.
44 Through, for example, the acceleration of the privatisation process and ironically, the reimpo-
   sition of VAT.
45 *VenEconomía 1995* (Caracas, 1995), pp. 53–6.
46 Economist Intelligence Unit, *Country Report, Venezuela 1996–7* (London, EIU, 1997).
47 Chávez was subject to a host of insults and allegations that he was attempting to spark a civil
   war in Venezuela. Former COPEI presidential candidate Eduardo Fernández claimed Chávez
   was the Venezuelan equivalent of the Libyan leader Colonel Gaddafi, and Pérez´s former
   Defence Minister Radames Muñoz León began mobilising top-level military figures in the event
   of a possible coup attempt by Chávez – or arguably, a coup if Chávez won the elections.
48 In the event of an organic constituent assembly being called, it would assume the powers of

Congress, unlike a derivative constituent assembly, which would work on redrafting the Constitution while Congress continued to sit.

49 D. Hojman, 'The Political Economy of Recent Conversion to Market Economics in Latin America', *Journal of Latin American Studies*, 26 (1994).

50 J. Navarro, 'Reversal of Fortune: The Ephemeral Success of Adjustment in Venezuela Between 1989 and 1993' (Caracas, World Bank Project on Governance and Successful Adjustment in Venezuela, 1994); and Naím, *Paper Tigers and Minotaurs*.

51 See Chapter 5.

52 A. Romero, 'Rearranging the Deck Chairs on the Titanic: The Agony of Democracy in Venezuela', *Latin American Research Review*, 32:1 (1997).

53 E. Baloyra and J. Martz, *Political Attitudes in Venezuela: Societal Cleavages and Political Opinion* (Texas, University of Texas Press, 1979).

54 Baloyra and Martz, *Political Attitudes in Venezuela*, p. 51.

55 Baloyra and Martz, *Political Attutudes in Venezuela*, p. 72.

56 Baloyra and Martz, *Political Attitudes in Venezuela*, p. 58.

57 Fundación Pensamiento y Acción, *Cultura democrática en Venezuela: Informe analítico de los resultados de una encuesta de opinión pública* (Caracas, FPA, January 1996). Mercanalysis poll in *El Nacional*, 21 June 1995.

58 For details of the extent of corruption in Venezuela see the three-volume *Diccionario de la corrupción en Venezuela* (Caracas, Ediciones Capriles, various years), which leaves the reader in no doubt as to the extent of corruption within the Venezuelan state and institutions.

59 According to a survey by Conciencia 21 of June 1995, 91 per cent of those surveyed believed the country was very rich. Romero, 'Rearranging the Deck Chairs', pp. 194–5.

60 For a discussion of these events see F. Sesto, *Pablo Medina en entrevista* (Caracas, Ediciones del Agua Mansa, 1993),

61 A retrospective analysis of abstention trends in Venezuela in Consejo Supremo Electoral (CSE), *Elecciones de 1995*, Caracas, CSE, 1995.

62 This translated into 9 mayoralties for the MAS in 1989 and 2 for LCR, 19 for the MAS and 5 for LCR in 1992.

63 H. Sonntag, 'Venezuela, el difícil curso de la transicíon', *Nueva Sociedad*, 151 (1997).

64 Buxton, *Venezuelan Party System*.

65 For evidence of electoral fraud and an analysis of how it is committed see Buxton, *Venezuelan Party System*, Chapter 3.

66 In May 1998, AD and the COPEI used their congressional majority to separate the national elections, so congressional elections would be held in November and the presidential elections in December. This was motivated by concern that running the elections conjuncturally would lead to a landslide victory by Chávez.

Appendix: Virtual Latin America

This section offers a guide to the various Web sites relevant to issues and subjects discussed in this book and the sister volume, *Developments in Latin American political economy: states, markets and actors*. Whilst clearly it would be impossible to be comprehensive in our listing, we hope to provide a general guide to some of the most important sites, to either complement Web sites already used by those studying the region or as a means of encouraging any remaining 'webphobes'. Given the paucity of attention Latin America receives in the British media, the Internet has become an invaluable source of information on the region and should be viewed as a critical tool of research. Whilst many of the country-specific Web sites are in Portugese and Spanish, there are also English sites which can be accessed. The addresses given were correct at the time of going to print and address changes should be taken as inevitable.

Perhaps the most useful and informative Web site for any Latin Americanist is the University of Texas LANIC page. This provides access to extensive links on a variety of Latin America-specific topics, which are broken down in a user-friendly manner either by country or subject. For a specific country, insert the name at the end of the address. So, for example, for Peru this would be:

www.lanic.utexas.edu/la/peru/

As an example of a search by topic, the human rights page, which provides links to international organisations and country-specific human rights groups, can be found at:

http://info.lanic.utexas.edu/la/region/hrights/

From this site you can access Amnesty International, Human Rights Watch, the Peacenet Directory of Human Rights resources, the US Department of State Country Report on Human Rights Practices and the DIANA international human rights database:

http://www.law.uc.edu:81/Diana/index.html.

The country-specific human rights pages are also extensive. See, for example, the Argentine human rights page, the Vanished Gallery, at:

http://www.yendor.com/vanished/

or the Colombian support network:

http://www.igc.apc.org/csn/index.html

For those interested in following up gender issues, we recommend you consult:

http://info.lanic.utexas.edu/la/region/women/

On the military, see:

http://info.lanic.utexas.edu/la/region/military/

On the environment:

http://info.lanic.utexas.edu/la/region/environment/

On indigenous groups, go to:

http://info.lanic.utexas.edu/la/region/indigenous/

And for access to the pages of financial and economic institutions see:

http://info.lanic.utexas.edu/la/region/economic/

In the government and political science section (which can be accessed directly at http://info.lanic.utexas.edu/la/region/government/) there is an extensive list of country resources. With links from this page to detailed sites on constitutions, political parties, Congress, government departments and the presidency, it is an invaluble site. As an example, the Argentine Constitution can be accessed through this site, or directly at:

http://reality.sgi.com/employees/.../argentina/Constitucion/ctoc.html

The Brazilian Constitution at:

http://www.rede-brasil.com/normas.html

For the Chilean Constitution, go to:

http://www.georgetown.edu/LatAmer...al/Constitutions/Chile/chile.html

For Peru, access:

http://www.georgetown.edu/LatAmer...al/Constitutions/Peru/peru.html

and for Uruguay:

http://www.georgetown.edu/LatAmer...al/Constitutions/Uruguay/uruguay.html

The government and political science page also provides links to recent election results in Latin America, a directory of all parties in the various countries and links to their home pages. The sites also provide information on public-opinion polling, pressure groups and laws governing political parties. See, for example:

wysiwyg://146/http://www.agora.stm.it/elections/election/argentina.htm
wysiwyg://157/http://www.agora.stm.it/elections/election/brazil.htm
wysiwyg://37/http://www.agora.stm.it/elections/election/chile.htm
wysiwyg://64/http://www.agora.stm.it/elections/election/colombia.htm
wysiwyg://81/http://www.agora.stm.it/elections/election/mexico.htm
wysiwyg://101/http://www.agora.stm.it/elections/election/peru.htm
wysiwyg://120/http://www.agora.stm.it/elections/election/uruguay.htm
wysiwyg://149/http://www.agora.stm.it/elections/election/venezuela.htm

If you require detailed psephological and political information, the above sites are complemented by the excellent Political Database of the Americas and the Lijphart Election Archive, the latter providing election results from the 1940s. The Political Database of the Americas can be found at:

http://www.georgetown.edu/pdba/

and the various country archives on the Lijphart site can be located at:

http://dodgson.ucsd.edu/lij/argn.html   for Argentina

http://dodgson.ucsd.edu/lij/chle.html   for Chile
http://dodgson.ucsd.edu/lij/clba.html   for Colombia
http://dodgson.ucsd.edu/lij/mxco.html   for Mexico
http://dodgson.ucsd.edu/lij/peru.html   for Peru

All Latin American countries covered in this book have developed their own 'virtual tours'of Congress and the presidency. These visually impressive Web sites provide detailed information on the relationship between the separate branches of the state, review forthcoming legislation, give historical information for visitors and provide graphs to demonstrate the breakdown of political power in the Legislative Assembly. Tour the Chilean, Colombian, Mexican and Peruvian Congresses at:

http//www.congreso.cl/camara/camara.html explanation of parl
http://www.camara-de-representantes.gov.co/
http://www.senado.gob.mx/
http://www.congreso.gob.pe/index.htm

The Venezuelan congresssional Web site, SAIL, allows surfers to request specific pieces of legislation:

http://www.internet.ve/sail/sv/home.html

In addition to congressional Web sites, there is extensive provision of government Web sites which give access to detailed information on government departments, legislation and budgets. A good example is the Peruvian government Web site at:

http://ekeko.rcp.net.pe/rcp/rcp-gob.shtml

For information on Latin American political personalities, we recommend a visit to the Cable News Network (CNN) profile page. Information on a specific president or politician can be accessed through the addition of the name at the end of the address. So, for example, information on Argentine President Carlos Menem can be found at:

http://cnn.com/resources/newsmakers/world/samerica/menem.html

The *Washington Post* has an extensive archive of back issues covering Latin American-related topics and news. This can be accessed at the following address, with the relevant country name inserted at the end of the address (here using Mexico as an example):

http://www/washingtonpost.com/wp-srv/inatl/longterm/wordlref/country/mexico.htm

The site also has links to back copies of Associated Press reports on Latin America, the CIA World Factbook and US State Department Notes. These latter two sites are particularly recommended as they provide detailed political, historical, geographic, social and economic information on all Latin American countries. For direct access to the CIA factbook page, use the following address with the relevant country abbreviation at the end, so for Peru, go to:

www.odci.gov/cia/publications/factbook/pe.html

For details of Latin American research centres and for access to exhaustive research findings on a broad range of topics and a variety of publications, visit the Consejo Latinoamericano de Ciencias Sociales (CLACSO, Latin American Council for the Social Sciences) at:

gopher://lanic.utexas.edu:70/00/la/region/clacso/about

and for the Centro Latinoamericano de Administración para el Desarrollo (CLAD, Latin American Administration Centre for Development) public-sector modernisation project go to:

gopher://lanic.utexas.edu:70/00/la/region/clad/about

CEPAL, the UN Economic Commission for Latin America and the Caribbean, is located at:

http://www.eclac.cl/

with this site providing access to CEPAL reports and archives.

In terms of the core political and economic international actors in Latin America, we can recommend the following sites for information on projects in the region and the role of the relevant external agent. For the Inter American Development Bank (IDB):

http://www/iadb.org/exr/english/index_english.htmv

or access the country directory at:

http://database.iadb.org/INT/_BRPTNET/brptpubframe.htm

The IDB site also has a site called 'Links to the Americas', which gives access to all sorts of relevant information:

http://iadb.org/common/links/links_americas.htm

The World Bank and International Monetary Fund (IMF) can be found at:

http://www.wordlbank.org/ and http://www.imf.org/

The UN Economic Commission for Latin America (ECLAC) has a really good site, with papers available for downloading:

http://www.eclac.cl

Information on the major trading blocs is abundant. For the NAFTA, go through LANIC to Mexico in the country index and access the section entitled 'NAFTA Resources'. The Mexican Embassy in London also has a site with a good range of links:
http://www.demon.co.uk/mexuk

For the Mercosur, try:

http://www.geocities.com/WallStreet/Floor/2089/Mercosurhome.html

as well as the country pages from LANIC.
For documents on the Summit of the Americas, go to:

http://www.miami.edu/nsc/summit/summit.htm

One of the great benefits of the Internet is that the daily newspapers in Latin America can be accessed and read on the day of publication. Whilst clearly the majority of these are in the domestic language, there are a number of excellent English language newspapers. For example, read the *Colombia Post* at:

http:/www.colombiapost.com/

The Argentine English Language daily the *Buenos Aires Herald* can be found at:

http://www.buenosairesherald.com/

and the Chilean English newspaper

http://www.chip.cl/

The main Colombian dailies *El Mundo*, *El País* and *El Tiempo* can be accessed at:

http://www.elmundo.com/
http://www.elpais-cali.com/actual/dia/diario.htm
http://www.eureka.com.co/noticias/

The Peruvian dailies *El Comercio* and *Expresso* are at:

http://www.elcomercioperu.com.pe/
http://www.expresso.com/pe/

The Mexican financial journal *Economista* and the daily *Excelsior* are at:

http://www.economista.com.mx/
http://www.excelsior.com.mx/

For the main Argentine dailies, see *Clarín* and *La Nación*:

http://www.clarin.com/
http://www.lanacion.com.ar/

and for Chile, *El Mercurio* and *La Epoca* are located at:

http://www.mercurio.cl/
http://www.laepoca.cl

The best method of accessing magazine and newspaper information for all Latin American countries is to use Yahoo, with the regional country page providing access to all publications. Yahoo country pages can be located at:

http://www.yahoo.com/Regional/countries/colombia
http://www.yahoo.com/Regional/countries/peru

etc.

The country pages also provide links to a range of sites such as universities, travel, social indices and government Web sites. Military Web sites can also be accessed from the country pages. These provide detailed organisational, expenditure and 'mission' information. See, for example, the Venezuelan navy and armed forces at:

http://www.armada.mil.ve/
http//ejercito.ven.net/

For information on military expenditure in the region, or for a discussion of 'military themes', visit:

http://www.sipri.se/projects/milex/introduction.html
http://info.lanic.utexas.edu/la/region/military/
http://www.geocities.com.capitolhill/7109/carlos.html

Search engines like Yahoo are also helpful in terms of tracking down relatively obscure pages such as those of guerrilla groups. For detailed information on the Mexican Zapatista movement, the Zapatista Net of Autonomy and Liberation is an informative, comprehensive Web site, with links to a range of Zapatista-related topics:

http://www.actlabe.utexas.edu/~zapatistas/guide.html

and

wysiwyg://89/http://spin.com.mx/~floresu/FZLN/

The EZLN web page can be found at:

http://www.ezln.org/

and for information on the Colombian FARC, visit:

http://www.constrast.org/mirrors/farc/

Extensive information on travel, social sciences, humanities and social indices can be accessed via Yahoo, and the country pages are also another method of accessing congressional and presidential Web pages, as well as information on the military, NGOs and human rights.

Another useful resource is the Stanford Virtual Library at:

http://vlib.stanford.edu//Overview.html

Select bibliography

Chapter 1: Brazil

Abranches, S. H., 'O dilema político–institucional brasileiro', in J. P. Dos Reis Velloso (ed.), *Modernização política e desenvolvimento*, Rio de Janeiro, José Olympio Editora, 1990.

Baer, W., *The Brazilian Economy: Growth and Development*, Westport, Praeger, 1995.

Barreto, C., 'Physiologism: A Political Disease Undermining Democratic and Economic Developments in Brazil', M.Sc. dissertation, Department of Government, London School of Economics and Political Science, 1997.

Berins Collier, R. and J. Mahoney, 'Adding Collective Actors to Collective Outcomes: Labor and Recent Democratization in South America and Southern Europe', *Comparative Politics*, 29 (1997).

M. C. Cacciamali, 'The Growing Inequality in Income Distribution in Brazil', in M. J. F. Willumsen and E. Gianetti da Fonseca (eds), *The Brazilian Economy: Structure and Performance in Recent Decades*, Miami, North–South Center, 1996.

Cammack, P., 'Resurgent Democracy: Threat and Promise', *New Left Review*, 157 (1986).

Cammack, P., 'Brazilian Party Politics, 1945–87: Continuities and Discontinuities', in V. Randall (ed.), *Political Parties in the Third World*, London, Sage, 1988.

Chaui, M. 'A quand la démocratie au Brésil?', in Centre National de la Recherche Scientifique, *Quel avenir pour la démocratie en Amérique Latine?*, Paris, Editions du CNRS, 1989.

Dos Santos, W. G., 'Modernização política: Algumas questões pós-Constituinte', in J. P. Dos Reis Velloso (ed.), *Modernização política e desenvolvimento*, Rio de Janeiro, José Olympio Editora, 1990.

Faoro, R., *Os donos do poder: Formação do patronato político brasileiro*, São Paulo, Editora Globo, 1975.

Ferreira, F. and J. Litchfield, 'Growing Apart: Inequality and Poverty Trends in Brazil in the 1980s', LSE / STICERD Discussion Paper 23 (1996).

Figueiredo, A. C. and F. Limongi, 'Mudança constitucional, desempenho do Legislativo e consolidação institucional', *Revista de Ciências Sociais*, 29:10 (1995).

Hagopian, F., *Traditional Politics and Regime Change in Brazil*, Cambridge, Cambridge University Press, 1996.

Keck, M., *The Workers' Party and Democratization in Brazil*, New Haven, Yale University Press, 1989.

Kinzo, M., 'Party Politics, Executive–Legislative Relations and the Constitutional Reforms in Brazil', paper presented at the conference on 'The Economic, Social and Political Consequences of the Stabilisation Plan in Brazil', London, Institute of Latin American Studies, (ILAS) 1996.

Lamounier, B., 'Brazil at an Impasse', *Journal of Democracy*, 5:3 (1994).

Levine, D., 'Paradigm Lost: Dependency to Democracy', *World Politics*, 40 (1987).

Macedo, R. and F. Barbosa, 'Brazil: Instability and Macroeconomic Policies', in M. J. F. Willumsen and E. Gianetti da Fonseca (eds), *The Brazilian Economy: Structure and Performance in Recent Decades*, Miami, North–South Center, 1996.

Mainwaring, S., 'Politicians, Parties and Electoral Systems: Brazil in Comparative Perspective', *Comparative Politics* (1991).

Mainwaring, S., 'Brazilian Party Underdevelopment in Comparative Perspective', *Political Science Quarterly*, 107:4 (1992).

Mainwaring, S., 'Brazil: Weak Parties, Feckless Democracy', in S. Mainwaring and T. Scully (eds), *Building Democratic Institutions: Party Systems in Latin America*, Stanford CA, Stanford University Press, 1995.

Mainwaring, S. 'Democracy in Brazil and the Southern Cone: Achievements and Problems', *Journal of Interamerican Studies and World Affairs*, 37:1 (1995).

Malan, P. and R. Bonelli, 'The Success of Growth Policies in Brazil', in S. Teitel (ed.), *Toward a New Development Strategy for Latin America*, Washington DC, Inter-American Development Bank ADB, 1992.

Martínez-Lara, J., *Building Democracy in Brazil: The Politics of Constitutional Change, 1985–95*, London, Macmillan, 1996.

Moreira Alves, M. H., 'Trade Unions in Brazil: A Search for Autonomy and Organization', in E. Epstein (ed.), *Labor, Autonomy and the State in Latin America*, Boston, Unwin Hyman, 1989.

Panizza, F. and A. Barahona de Brito, 'The Politics of Human Rights in Democratic Brazil', *Democratization*, 5:4 (1998).

Payne, L., *Brazilian Industralists and Democratic Change*, Baltimore, Johns Hopkins University Press, 1993.

Power, T., 'Why Brazil Slept: The Search for Political Institutions, 1985–1997', paper prepared for delivery at the meeting of the Latin American Studies Association, Gudalajara, Mexico, 1997.

Rabello de Castro, P. and M. Ronci, 'Sixty Years of Populism in Brazil', in R. Dornbusch and S. Edwards (eds), *The Macroeconomics of Populism in Latin America*, Chicago and London, University of Chicago Press, 1991.

Rezende, F., 'The Brazilian Economy: Recent Developments and Future Prospects', *International Affairs*, 74:3 (1998).

Roett, R., *Brazil: Politics in a Patrimonial Society*, New York, Praeger, 1984.

Roett, R. and S. Kaufmann (eds), *Brazil Under Cardoso*, Boulder, Lynne Rienner, 1997.

Schneider, R., *Brazil: Culture and Politics in a New Industrial Powerhouse*, Boulder, Westview, 1996.

Schönleitner, G., 'Poverty and Inequality in Brazil: Obstacles to Economic Development and Democratic Consolidation?', mimeo, London School of Economics, 1997.

Selcher, W., 'Contradictions, Dilemmas and Actors in Brazil's *Abertura*, 1979–1985', in W. A. Selcher (ed.), *Political Liberalization in Brazil*, Boulder and London, Westview, 1986.

Selcher, W. A. (ed.), *Political Liberalization in Brazil*, Boulder and London, Westview, 1986.

Share, D. and S. Mainwaring, 'Transitions Through Transaction: Democratization in Brazil and Spain', in W. A. Selcher (ed.), *Political Liberalization in Brazil*, Boulder and London, Westview, 1986.

Skidmore, T., *Politics in Brazil, 1930–1964: An Experiment in Democracy*, New York, Oxford University Press, 1967.

Skidmore, T., *The Politics of Military Rule in Brazil, 1964–85*, New York, Oxford University Press, 1988.

Sola, L., 'Heterodox Shock in Brazil: Técnicos, Politicians and Democracy', *Journal of Latin American Studies*, 23 (1991).

Sola, L., 'The State, Structural Reform and Democratization in Brazil', in W. C. Smith, C. H. Acuña and E. Gamarra (eds), *Democracy, Markets and Structural Reform in Latin America*, Miami, North–South Center and Transaction, 1993.

Stepan, A., *Democratizing Brazil: Problems of Transition and Consolidation*, New York / Oxford, Oxford University Press, 1989.

Stepan, A., *Rethinking Military Politics: Brazil and the Southern Cone*, Princeton, Princeton University Press, 1988.

Weyland, K., 'The Rise and Fall of President Collor and its Impact on Brazilian Democracy', *Journal of Interamerican Studies and World Affairs*, 35:1 (1993).

Weyland, K., *Democracy Without Equity: Failures of Reform in Brazil*, Pittsburgh, Pittsburgh University Press, 1996.

Chapter 2: Argentina

Acuña, C. H., 'Politics and Economics in the Argentina of the Nineties (Or, Why the Future Is No Longer What It Used To Be', in W. C. Smith, C. H. Acuña and E. A. Gamarra (eds), *Democracy, Markets and Structural Reform in Latin America: Argentina, Bolivia, Brazil, Chile and Mexico*, North–South Center, Miami, University of Miami and Transaction, 1994.

Acuña, C. H. (ed.), *La nueva matriz política argentina*, Buenos Aires, Ediciones Nueva Visión, 1995.

Adelman, J. (ed.), *Essays in Argentine Labour History, 1870 to 1930*, London, Macmillan, 1992.

Azpiazu, D., E. Basualdo and M. Kavisse, *El nuevo poder económico en la Argentina de los años 80*, Buenos Aires, Editorial Legasa, 1986.

Azpiazu, D. and B. Kosacoff, *La industria argentina: Desarrollo y cambios estructurales*, Buenos Aires, Centro Editor de América Latina, 1989.

Azpiazu, D. and A. Vispo, 'Some Lessons of the Argentine Privatization Process', *CEPAL Review*, 54 (1994).

Bustos, P. (ed.), *Más allá de la estabilidad: Argentina en la epoca de la globalización y la regionalización*, Buenos Aires, Fundación Friedrich Ebert, 1995.

Calvert, P., 'Privatisation in Argentina', *Bulletin of Latin American Research*, 15:2 (1996).

Calvert, P. and Calvert, S., *Argentina: Political Culture and Instability*, Basingstoke, Macmillan, 1989.

Canitrot, A., 'Teoría y práctica del liberalismo: Política anti-inflacionaria y apertura económica en la Argentina', *Desarrollo Económico*, 21:82 (1981).

Canitrot, A., 'Crisis and Transformation of the Argentine State (1978–1992)', in W. C. Smith, C. H. Acuña and E. A. Gamarra (eds), *Democracy, Markets and Structural Reform in Latin America: Argentina, Bolivia, Brazil, Chile and Mexico*, North–South Center, Miami, University of Miami and Transaction, 1993.

Cavallo, D. and R. Domenech, 'Las políticas macroeconómicas y el tipo de cambio real: Argentina, 1913–84', *Desarrollo Económico*, 28:3 (1988).

Ciría, A., *Parties and Power in Modern Argentina, 1930–1946*, Albany, State University of New York Press, 1974.

Ciría, A. (ed.), *New Perspectives on Modern Argentina*, Bloomington, Latin American Studies Program, Indiana University, 1972.

Cortés Conde, R., *La economía argentina en el largo plazo (siglos XIX y XX)*, Buenos

Aires, Sudamericana, 1997.

De Imaz, J. L., *Los Que Mandan (Those Who Rule)*, Albany, State University of New York Press, 1970.

De la Balze, F. A. M. (ed.), *El comercio exterior argentino en la década de 1990*, CARI, Buenos Aires, Ediciones Manantial, 1991.

De la Balze, F. A. M. (ed.), *Reforma y convergencia: Ensayos sobre la transformación de la economía Argentina*, ADEBA and CARI, Buenos Aires; Ediciones Manantial, 1993.

Di Tella, G., *Perón–Perón, 1973–1976*, Buenos Aires, Sudamericana, 1983.

Di Tella, G. and R. Dornbusch (eds), *The Political Economy of Argentina, 1946–1983*, Pittsburgh, Pittsburgh University Press, 1989.

Dodson, M., 'The Catholic Church in Contemporary Argentina', in A. Ciría (ed.), *New Perspectives on Modern Argentina*, Bloomington, Latin American Studies Program, Indiana University, 1972.

Dorfman, A., *Cincuenta años de la industrialización argentina, 1930–1980*, Buenos Aires, n.p., 1983.

Economist Intelligence Unit, *Country Report: Argentina*, London, EIU; various years.

Ferreira Rubio, D. and M. Goretti, 'Cuando el Presidente gobierna solo: Menem y los decretos de necesidad y urgencia hasta la reforma constitucional (julio 1989–agosto 1994)', *Desarrollo Económico*, 36:141 (1996).

Frenkel, R. and J. M. Fanelli, *Políticas de estabilización e hiperinflación en Argentina*, Buenos Aires, Tesis, 1990.

Ghio, J. M., 'The Argentine Church and the Limits of Democracy', in A. Stuart-Gambino and E. Cleary (eds), *The Latin American Church and the Limits of Politics*, Boulder, Lynne Rienner, 1991.

Horowitz, J., *Argentine Unions, the State and the Rise of Peron, 1930–1945*, Berkeley, University of California Press, 1990.

James, D., *Resistance and Integration: Peronism and the Argentine Working Class, 1946–1976*, Cambridge, Cambridge University Press, 1988.

Jones, M. P., 'Evaluating Argentina's Presidential Democracy, 1983–1995', in S. Mainwaring and M. Soberg Shugart (eds), *Presidentialism and Democracy in Latin America*, Cambridge, Cambridge University Press, 1997.

Kosacoff, B., *La industria argentina: un proceso de reestructuración desarticulada*, Buenos Aires, Comisión Económica para América Latina and Centro Editor de América Latina, 1994.

Lewis, C. M. and N. Torrents (eds), *Argentina in the Crisis Years (1983–1990): From Alfonsín to Menem*, London, Institute of Latin American Studies (ILAS), 1993.

Lewis, P., *The Crisis of Argentine Capitalism*, Chapel Hill, University of North Carolina Press, 1989.

Llach, J., 'El Plan Pinedo de 1940: Su significado histórico y los orígenes de la economía política del peronismo', *Desarrollo Económico*, 92 (1984).

Machinea, J., *Stabilization Under Alfonsin's Government: A Frustrated Attempt*, Buenos Aires, CEDES, 1990.

Machinea, J. L., 'Stabilisation under Alfonsin', in C. M. Lewis and N. Torrents (eds), *Argentina in the Crisis Years (1983–1990): From Alfonsín to Menem*, London, Institute of Latin American Studies (ILAS), 1993.

Mallon, R. and J. Sourrouille, *Economic Policy-making in a Conflictive Society: The Argentine Case*, Cambridge, MA, Harvard University Press, 1975.

Manzetti, L. And M. Dell'Aquila, 'Economic Stabilization in Argentina: The Austral Plan', *Journal of Latin American Studies*, 35:4 (1993–94).

Menem, C. and M. Baizán, *Conversaciones con Carlos Menem: Como consolidar el modelo*, Buenos Aires, Editorial Fraterna, 1993.

Menem, C. and M. Baizán, *Desde el poder: Carlos Menem responde*, Buenos Aires, Corregidor, 1994.

Menem, C. and R. Dromi, *El estado hoy: Integración, participación, solidaridad*, Buenos Aires, Ediciones Ciudad Argentina, 1996.

Molinelli, G., 'Las relaciones Presidente Congreso en Argentina, 1983–1989', *Post Data*, 2 (November 1996).

Munck, R., 'The Democratic Decade: Argentina since Malvinas', *Bulletin of Latin American Research*, 11:2 (1992).

Mundlak, Y., D. Cavallo and R. Domenech, *Agriculture and Economic Growth in Argentina, 1913–84*, Washington, DC, International Food Policy Research Institute, 1989.

Murmis, M. and J. C. Portantiero, 'Crecimiento industrial y alianza de clases en la Argentina, 1930–40', in M. Murmis and J. C. Portantiero (eds), *Estudios sobre los origenes del peronismo*, Buenos Aires, Siglo XXI, 1971.

Mustapic, A. M. and N. Ferretti, 'El veto presidencial bajo Alfonsín y Menem (1983–1995)', mimeo, Buenos Aires, 1997.

Norden, D., *Military Rebellion in Argentina: Between Coups and Consolidation*, Lincoln, University of Nebraska Press, 1996.

Palermo, V. and M. Novaro, *Política y poder en el gobierno de Menem*, Buenos Aires, Grupo Editorial Norma, 1997.

Peralta Ramos, M., *The Political Economy of Argentina: Power and Class Since 1930*, Boulder, Lynne Rienner, 1992.

Potash, R., *The Army and Politics in Argentina, 1928–1945*, Stanford, Stanford University Press, 1969.

Potash, R., *The Army and Politics in Argentina, 1945–1962*, Stanford, Stanford University Press, 1980.

Potash, R., *The Army and Politics in Argentina, 1962–1973*, Stanford, Stanford University Press, 1992.

Rock, D., *Politics in Argentina, 1890–1930: The Rise and Fall of Radicalism*, Cambridge, Cambridge University Press, 1975.

Rock, D., *Argentina, 1516–1982: From Spanish Conquest to the Falklands War*, Berkeley, University of California Press, 1985.

Rouquié, A., 'Argentina: The Departure of the Military – End of a Political Cycle or Just Another Episode?', *International Affairs*, 59:4 (1983).

Schvarzer, J., *Martínez de Hoz: La lógica política de la política económica*, Buenos Aires, Centro de Investigaciones Sociales sobre el Estado y la Administración, 1983.

Schvarzer, J., *La industria que supimos conseguir: Una historia política-social de la industria argentina*, Buenos Aires, Planeta, 1996.

Sikkink, K., *Ideas and Institutions: Development in Brazil and Argentina*, Ithaca, Cornell University Press, 1991.

Smith, P., *Politics and Beef in Argentina: Patterns of Conflict and Change*, New York, Columbia University Press, 1969.

Smith, W., *Authoritarianism and the Crisis of the Argentine Political Economy*, Stanford, Stanford University Press, 1989.

Smith, W. C., 'State, Market and Neoliberalism in Post-Transition Argentina: The Menem Experiment', *Journal of Interamerican Studies and World Affairs*, 33:4 (1991).

Szusterman, C., *Frondizi and the Politics of Developmentalism in Argentina, 1955–1962*, London, Macmillan, 1993.

Torre, J. C., *La vieja guardia sindical y Perón: Sobre los origenes del peronismo*, Buenos Aires, Sudamericana and Instituto Torcuato Di Tella, 1990.

Torre, J. C., 'Conflict and Co-operation in Governing the Economic Emergency', in C. M. Lewis and N. Torrents (eds), *Argentina in the Crisis Years (1983–1990): From Alfonsín to Menem*, London, Institute of Latin American Studies (ILAS), 1993.

Torre, J. C. and L. de Riz, 'Argentina since 1946', in L. Bethell (ed.), *The Cambridge History of Latin America. Volume VIII: 1930 to the Present*, Cambridge, Cambridge University Press, 1991.

Waisman, C., *The Reversal of Development in Argentina: Post-War Counterrevolutionary Policies and Their Structural Consequences*, Princeton, Princeton University Press, 1987.

Waldmann, P., *El Peronismo, 1943–1955*, Buenos Aires, Sudamericana, 1981.

Waldman, P., 'The Peronism of Peron and Menem: From Justicialism to Liberalism', in C. M. Lewis and N. Torrents (eds), *Argentina in the Crisis Years (1983–1990): From Alfonsín to Menem*, London, Institute of Latin American Studies (ILAS), 1993.

World Bank (International Bank for Reconstruction and Development), *Argentina: From Insolvency to Growth*, Washington DC, World Bank, 1993.

Wynia, G., *Argentina in the Postwar Era: Politics and Economic Policy Making in a Divided Society*, Albuquerque, University of New Mexico Press, 1978.

Wynia, G., *Argentina: Illusions and Realities*, New York, Holmes and Meier, 1986.

Chapter 3: Chile

Angell, A. and B. Pollack, 'The Chilean Elections of 1989 and the Politics of the Transition to Democracy', *Bulletin of Latin American Research*, 9:1 (1990).

Angell, A. and B. Pollack, 'The Chilean Elections of 1993: From Polarisation to Consensus', *Bulletin of Latin American Research*, 9:1 (1995).

Bermejo, N., 'Democracy and the Lessons of Dictatorship', *Comparative Politics*, 24:3 (1992).

Caistor, N., *Chile in Focus*, London, Latin America Bureau, 1997.

Chavkin, S., *Storm over Chile: The Junta Under Siege*, New York, Lawrence Hill, 1993.

Collier, S. and W. Sater, *A History of Chile, 1808–1994*, Cambridge, Cambridge University Press, 1997.

Collins, J. and J. Lear, 'Free Market Miracle or Myth: Chile's Neo-Liberal Experiment', *The Ecologist*, 26:4 (1996).

Constable, P. and A. Valenzuela, *A Nation of Enemies, Chile Under Pinochet*, New York, Norton, 1991.

De Kadt, E., 'Poverty-Focused Policies: The Experience of Chile', Institute of Development Studies (Sussex, UK) Discussion Paper 319 (1993).

Drake, P. and I. Jaksic, *The Struggle for Democracy in Chile, 1982–1990*, Lincoln, University of Nebraska Press, 1991.

Fazio, H., *Mapa actual de la extrema riqueza en Chile*, Santiago, LOM-ARSIS, 1997.

Fontaine, J. A., 'Transición económica y política en Chile: 1970–1990', *Estudios Públi-*

cos, 50 (1993).

Godoy, O., 'Algunas claves de la transición política en Chile', *Estudios Públicos*, 38 (1990).

Gwynne, R., 'Non-Traditional Export Growth and Economic Development: The Chilean Forestry Sector since 1974', *Bulletin of Latin American Research* (May 1993).

Gwynne, R., 'Regional Integration in Latin America: The Revival of a Concept', in R. Gibb and W. Michalak (eds), *Continental Trading Blocs: The Growth of Regionalism in the World Economy*, New York, Wiley, 1994.

Hojman, D., 'Chile after Pinochet: Aylwin's Christian Democrat Economic Policies for the 1990s', *Bulletin of Latin American Research*, 9:1 (1990).

Hojman, D., 'Employment- and Earnings-generating Potentials of the Neo-liberal Model', in D. Hojman (ed.), *Neo-liberal Agriculture in Rural Chile*, Basingstoke, Macmillan, 1993.

Hojman, D., 'Chile under Frei (Again): The First Latin American Tiger – or Just Another Cat?', *Bulletin of Latin American Research*, 14:2 (1995).

Hojman, D., 'Poverty and Inequality in Chile: Are Democratic Politics and Neoliberal Economics Good for You?', *Journal of Interamerican Studies and World Affairs*, 38:2 (1996).

Latin America Bureau (LAB), *Chile: The Pinochet Decade*, London, 1983.

Leftwich, A., 'Governance, Democracy and Development in the Third World', *Third World Quarterly*, 14:3 (1993).

Martínez, J. and A. Díaz, A., *Chile: The Great Transformation*, Geneva, UNRISD and Brookings Institution, 1996.

Meller, P., 'La apertura comercial chilena: Lecciones de política', *Estudios CIEPLAN*, 35 (1992).

Meller, P., *Un siglo de economía política chilena (1890–1990)*, Santiago, Editorial Andrés Bello, 1996.

Meller, P. and R. Sáez, 'Lecciones y desafíos futuros del auge exportador chileno', in P. Meller and R. Sáez (eds), *Auge exportador chileno: Lecciones y desafíos futuros*, Santiago, CIEPLAN and Dolmen, 1997.

MERCOSUL: Revista de Negocios, various issues.

Munck, G., 'Algunas Claves de la Transición Política en Chile', *Latin American Research Review*, 29:2 (1994).

Munck, G., 'Democratic Stability and its Limits', *Journal of Interamerican Studies and World Affairs* (Summer 1994).

Muñoz, O., 'Economy and Society in Chile: Frustration and Change in the Historical Process', *International Social Science Journal*, 134 (1992).

Muñoz, O. and C. Celedón, 'Chile en transición: Estrategia económica y política', *Estudios CIEPLAN*, 37 (1993).

Oppenheim, L., *Politics in Chile: Democracy, Authoritarianism, and the Search for Development*, Boulder, Westview, 1993.

Oxhorn, P. (1994), 'Understanding Political Change after Authoritarian Rule: The Popular Sectors and Chile's New Democratic Regime', *Journal of Latin American Studies*, 26:3 (1994).

Petras, J., 'Alternatives to Neoliberalism in Latin America', *Latin American Perspectives*, 92:24 (1997).

Petras, J. and F. Leiva, *Democracy and Poverty in Chile: The Limits to Electoral Politics*,

Boulder, Westview, 1994.

Pollack, B. and A. Angell, *The Legacy of Dictatorship: Political, Economic and Social Change in Pinochet's Chile*, Liverpool, Institute of Latin American Studies (ILAS), 1993.

Rabkin, R., 'The Aylwin Government and "Tutelary" Democracy: A Concept in Search of a Case?', *Journal of Inter-American Studies and World Affairs*, 34:4 (1992).

Richards, D., 'The Political Economy of the Chilean Miracle', *Latin American Research Review*, 32:1 (1997).

Sánchez Otero, G., 'Neoliberalism and its Discontents', in F. Rosen and D. McFadyen (eds), *Free Trade and Economic Restructuring in Latin America*, New York, Monthly Review Press, 1995.

Schmitter, P., G. O'Donnell and L. Whitehead, *Transitions from Authoritarian Rule*, Baltimore, Johns Hopkins University Press, 1986.

Silva, E., 'Capitalist Regime Loyalties and Redemocratization in Chile', *Journal of Inter-American Studies and World Affairs*, 34:4 (1992).

Silva, E., 'From Dictatorship to Democracy: The Business–State Nexus in Chile's Economic Transformation, 1975–1994', *Comparative Politics*, 28:3 (1996).

Sunkel, O., 'Consolidation of Chile's Democracy and Development: The Challenges and the Tasks', Institute of Development Studies (Sussex, UK) Discussion Paper 317 (1993).

Velasco, A. and M. Tokman, 'Opciones para la política comercial chilena en los 90', *Estudios Públicos*, 52 (1993).

Weyland, K., 'Growth with Equity in Chile's New Democracy', *Latin American Research Review*, 32:1 (1997).

Wilhelmy, M. and R. Lazo, 'La política multilateral de Chile en Asia–Pacífico', *Estudios Internacionales*, 30:117 (1997).

Chapter 4: Uruguay

Abreu Bonilla, S., *Mercosur e integración*, Montevideo, Fundación de Cultura Universitaria, 1991.

Butler, D. and A. Ranney, *Referenda Around the World: The Growing Use of Direct Democracy*, London, Macmillan, 1994.

Cocchi, A. (ed.), *Reforma electoral y voluntad política*, Montevideo, Ediciones de la Banda Oriental, 1988.

Comisión Intercameral Empresarial (CIE), *Hacia un Uruguay con futuro: Análisis y propuestas del sector empresarial privado*, Montevideo, CEI IE, 1989.

Díaz, O., *Relaciones laborales y convenios en el Uruguay: Los sindicatos ante la reestructura productiva*, Montevideo, Centro Uruguay Independiente, 1995.

Finch, H., *Towards the New Economic Model: Uruguay 1973–97*, University of Liverpool, Institute of Latin American Studies (ILAS) Research Paper 22 (1998).

Gillespie, C., *Negotiating Democracy: Politicians and Generals in Uruguay*, Cambridge, Cambridge University Press, 1991.

Márquez Mosconi, G., *An Assessment of Pension System Reform in Uruguay in 1995*, Washington, DC, Social Programs Division, Inter-American Development Bank (IDB), 1997.

Nohlen, D. and J. Rial (eds), *Reforma electoral: Posible? Deseable?*, Montevideo, Ediciones de la Banda Oriental, 1986.

Pareja, C. and A. Romeo Pérez, 'Hacia otra reforma política', *Cuadernos del CLAEH*, 71 (1994).

Ures, J., 'La relación clase–voto en Montevideo', *Revista Uruguaya de Ciencias Sociales*, 1:1 (1972).

Chapter 5: Peru

Balbi, C., 'Politics and Trade Unions in Peru', in M. Cameron and P. Mauceri (eds), *The Peruvian Labyrinth: Polity, Society, Economy*, University Park, Pennsylvania State UniversityPress, 1997.

Cameron, M. and P. Mauceri (eds), *The Peruvian Labyrinth: Polity, Society, Economy*, University Park, Pennsylvania State University Press, 1997.

Carbonetto, D., *El Perú heterodoxo*, Lima, INP, 1986.

Cotlear, D., H. Martínez, J. León and J. Portugal, *Perú: La población migrante*, Lima, Amidep, 1987.

Crabtree, J., *Peru under García: An Opportunity Lost*, Basingstoke, Macmillan, 1992.

Crabtree. J., 'The 1995 Elections: End of the Line for the Party System?', Institute of Latin American Studies (ILAS), London, Occasional Papers, 1995.

Crabtree, J., 'Populismo y neopopulismo: La experiencia peruana', *Apuntes*, 40, 1st semester (1997).

Crabtree, J. and J. Thomas (eds), *Fujimori's Peru*, London, Institute of Latin American Studies (ILAS), 1998.

Dancourt, O., *Reformas estructurales y política macroeconómica en el Perú, 1990–1996*, Lima, PUCP, 1997.

Degregori, C., *Sendero Luminoso I. Los hondos y mortales desencuentros II. Lucha armada y utopia autoritaria*, Lima, IEP, 1986.

Degregori, C. and R. Grompone, *Elecciones 1990, demonios y redentores: Una tragedia en dos vueltas*, Lima, IEP, 1991.

Durand, F. and R. Thorp, 'Tax Reform: the SUNAT Experience', in J. Crabtree and J. Thomas, *Fujimori's Peru*, London, Institute of Latin American Studies (ILAS), 1998.

Fitzgerald, E. V. K., 'State Capitalism in Peru: A Model of Economic Development and its Limitations', in C. McClintock and A. Lowenthal (eds), *The Peruvian Experiment Reconsidered*, Princeton, Princeton University Press, 1983.

Gonzáles de Olarte, E., 'Economic Stabilization and Structural Adjustment under Fujimori', *Journal of Interamerican Studies and World Affairs*, 35:2 (1993).

Gorriti, G., *Sendero: Historia de la guerra milenaria en el Perú*, Lima, Apoyo, 1990.

Graham, C., *Peru's APRA: Parties, Politics and the Elusive Quest for Democracy*, Boulder, Lynne Rienner, 1991.

Graham C. and C. Kane, 'Opportunistic Government or Sustaining Reform? Electoral Trends and Public Expenditure Patterns in Peru, 1990–95', *Latin American Research Review*, 33:1 (1998).

Infante R., *Perú: Ajuste del mercado laboral urbano y sus efectos sociales*, Lima, OIT, 1995.

Kay, B. H., 'Fujipopulism and the Liberal State in Peru', *Journal of Interamerican Studies and World Affairs*, 38:4 (1996).

Lowenthal, A., *The Peruvian Experiment: Continuity and Change under Military Rule*, Princeton, Princeton University Press, 1975.

McClintock, C. and A. F. Lowenthal (eds), *The Peruvian Experiment Reconsidered*,

Princeton, Princeton University Press, 1983.

Matos Mar, J., *Desborde popular y crisis del estado*, Lima, IEP, 1984.

Matos Mar, J. and J. Mejía, *La reforma agraria en el Peru*, Lima, IEP, 1980.

Mauceri, P., 'Military Politics and Counter-Insurgency in Peru', *Journal of Interamerican Studies and World Affairs* (Winter 1991).

Mauceri, P., 'State Reform, Coalitions and the Neoliberal Autogolpe in Peru', *Latin American Research Review*, 30:2 (1995).

Mauceri, P., *State under Siege: Development and Policy Making in Peru*, Boulder, Westview, 1996.

Morales, E., *Cocaine: White Gold Rush in Peru*, Tuscon, University of Arizona Press, 1985.

Obando, E., 'Fujimori and the Military', in J. Crabtree and J. Thomas (eds), *Fujimori's Peru*, London, Institute of Latin American Studies (ILAS), 1998.

Palmer, D. S. (ed.), *The Shining Path of Peru*, London, Hurst, 1992.

Panfichi, A. and C. Sanborn, 'Democracia y neopopulismo en el Perú contemporáneo', *Márgenes*, 13/14 (1995).

Perú Económico, 'Privatización en el Perú', 27:6 (1994).

Philip, G., *The Rise and Fall of the Peruvian Military Radicals 1968–78*, London, Athlone, 1978.

Poole, D and G. Reñique, G., *Peru – Time of Fear*, London, Latin America Bureau, 1992.

Scheetz, T., *Peru and the International Monetary Fund*, Pittsburgh, Pittsburgh University Press, 1986.

Schmidt, G. D., 'Fujimori's 1990 Upset Victory in Peru: Electoral Rules, Contingencies, and Adaptive Strategies', *Comparative Politics*, 28:3 (1996).

Seminario, B., *Reformas estructurales y política de estabilización*, Lima, CIUP, 1995.

Stark, O., *The Peru Reader: History, Culture, Politics*, London, Latin America Bureau, 1993.

Stein, S. and C. Monge, *La crisis del estado patrimonial en el Perú*, Lima, IEP, 1988.

Stepan, A., *The State and Society: Peru in Comparative Perspective*, Princeton, Princeton University Press, 1978.

Strong, S., *Shining Path: The World's Deadliest Revolutionary Force*, London, HarperCollins, 1992.

Sulmont, D., *Movimiento obrero peruano 1890–1980*, Lima, Tarea, 1981.

Tanaka, M., 'From Movimientismo to Media Politics: The Changing Boundaries between Society and Politics in Fujimori's Peru', in J. Crabtree and J. Thomas (eds), *Fujimori's Peru*, London, Institute of Latin American Studies (ILAS), 1998.

Taylor, L., 'Counter-Insurgency Strategy, the PCP–Sendero Luminoso and the Civil War in Peru, 1980–1996', *Bulletin of Latin American Research*, 17:1 (1998).

Thorp, R. and G. Bertram, *Peru, 1890–1977: Growth and Policy in an Open Economy*, New York, Columbia University Press, 1978.

Tulchin, J. and G. Bland (eds), *Peru in Crisis: Dictatorship or Democracy*, Boulder, Lynne Rienner, 1994.

Vargas Llosa, M., *El pez en el agua*, Barcelona, Seix Barral, 1993.

Webb, R., *Government Policy and the Distribution of Income in Peru*, Cambridge, Harvard University Press, 1977.

Webb, R. and A. Figueroa, *Distribución del ingreso en el Perú*, Lima, IEP, 1975.

Wise, C., 'The Politics of Peruvian Economic Reform', *Journal of Interamerican Studies and World Affairs* (Spring 1994).

Chapter 6: Mexico

Bailey, John: *Governing Mexico: The Statecraft of Crisis Management*, 1988.

Banco de México, *The Mexican Economy*, Mexico City, Banco de México, various years.

Camp, R. A., *Intellectuals and the State in Twentieth-Century Mexico*, Austin, University of Texas Press, 1985.

Camp, R. A., *Politics in Mexico*, 2nd edn, New York, Oxford University Press, 1996.

Cansino, C., 'Mexico: The Challenge of Democracy', *Government and Opposition* 30:1 (1995).

Comision Federal Electoral and Instituto Federal Electoral, *Reporte de Resultados Electorales: 1976 – 1991*, Mexico, IFE, 1992.

Coppedge, M., 'Parties and Society in Mexico and Venezuela: Why Competition Matters', *Comparative Politics*, 25:3 (1993).

Cornelius, W. and A. Craig, *The Mexican Political System in Transition*, San Diego, Center for US–Mexican Studies, University of California, 1991.

Cornelius, W., A. Craig and J. Fox, 'Mexico's National Solidarity Program: An Overview', in W. Cornelius *et al.* (eds), *Transforming State–Society Relations in Mexico: The National Solidarity Strategy*, San Diego, Centre for US–Mexican Studies, University of California, 1994.

Domínguez, J. I., 'Mexico's New Foreign Policy: States, Societies and Institutions', David Rockefeller Center for Latin American Studies Working Papers 96–5 (1997).

Dwyer, A., *On the Line: Life on the US–Mexican Border*, London, Latin America Bureau, 1994.

Foweraker, J. and A. L. Craig (eds), *Popular Movements and Political Change in Mexico*, Boulder, Lynne Rienner, 1990.

Gates, M., *In Default: Peasants, the Debt Crisis and the Agricultural Challenge in Mexico*, Boulder, Westview, 1993.

Handelman, H., *Mexican Politics: The Dynamics of Change*, New York, St Martin's Press, 1997.

Harvey, N. and M. Serrano, *Party Politics in an 'Uncommon Democracy': Political Parties and Elections in Mexico*, London, Institute of Latin American Studies (ILAS), 1994.

Hellman, J. A., *Mexico in Crisis*, New York, Holmes and Meier, 1983.

Knight, A., 'Solidarity: Historical Continuities and Contemporary Implications', in W. Cornelius *et al.* (eds), *Transforming State–Society Relations in Mexico: The National Solidarity Strategy*, San Diego, Centre for US – Mexican Relations, 1994.

Lustig, N., 'México, el Pacto de Solidaridad Económica: La heterodoxia puesta en marcha', in G. Rozenwurcel (ed.), *Elecciones y política económica en América Latina*, Buenos Aires, Grupo Editorial Norma, 1991.

Lustig, N., *Mexico: The Remaking of an Economy*, Washington, DC, Brookings Institution, 1992.

Morris, S. D., *Political Reformism in Mexico: An Overview of Contemporary Mexican Politics*, Boulder, Lynne Rienner, 1995.

Otero, G. (ed.), *Neo-Liberalism Revisited: Economic Restructuring and Mexico's Political Future*, Boulder, Westview, 1996.

Pastor, M., 'Post-Revolutionary Mexico: The Salinas Opening', *Journal of Interamerican Studies and World Affairs*, 1:3 (1990).

Pastor, M. and C. Wise, 'The Origins and Sustainability of Mexico's Free Trade Policy', *International Organization*, 48:3 (1994).

Philip, G., *The Presidency in Mexican Politics*, London, Macmillan, 1992.

Philip, G., 'Democracy in Mexico', *Democratisation*, 3:1 (1996).

Quintana, E., 'Empresas privatizadas: Divorcios y conflictos', *Este País*, 9 (December 1991).

Riding, A., *Distant Neighbours*, New York, Vintage, 1984.

Roett, R. (ed.), *The Challenge of Institutional Reform in Mexico*, Boulder, Lynne Rienner, 1995.

Russell, P. L., *Mexico Under Salinas*, Austin, Mexico Resource Center, 1994.

Simon, J., *Endangered Mexico: An Environment on the Edge*, London, Latin America Bureau, 1998.

Smith, P. H., *Labyrinths of Power: Political Recruitment in Twentieth-Century Mexico*, Princeton, Princeton University Press, 1979.

Springer, G. L. and J. L. Molina, 'The Mexican Financial Crisis: Genesis, Impact and Implications', *Journal of Interamerican Studies and World Affairs*, 37:2 (1995).

Chapter 7: Colombia

Agudelo Villa, H., *La revolución liberal: Un proyecto político inconcluso*, Bogotá, Tercer Mundo Editores, 1996.

Buitrago, L. and L. Zamosa (eds), *Al filo del caos: Crisis política en la Colombia de los años 80*, Bogotá, Tercer Mundo Editores, 1991.

Cárdenas, M., *Coffee Exports, Endogenous State Policy and the Business Cycle*, Berkeley, University of California Press, 1991.

Cárdenas, M. and R. Córdoba, *Recent Economic Policy in Colombia: The View from Outside*, mimeo, Institute of Latin American Studies (ILAS), London (1996).

Child, J., 'Apertura y privatización', in J. Child (ed.), *Neoliberalismo y subdesarrollo: Un analisis crítico de la apertura económica*, Bogotá, El Ancora Editores, 1995.

Harding, C., *Colombia in Focus*, London, Latin American Bureau, 1997.

INCOMEX, *Material seleccionado. Proceso de modernización de la economía colombiana*, mimeo, Bogotá, 17 April 1990.

McBeth, B. (ed.), *Colombia*, London, Euromoney Publications, 1993.

Ocampo, J., 'The Economic Policy of the Samper Administration', mimeo, Institute of Latin American Studies (ILAS), London (1996).

Palacios, M., *Coffee in Colombia, 1850–1970: An Economic, Social and Political History*, Cambridge, Cambridge University Press, 1979.

Restrepo, L., 'Colombia; una nación en peligro', in IEPRI, Universidad Nacional, *Síntesis '97: Anuario social político y económico de Colombia*, Bogotá, IEPRI, Universidad Nacional, 1997.

Revéiz, E., *El estado como mercado. La gobernabilidad económica y política en Colombia antes y después de 1991*, Bogotá, Fonade, Carlos Valencia Editores, 1996.

Richani, N., 'The Political Economy of Violence: The War System in Colombia', *Journal of Interamerican Studies and World Affairs*, 39:2 (1997).

Rojas Morales, E., *Colombia a la deriva. Una mirada ética a la política y un juicio moral a la campaña 'Samper Presidente'*, Bogotá, Fundación para la Investigación y Desarrollo de la Ciencia Política (FIDEC), 1997.

Salamanca, G., *Colombia y la crisis de la deuda*, Bogotá, CINEP, 1991.

Salazar, A., *Born to Die in Medellín*, London, Latin America Bureau, 1990
Sarmiento Palacio, E., *Apertura y crecimiento económico: de la desilución al nuevo estado*, Bogotá, Tercer Mundo Editores, 1996.
Smith, P., *Drug Policy in the Americas*, Boulder, Westview, 1992.

Chapter 8: Venezuela

Alexander, R., *The Venezuelan Democratic Revolution*, New Brunswick, Rutgers University Press, 1964.
Alexander, R., *Rómulo Betancourt and the transformation of Venezuela*, New Brunswick, Transaction, 1982.
Baloyra, E. and J. Martz, *Political Attitudes in Venezuela, Societal Cleavages and Political Opinion*, Texas, University of Texas Press, 1979.
Barrios, A. and R. de la Cruz, *El costo de la descentralización en Venezuela*, Caracas, Nueva Sociedad, 1994.
Bergquist, C., *Labour in Latin America*, Stanford, Stanford University Press, 1986.
Betancourt, R., *Venezuela's Oil*, London, Allen and Unwin, 1978.
Buxton, J., 'The Venezuelan Party System 1988–1995', Ph.D. thesis, London School of Economics, 1998.
Catala, J. (ed.), *El juicio politico al ex-presidente de Venezuela Carlos Andres Pérez, verdades y mentiras en el juicio oral*, Caracas, Centauro, 1995.
Coppedge, M., 'Parties and Society in Mexico and Venezuela: Why Competition Matters', *Comparative Politics*, 25:3 (1993).
Coppedge, M., *Strong Parties and Lame Ducks: Presidential Partyarchy and Factionalism in Venezuela*, Stanford, Stanford University Press, 1994.
Coppedge, M., 'Prospects for Democratic Governability in Venezuela;, *Journal of Interamerican Studies and World Affairs*, 36:2 (1994).
Diccionario de la corrupción en Venezuela, Caracas, Ediciones Capriles, various years.
Economist Intelligence Unit (EIU), *Country Report, Venezuela*, London, EIU, various years.
Ellner, S., *Organised Labour in Venezuela, 1958–1991*, Wilmington, Scholarly Resources, 1993.
Fundación Pensamiento y Acción (FPA), *Cultura democrática en Venezuela: Informe analítico de los resultados de una encuesta de opinión pública*, Caracas, FPA, 1996.
García, L., *La máscara del poder*, Caracas, Tropicos, 1988.
Goodman, L. (ed.), *Lessons of the Venezuelan Experience*, Washington, DC, Woodrow Wilson Centre Press, 1995.
Granier, M. and G. Yepes, *Más y mejor democracia*, Caracas, Roraima, 1987.
Hellinger, D., *Venezuela: Tarnished Democracy*, Boulder, Westview, 1991.
Hellinger, D., 'Causa R and Nuevo Sindicalismo in Venezuela', *Latin American Perspectives*, 90:23, no. 3 (1996).
Hojman, D., 'The Political Economy of Recent Conversion to Market Economics in Latin America', *Journal of Latin American Studies*, 26 (1994).
Jongkind, F., 'Venezuelan Industry Under the New Conditions of the 1989 Economic Policy', *European Review of Latin American and Caribbean Studies*, 54 (1993).
Karl, T., 'Petroleum and Political Pacts; The Transition to Democracy in Venezuela', *Latin American Research Review*, 23:3 1998.
Kornblith, M., 'La crisis del sistema político venezolano', *Nueva Sociedad*, 140 (1996).

Léon, R., *Los efectos perversos del petroleo*, Caracas, Capriles, 1990.

Levine, D., *Conflict and Political Change in Venezuela*, Princeton, Princeton University Press, 1973.

Levine, D., 'The Transition to Democracy in Venezuela: Are There Lessons to be Learnt ?', *Bulletin of Latin American Research*, 4:2 (1985).

McCoy, J., 'The Politics of Adjustment: Labour and the Venezuelan State', *Journal of Interamerican Studies and World Affairs*, 28:4 (1987).

McCoy, J., 'Labour and the State in a Party Mediated Democracy', *Latin American Research Review*, 24 (1988).

McCoy, J. *et al.*, *Venezuelan Democracy Under Pressure*, New Brunswick, North–South Center, 1995.

Mainwaring, S and T. Scully, *Building Democratic Institutions in Latin America*, Stanford, Stanford University Press, 1995.

Mommer, B and A. Baptista, *El petróleo en el pensamiento ecónomico de Venezuela. Un ensayo*, Caracas, Ediciones IESA, 1992.

Naím, M., *Paper Tigers and Minotaurs: The Politics of Venezuela's Economic Reforms*, Washington, DC, Carnegie Endowment for International Peace, 1993.

Naím, M. and R. Pinango, *El caso venezolano: Una ilusión de armonía*, Caracas, Ediciones IESA, 1984.

Navarro, J., 'Reversal of Fortune: The Ephemeral Success of Adjustment in Venezuela Between 1989 and 1993', Caracas, World Bank Project on Governance and Successful Adjustment in Venezuela, 1994.

Philip, G., 'Venezuelan Democracy and the Coup Attempt of February 1992', *Government and Opposition*, 27:4 (1992).

Romero, A., *Decadencia y crisis de la democracia: ¿A dónde va la democracia venezolana?*, Caracas, Panapo, 1994.

Romero, A., 'Rearranging the Deck Chairs on the Titanic: The Agony of Democracy in Venezuela', *Latin American Research Review*, 32:1 (1997).

Salamanca, L., 'Venezuela, la crisis del rentismo', *Nueva Sociedad*, 131 (1994).

Sesto, F., *Pablo Medina en entrevista*, Caracas, Ediciones del Agua Mansa, 1993.

Smith, W. and J. McCoy, 'Deconsolidácion o reequilibrio democrático en Venezuela', *Nueva Sociedad*, 140 (1995).

Sonntag, H., 'Venezuela, el díficil curso de la transicíon', *Nueva Sociedad*, 151 (1997).

Torres, A., *La experiencia política en una democracia partidista joven: El caso de Venezuela*, Universidad Simón Bolívar (Caracas) (1980) paper 29.

Tulchin, J. and G. Bland, *Venezuela in the Wake of Radical Reform*, Boulder, Lynne Reiner, 1993.

Urbaneja, D., *Pueblo y petróleo en la política venezolana del siglo XX*, Caracas, CEPET, 1992.

Walsh, F., Attitudinal Survey, *Nueva Sociedad*, 121 (1992).

Index